D1565428

Walk With Me

*The Story of One Man's Life
with Muscular Degeneration
and His 1,700-Mile Walk Through
California*

by
Martin McCorkle

PublishAmerica
Baltimore

© 2004 by Martin McCorkle.
All rights reserved. No part of this book may be reproduced, stored in a retrieval system or transmitted in any form or by any means without the prior written permission of the publishers, except by a reviewer who may quote brief passages in a review to be printed in a newspaper, magazine or journal.

First printing

ISBN: 1-4137-3043-4
PUBLISHED BY PUBLISHAMERICA, LLLP
www.publishamerica.com
Baltimore

Printed in the United States of America

Dedication

To my friends and family who walked with me through California:

Pat McCorkle
Don
Sally
Cindy
Rich Wilkinson
Roger Haugen
Brian Thiessen
Ann McKay
Danette Morris
Steve Unversaw
Kurt Steen
Jennifer
Max McCorkle
Nick Hill
Jeanine Thiessen

Foreword

It is a great pleasure to introduce Martin McCorkle's *Walk With Me: The Story of One Man's Life with Muscular Degeneration and His 1,700-Mile Walk Through California*.

John Muir, my great-grandfather, encouraged people to "climb the mountains and get their good tidings. Nature's peace will flow into you as sunshine flows into trees. The winds will blow their own freshness into you, and the storms their energy, while cares will drop off like autumn leaves."

Martin McCorkle took these words to heart. The inspirational story that follows tells about a man who will not be limited by the challenges he faces. He challenges his limits. His example shows us all how the world can be a richer place.

Michael Muir, President
United States Driving for the Disabled, Incorporated

The

Pacific Crest
Trail

through

California

CASCADE MOUNTAINS

Eureka

Redding

Lake
Tahoe

0   50   100 miles

Sacramento

SIERRA NEVADA MOUNTAINS

San
Francisco

San
Jose

Fresno

Forester
Pass

Bakersfield

Mojave

N

W — E

S

Los
Angeles

San
Diego

Day 73:
Forester Pass

Late June 1982

About 750 miles north of the Mexican border on the Pacific Crest Trail, just south of Forester Pass in the Sierra Nevada Mountains of California

Awakened by light, my warm fingers searched for cold zippers. I squirmed out of my cocoon-like sleeping bag and crisp air pricked my exposed skin.

Man, it's cold.

I unrolled my pillow, which consisted of a smelly tee shirt, a tattered green wool shirt and my hiking shorts and quickly put on my clothes.

Well, this is it. This is the day.

I looked at my boots next to my ground cloth. They were frozen solid. The day before, I had worn them during the ford of raging Tyndale Creek. They hadn't had time to dry out before I had made camp. To my left, the creeklet that I had used to provide water for supper had ceased to flow. Sheets of ice covered small pools.

Hard freeze last night. That's good, very good.

I searched inside my sleeping bag for my wool socks. Throughout the night my body heat had helped to evaporate some of the water out of my socks. Now they were clammy, but not wet.

I rubbed my feet and examined them. They were in good shape. My custom-made boots had kept my blisters to a minimum.

I love my boots.

After I had pulled on my socks, I worked my boots until they were somewhat pliable and put them on. I felt their icy grasp as I laced them high up my bony, diseased calves.

Okay, I've got to stand up.

Standing up for the first time in the morning is always hard. When I'm lying down or sitting, I can still believe that I am normal, even strong, but all I have to do is stand up and reality is back.

The muscles in my feet, ankles and calves are dying. I clutched my staff and, using it as a lever, pushed myself up until my healthy quadriceps could engage and give me strength. I stood uneasily, grasping my staff for balance.

How am I going to climb this pass? I shouldn't be here. I'm not going to make it.

For over eight weeks, I had walked north on the Pacific Crest Trail (PCT)—a continuous trail tracing the highest mountain ranges from Mexico to Canada. I had pushed my boots through a border fence and touched Mexican sand, and then I walked. Smaller mountain ranges, desert valleys and a handful of rattlesnake sightings were behind me. Through all of that I had carried a fear of this day like a 20-pound dumbbell in my pack. Today I would attempt to cross over Forester Pass. At 13,015 feet, Forester was the highest, snowiest and most dangerous pass on my 1,700-mile trek to Oregon.

Every report I had heard was the same: Forester Pass was impassable. The late, heavy winter snows still covered the high places. No one was getting through. Hikers detoured around it.

Camped with me were my older brother Pat and a new friend named Cindy. Pat had recently served a few years with the army and had jumped at the opportunity to hike through California with me. He was a great trail partner. He rarely complained, though there was much to complain about. He was fastidiously clean, brushing and flossing his teeth without fail every night. His green pants kept their press through the whole route.

Cindy had met up with us along the trail about 20 days before. Our pace and temperaments matched, so we decided to stay together through this difficult stretch. She tied her black hair in pigtails and carried fresh vegetables, such as whole lettuce heads, to eat. She had such a sisterly demeanor that we easily folded her into our family group. Pat and I were used to having a sister around and we enjoyed the new company.

Our camp stirred to life. We made breakfast, but the oatmeal-like

8

substance was bad and we didn't eat it. Guided by experience and powered by anxiety, we packed up in a few short minutes. As I finished my morning routine, I took a long, hard look at the pass.

Forester Pass reminded me of a medieval castle. A frozen moat of snow surrounded a granite wall that shot thousands of feet straight up into the clear sky. The small, jagged notch of the pass seemed like a portal where boulders and hot oil could be thrown down at any who dared to ascend. I couldn't imagine that a trail ran up that sheer face of ice and granite. I searched for the characteristic zigzag pattern of switchbacks, but I couldn't find them. There was only snow, rock and sky.

We wanted to get going. Because the High Sierra nights often bring sub-freezing temperatures, the refrozen snowpack is easier to walk on in the early morning. We hoped to crunch right along the top of the snow and not break through. For the next mile, the solid snow didn't give an inch. The only indication of my passing was the waffle-like grid left behind by the soles of my custom-made boots. My spirits lifted. With hardly a problem at all, we came to the wall, the final ascent of the pass. We found a few small sections of trail and had to cut a few steps with our ice axes, but the ascent was going splendidly. For a time, I laughed at how I had worried about this day. I started to enjoy the beauty, the rhythm of the walk, the glory of a Sierran morning. This was hiking at its best.

About 100 feet below the pass, we turned a corner and saw what I had dreaded. Our trail was covered with a fifteen-yard section of pure snow and ice sloping at a deadly angle. Our eyes followed the chute down to where it disappeared over an edge, like the lip of a waterfall captured in a photograph. Thoughts flew quickly: We couldn't go back. That would take days. It would take even more days—perhaps weeks—to walk around Forester on the Sierra's snowless eastern slopes and eventually regain the PCT.

But if I fell here, if I slipped, I was dead. Or perhaps worse, I'd wind up jammed between ice and rock at 13,000 feet with a broken leg—my last breaths spent watching my life-blood soak into the ice, like a gruesome snowcone.

I can't explain why, but there was never a question about turning back. We all knew we would go north. A fifteen-yard ice chute would not stop a 1,700-mile hike. We had a rope with us—if our pencil-thin string could be called a rope. We knew that, if we fell, the rope would probably break. If the rope did hold the weight of a body and a pack, the knife-sharp granite surrounding the chute would surely slice it. We used it anyway. Somehow our thin rope helped us to feel connected. We needed all the help we could get.

Our first plan was for me to cut steps across, then Cindy and Pat would follow. I got out my ice ax, reshouldered my pack and tied the rope around my waist. As soon as I stepped out on the ice, I knew that I couldn't get across. I couldn't feel anything underneath my feet. I saw my feet and willed them to stay still, but they moved. When I wanted them to move, they wouldn't. Before I took one full step, I came back to solid ground.

"I can't do this." I looked at Pat. He was our strongest hiker—he had power that I did not have. "You've got to do this. When you get across, Cindy will follow your steps, and then I'll come last."

Pat looked across and said simply, "Okay."

My brother hacked at ice, taking sure, confident steps, making his way across this deathfall ice chute. I took great joy in letting out each handful of rope. The rhythm was mesmerizing—chop, chop, chop, chop, step, chop, chop, chop, chop, step. I was proud of him. A picture of this belonged on the cover of *Mountain Magazine*. With a final step, his boots met the iceless trail.

Cindy was next, with both Pat and me holding on to the rope. This chivalrous plan, however, had one problem. The rope was too short; there was very little slack between us. My brother's steps formed a sort of arch reaching from one side to the other. Cindy couldn't follow this route because the rope threatened to pull her down. She had to start all over and cut a new route straight across. She joined Pat on the other side.

Now I was alone. Pat looked at me across the chute and yelled, "Now it's your turn. You can do this."

By this time I was in bad shape. I had been sitting in the shade and wind for a long time. I was really cold. With shivering hands, I shouldered my pack and tried to grab my ice ax. I couldn't get my hand to grip. I saw a hand on top of the ax and said to this hand, "close—grip", but no connection was made. Finally, I reached over with my other hand and wrapped the lifeless one around the top of my ax.

The obvious presence of death is a great motivator. Each step was a labor. So much had to be done. The first foot had to find solid purchase in the newly cut steps. Then I had to balance on that foot while I brought my ax forward, ensuring that it too was securely wedged in the snow and ice. Then, the back foot had to go that perilously long distance from the back to the front, where I had to do all this again. Any problem anywhere and ZING! I was very cold, hovering between life and death, between north and south. Step, ax, step, rest. *I shouldn't be here.* Step, ax, step, rest. *I have no business in these mountains.* Step, ax, step, rest. *I could be dead in ten seconds.* Step, ax, step . . . .

I fell into Cindy's arms.

"Hey, good job," my brother said.

As I let go of Cindy, I tried to unbuckle my belt strap, but my hands were useless.

"I can't do this."

Pat saw my struggle and looked at Cindy, "Let's get his pack off." He unbuckled my strap and they lifted my burden.

As I sat down, I said slowly, "I don't feel very good."

Cindy said to Pat, "He's cold. Come on, let's hug him."

So we embraced, gently swaying against the wind. Their warmth flowed to me. Sandwiched between them, I could see the chute. After several minutes, I managed a smile.

When I felt a bit better, we shouldered our packs and scaled the last few switchbacks to the pass. Without a glance back at the highlands of Sequoia National Park, we looked north into the fresh, new wilderness of Kings Canyon. We walked down from the pass a few yards. The wall of Forester Pass, so recently our adversary, now became a shelter against the southern winds.

At a wide bend in the trail, we stopped again to warm our bodies and spirits with a boiling cup of miso soup. Miso soup was one of the many supposedly healthy soups we took along on this trip. Whether miso soup is healthy or not, I don't know, but I didn't like the sharp, bitter taste. Tiny freeze-dried fish, which were the main substance in the soup, floated to the top of each cup. Their blank eye sockets stared up at me as I drank. But I didn't care—the soup was warm; it soothed me. The warmed cup restored my hands. The three of us sat in a tight group, grinning like fools who have conquered a common foe. And then, of course, there was the Sierra Nevada.

I've hiked thousands of miles in many places. I've rested by the red shores of the Colorado River, gazing up at the weight of the Grand Canyon. I've seen the glory of the Rocky Mountains from her high places. I've tasted the ancient flavor of the Appalachians. As I enjoyed my soup, my eyes drank of a different drought. Nothing rivals the beauty and majesty of the High Sierra.

To the east, the ragged, torn granite crest of the Sierra stretched up to the skies, wishing to outdo the clouds by sheer will. To the west lay the Great Western Divide—a set of mountain peaks and passes that alone would sing of glory, but here played only a minor part in this alpine song. To the north, straight down from Forester Pass, was a land of snow, ice, rock and air. In another time, glaciers ruled this land. Their weight and power had carved out distinctive U-shaped canyons and left the land dotted with lakes.

One of these lakes was stranded at the top of Bubb's Creek Canyon and rested, frozen, beneath us. The canyon walls embraced the lake as a mother embraces a child. But here, this mountainous embrace did not bring warmth, but blocked out all sun and light—a cold embrace, reminding the lake of its glacial birth. My eyes searched beyond this lake and, looking down the canyon, I could see a small section of trail through a break in the snowpack. Small wisps of fog and cloud drifted upward and began to fill Bubb's Canyon. From there, I looked as far north as I could see. Mountain peaks and passes crowned with snow looked like the waves of a vast, endless sea. That I was alive and would walk through this land was a holy thing.

I said hopefully, "Let's head for that piece of trail. Maybe the snow won't be so bad down there and we can make camp."

Much of the day, however, had been spent. We didn't carry watches; we preferred to measure our days against the course of the sun. All through the morning, the snow was melting, and was now slush, which would not hold our weight. Instead of crunching along the top, we crushed, in irregular and unpredictable fashion, right through to the rocks underneath. It was terribly unnerving to realize that, while the snow on top looked relatively uniform, the rocks, gaps, crevices and holes underneath were not. Sometimes I only broke through a few inches to level rock. Other times I broke through up to my waist. But what I feared most was breaking through to slanted, jagged rock and breaking an ankle. I broke through more times than I could count. This took its toll in my head. I didn't want to walk anymore. I was certain that the next time I broke through would be the last.

As we neared the frozen cirque lake below Forester Pass, the snowfields grew steeper. The canyon walls blocked the sun and the snow turned icy. Not so hard as to require an ice ax to cut steps, but hard enough to demand several kick-ins for each step. I got behind Pat and walked in his steps. The lake grew near. It was beautiful; completely frozen except for a small pool of emerald blue melting in the center. I focused on each step. Follow Pat—one step at a time.

I placed my boot in one of his steps, the snow below the step gave way and I fell, sliding quickly on the icy slope. *Turn over! Get on your stomach! Drive your staff into the snow. You've got to stop. The lake! The lake! Now! Now!*

I stopped a few dozen yards below Pat and Cindy. The walls were steeper, the lake was closer. I carefully got back to my feet.

Pat yelled to me, "Good stop. We'll contour down a little more and meet you."

I nodded in agreement and set out to kick-in my own steps and immediately fell again.

"Ahhhh!"

Pat yelled down to me, "Martin, self arrest! Self arrest!"

I somehow managed to stop again. I was too far away from the others to receive assistance. I was now only a hundred yards or so from the lake's icy shores. *I'm going to slide to that lake, glide to the middle, fall through the ice and drown.*

I heard my brother above me. "Get up! Come on, let's go!"

I got back up and started again. I fell twice more. Each time growing further from the group and closer to the lake. Fatigue was extreme; advancement so difficult. Each step required five or six kick-ins. And always, the lake was waiting for me.

I was about 20 yards above the lake on the steepest portion. I had walked 30 yards without falling. The canyon wall moderated only 20 yards ahead. *You're going to make it.* Kick, kick, kick, kick, kick, step. *Only a few more feet.* Kick, kick, kick, kick, kick, step. *Take it slow, Do it righ . .*

"Ahhh!" I fell.

13

You've got to stop! You've got to stop! You're too close! The lake! The lake!

With a final burst of strength, I jammed my staff into the snow, hanging on as I continued to slide. *Push! Push!* I leaned all my weight into the staff and stopped five yards from the icy shore.

I sighed. *What am I doing here?*

I stood up. So near to the lake, the slope was now manageable. I walked fifteen yards along the snow-covered shore and turned around at the head of the lake. Tender, late-afternoon sun rays cast shadows over gray rock and white snow. Forester Pass stood passionless 1,000 feet above me. I saw our footprints and the skids left by my slides all the way down. The emerald pool at the lake's center echoed the clear, high sky. Lethal majesty surrounded me.

Pat and Cindy worked down the ridge. "Hey, you made it," said Pat.

"Uh huh," was all I could say.

By now, three-fourths of the day had passed. We had only a short walk to the trail fragment we had seen during our break. Our spirits were high, with the expectation that we would find the trail and that the snow would give way quickly. But Forester had one more test for us. The wisps of fog that we had seen down canyon pushed up and quickly gathered into dense pea soup. The winds, which earlier had raged to the north, now blew south, right into our wind-burned, sun-scorched faces. Then, in late June, it began to snow! Not only did we have to contend with snow on the ground; we had to fight it in the air. This was not fair. My brother muttered something about the absurdity of it all and quipped, "Admiral Byrd will be meeting us shortly."

I replied with a disgusted, "Yeah, right."

I was tired. I wanted to get to a dry place by the trail, eat a warm, voluminous dinner and sleep the blessed sleep of the weary. But instead, visibility was down to a dozen yards. In a mindless fashion, we walked to the trail fragment and found it to be only that—a small piece of trail surrounded by endless snow.

At such a time as this, there is only one remedy—just walk. And so, beyond fatigue and weariness, we walked. Time had no meaning. Distance had no significance. As we descended into the canyon, Bubb's Creek grew larger and louder as it rejoiced to splash down its course. The snow below our feet gave way to land. The snow above became gentler, and the storm's winds relaxed. After a creek ford, we decided to move up the side of the canyon a bit to see if we could pick up the trail. Contouring up the canyon, we found the PCT, a tread about one foot wide running through this open, wild land. We wanted to make sure that snow would not again overtake the trail, so we followed it for about half a mile. Finally, with the snowpack behind us, we made camp.

I don't know what we ate, but we ate our food hot and fast. All three of us crammed into a two-man tent. I watched my stork-like legs slip into my sleeping bag. *I don't know how, but I walked this trail another day.* I closed my eyes and was taken by darkness.

Part 1:
Base Camp

Chapter 1:
What's Wrong With Him?

Please stop . . . Oh, please, please stop . . . Don't turn it up . . . It hurts . . . It really, really hurts . . . Don't make it hurt more. I wanted to scream. Yet I did not make a sound. The people in the medical building were important people. The people wearing the white clothes with pockets filled with odd tools, carrying clipboards, could not be bothered. They had important work to do. One of these white-coated people was hurting me, hurting me badly. I wanted to cry. I wanted to run, but I couldn't. They were important. I had to do what they asked. Besides, my legs were covered with needles.

My parents had raised two children before me. Dad had been through the sit-crawl-stand-walk-run thing twice already. He knew what to expect, but he was uneasy with my development. I fell a lot, and I couldn't run at all. I walked funny. He sensed that something was wrong, but no one seemed to know what was the matter with me. When I entered grammar school, he still didn't know. I had seen lots of doctors. They agreed that something wasn't right, but they couldn't tell us what.

Finally a consensus grew that my problem was neurological. That meant that I needed to undergo an electromyogram (EMG). In today's world of MRIs and CAT scans, one would think that an EMG was an innocuous thing. But that test is one of my life's worst memories. By the time I came in for the test, I was in the third grade. I had already been poked and prodded a whole lot more than most kids and had developed a fear of all things medical. Yet nothing that I had experienced so far came close to what awaited me that day.

I was alone in a medical room sitting on an examination table surrounded by sleek space-age equipment. Someone important came in. He took small amounts of jelly and rubbed it in small circles all over both of my legs. Then, at the center of each jelly circle, he inserted a small needle attached to a wire leading to a machine. Sharp pain shot through me with each prick.

But this was only the beginning. Electricity was then pulsed through these needles. The pulses got stronger and stronger and stronger and stronger, seeking some reaction that I did not understand or care about. In some areas, the jolts weren't so bad, but in others, the surge just kept coming, an unstoppable tide of pain. I never knew how strong the shocks would become or how long they would last.

During the worst part of this test, I felt my entire body jerking as it sought to absorb this foreign strength raping my nervous system. After a while, all I did was lie there and hope for the end. Electrical spasms were the only sign of life.

The EMG is a test designed to measure nerve conduction velocity. The increasing strength of the electric shocks is needed to find the maximum velocity of nerve conduction. What all this meant was this: They finally knew what I had. The test was conclusive. You could find it in a book. There were doctors who specialized in it.

A few weeks later, I was in a different office waiting for yet another doctor. This new doctor was a specialist and was going to tell us about my condition. We waited a long time before he came in.

"Hello, I'm Dr. Horn . . . and you must be Martin." He seemed genuinely happy to see me. He was older and kinder than the other white-clad people. But he still had lots of creepy looking things in his pocket.

"Hi."

My dad asked, "What's the matter with my son?"

"He has Charcot-Marie-Tooth or simply CMT. The names don't mean anything—they were the first doctors to research the condition in the late 1800s."

He went on and told us more about CMT. CMT is an inherited neurological condition that affects the lower legs, feet, and hands. CMT is progressive, meaning that it gets worse over time. It causes nerve cells in the extremities to degenerate. When the nerve cells die, the muscles weaken and die due to loss of stimulation from the affected nerves. CMT is the most common inherited neurological

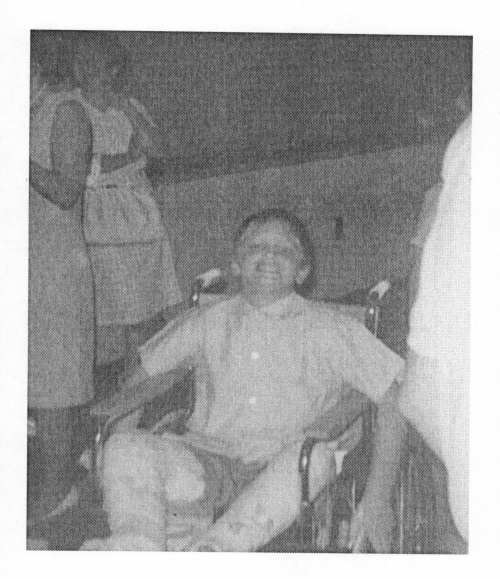

Truckin' around in my wheelchair

disorder and affects about 150,000 Americans.

He finished by saying, "CMT usually manifests itself in adults, which is part of the reason why it was tough to diagnose in your son. There is no treatment for CMT. Martin will have CMT his whole life. But there are surgeries, splints, and activities that can help him along the way."

"Will he ever be able to run?"

"No, but if he keeps his general health up and his weight down, he should be able to keep walking."

My dad seemed shaken by this answer. He swallowed and gathered himself for another question. "Will he be able to drive?"

"Yes, I think so." My dad relaxed.

"What should we do now?"

"There are a few surgical procedures that may help."

I didn't like that answer.

My mom stood in our living room. She had talked with my surgeon, and agreed that it was best to begin the surgeries right away. She asked me if going to the hospital next week would be all right. With all the bravery that I could muster, I said, "Okay." Going to the hospital is scary for anyone, but it's really terrifying for kids. The first day was an endless parade of tests. Vampires, dressed in white, took my blood. Another man pricked some part of my body to check my clotting capability. There were examiners and other tests. By the end of the day, I felt like a pincushion at a quilting bee.

Surgeons like to start early. I was awakened at first light and denied breakfast. I wasn't hungry anyway. I had to have these shots in both of my thighs half way between my knees and waist. Those needles were MASSIVE, about two inches long. They hurt when they went in, and I could feel the stuff inside being pushed into me. They called them "cocktails." After that, things got fuzzy. I was moved to a gurney, wheeled to a preparation area, wheeled again into the operating room. Someone gave me the gas and asked me to count backwards from 100. I don't think I got past 96.

Two times during grammar school I went under the knife. The first operation was to fuse my ankles. Because there is little or no muscle in the feet and calves of people with CMT, fine control of the feet is not possible. Surgeons had learned to restrict motion of the foot by fusing the many smaller foot bones into a few. The second operation was to lengthen my Achilles tendons. My tendons were lengthened because as muscles atrophy, they tend to tighten. The hands and feet of CMT victims can look like claws. Although these surgeries had different goals, they felt the same to me. I don't remember two surgeries, just one.

The haze lifted, and I began to regain consciousness. My parents were there. Both of my legs were covered with shining white casts all the way up my legs. Suspended in the air, my legs looked like the wings of some awkward, clumsy bird. For the next few days, I needed a lot of pain medication and didn't stay awake much. At first, my casts were pure and unstained. But since I was bleeding from my incisions, every time I woke up, I saw a bigger pattern of dark red spreading, like a disease, from where my ankles bled. Nurses would come and trace the stain and mark the time. I imagined that the red stain would grow and cover my whole cast.

I couldn't do much while suspended in traction. But it wasn't all bad. I liked to order my own meals. I really liked that I could get ice cream and juice pretty much whenever I wanted. Some of the nurses were really nice. Most of my energy went into the pursuit of moving my bowels. I understood that I couldn't get out until that happened. So I ate the right food, hoping for a full bedpan. Finally, after ten days in my hospital bed, with the help of a suppository, I accomplished this one goal and got to go home.

Each operation required that I spend three months in a wheelchair. Two memories stand out. My grammar school had these really excellent ramps that were hundreds of yards long. I loved to tear down those ramps. I raced my friends down them and often won. I also remember ripping through the kitchen and scratching the refrigerator after I didn't quite make a tight turn. My mom was not pleased.

After three months, my longer casts were replaced with new ones. In these knee length casts I could walk around with crutches. Then, finally, after another three months, I was freed from my plaster shackles.

The last part of this long ordeal was the removal of my stitches. My dad and I went to the doctor, and my casts were removed. I looked at my now *really* thin legs with a kind of disgust. There was no muscle on my lower leg. Because I had gained a little weight while sitting around so much, I looked like a stork. I turned onto my stomach so that my physician had easy access to the stitches along my Achilles tendon.

And then I just started to cry. I had fought against such pain. I had sat around for so long. I had endured the funny looks, the missed play times. My spirit just couldn't keep it in anymore. I cried, wetting the paper sheet on the examination table. My dad seemed embarrassed, and the doctor didn't get it. I remember him saying that this part of the process was the easiest, that it didn't hurt much at all. That moment was one of the loneliest in my life.

I stopped crying.

I had one last surgery as a freshman in high school, but my doctor only did one foot and I didn't have to use a wheelchair. Having received all that medicine could offer, it was now up to me to do what I could with CMT.

Chapter 2:
Being a Boy

I was born in Marysville, a small city in northern California. My parents moved to an even smaller town in the foothills of the Sierra Nevada when I was in the second grade. Penryn, besides having a funny name, had a population of about 600, a corner grocery, a barber, a gas station, a library, a constable and a grammar school.

We built a house on three acres of land that were surrounded by open space. The open space was the ticket. Empty places are magical to a boy, and I found a few in my wanderings.

Just outside my front door, I followed a dirt road that led up to an asphalt road that served about five families. But to stay on the road was not this boy's intention. If I left the road, a forest of scrub oak and digger pine soared up around me. There were surely rattlesnakes there, maybe even bears. When I dared, I pressed on through the woods until I found a man-made clearing, long abandoned but littered with rusting, brown steel, like the ancient bones of a dinosaur. A hush fell over the whole forest as I moved on. The birds seemed to stop singing, the grasshoppers, once numerous, were now few. The trees around the clearing grew thin, exposing nothing but air beyond their thin veil. I approached those trees carefully, watching my footing, lest the ground should suddenly crumble. Finally, grabbing a sturdy branch for comfort, I leaned forward and gazed DOWN into a deep wound in the earth. I had come to the quarry.

The quarry was a place of mystery. In Penryn's ancient past, men sweated here, carving granite from the hills. Now the quarry resembled a turkey carcass after Thanksgiving, spent and eerie. Dark water filled the quarry to the brim. A foul odor camped around it. I was certain that there was no bottom, only water forever. I knew that some form of terrible life haunted those evil waters—a boa constrictor one day, a monstrous alligator the next. They waited patiently for me to wander too close to their dark kingdom.

Behind our house was a small forest of scrub oaks dotted with granite boulders the size of trucks. If I followed the lay of the land downhill from there, I came to a small creek—the sheer joy of a young boy's heart. I built dams to save imaginary cities from raging flash floods. Waterskippers were chased with the endless energy of youth. But that still wasn't the best place. I had to go upstream to the spring beds that fed this infant creek. I knew just where to go and what faint paths to follow, and came to the Buckeye Grove.

The grove was a place of wonder. Buckeye trees are common in the foothills of the Sierra, but this was different. It seemed as if these buckeye trees had been planted in a tight group and as they grew, someone pushed the main branches outward, like the spokes of a bike radiating from the hub. I knew that Indians had done this. There were many branches to climb and hang from as the buckeye canopy protected me from the world outside.

The fruit of the buckeye tree was also a wonderful gift. When newly ripe, the buckeye fruit sits comfortably in a boy's hand and is the perfect size and weight for throwing. Even better, when the inside rots out, you can wedge a firecracker inside it, light the fuse and throw. Not only do you get the most satisfying POP from the cracker, but the disintegrating buckeye fruit produced a most excellent shrapnel effect. Oh, the foes that were vanquished by my secret weapon!

When hunger would strike me, blackberry bushes surrounded the grove. In season, the best, biggest, juiciest blackberries hung from deep within these bushes. I could often see them hanging, full, ready to be picked about a foot or so inside. But I had seen the spiders that lurked in those bushes. They were hairy and brown, with pulsing fangs. They guarded the choicest of berries. Their multiple eyes were always watching. But when I was hungry, I took the risk. Those berries, plucked from danger, stained my fingers and my mouth a bright purple.

So, when I could have been sitting around, I was outside. Granted, I did watch a lot of TV. I did sit around a lot. But there was something to being outside that moved me. Something that drew me—even when I was slow—even when I fell. Even when the other kids always got there first.

Kids can be cruel. And they were from time to time. I was tripped a lot and given a variety of descriptive nicknames. But my memories of dealing with CMT as a child are mostly filled with astonishing acts of kindness and understanding from my friends and my school.

I obviously could not do a lot of things that other kids could. I couldn't run or stand on my toes. My balance was wretched. I was overweight from all the time spent sitting in wheelchairs and watching TV. These things all conspired against me in PE class. PE met outside, where we did basic exercises on the blacktop. I did okay there. But PE finished up with running a few laps around the grassy football field in the middle of the playground. I simply couldn't do it. I could walk and walk a little faster, but top speed was not even a trot. I do recall a few wisecracks shot at me as my classmates sped past me, resenting the fact that they had to run and I got by with walking. Most kids finished lots of laps before I finished one. But as they completed their required laps, some would always stop and walk with me the last portion of the way. This touched something deep in me. I often told my parents that kids waited for me. They stopped so that I wouldn't always finish last.

In competitive sports, life got a little tougher. Penryn Elementary School was a small school and our coaches needed all the help they could get, even if help had to come from me. Believe it or not, I played basketball for the Penryn Panthers.

My father set up a basketball hoop mounted on a piece of plywood, rooted in the ground with an old pipe. As I was tall for my age and couldn't move much, he saw the center position as my only hope. He worked with me on my hook shot and free throws. He taught me how to use my body to block out and rebound. I could shoot a little, so I kept shooting and shooting and shooting.

In a school with only about 20 boys in each class and fifteen who couldn't shoot a basket to save their souls, I made the team. Now since I could shoot, but not run, my coach had the team feed me the ball. Our point guard, Dacher, his long blond hair barely restrained by his red, white and blue headband, pushed the ball up court. He faked a pass to the forward and bounce-passed to me for a hook shot. But I could only walk/trot down the basketball court two or three times before I could go no further. Then I stayed down by our basket and the team threw me the ball after a rebound or on a quick inbound pass. I scored four to eight points a game doing this.

It was embarrassing, though. My uniform was too small and it had a hole in the crotch. I was fat, and my stomach bulged over my skintight trunks. The worst thing was my stork legs prominently displayed below the shorts. I felt really uncomfortable, but I wanted to play.

As fortunate as I was in my childhood, there were still problems. I learned fast to avoid fights. I lost badly in my first battles. My adversaries went for my legs and knocked me down. CMT robbed me of any balance or maneuverability. Once on the ground, like a beached whale, I was easy pickings. Even smaller kids could beat me up by taking me down. In the Darwinian world of young boys, I realized that I needed a new strategy or I was going to be in fights all the time. Little kids loved to fight big kids—so long as they knew they could win. So I got very good at keeping myself out of fights.

This worked for me until high school, where I met Steve. There are some kids who are just mean. They see other kids as oysters. They seek the weak spot in the shell. They find it and poke, prod, pick and tug until that shell is cracked and a child's inner life is revealed. Then, with a ravenous appetite, they tear into that tender flesh, scraping for the pearl—the soul. The meanest of these kids seem to wear warrior necklaces made of such priceless pearls. Steve was such a one to me.

While a freshman, I went through my final surgery. Then I joined the gimp PE class—a small group of kids with problems that kept us from regular PE. On the first day of this class, I met Steve, and from the beginning he hated me.

Steve had been cruising out with some of his friends and ended up with a broken arm when they couldn't quite make a turn and rolled their car. Every day Steve cooked up some new way to harass me. Sometimes, he would simply mouth every possible derogatory name a derelict teenager can think of right straight at me. He tripped me more times than I could count. I was "bumped" during our sessions constantly. He rallied the other kids to take potshots at my skinny legs. Though his assault was endless, our teacher never saw him. He was kind when she was watching. Outside of class, he always waited for me and continued his barrage of insults and petty physical attacks. I got pushed into my locker, had my books knocked away and was tripped in the hallways.

One or two of these things would not have done much, but as he pursued them day after day, I started to hate him. I was scared to be at school. Then, I started to get mad. We were outside, on some kind of field, when Steve began his patient, crafty attacks, and I just lost it. With as much power as I could muster, I kicked Steve in the shins. My revenge, however, was not to be sweet. I missed his leg, only grazing his calf. Our teacher had turned to speak to us and saw me kick Steve for no apparent reason. As she ran to Steve's aid and read me the riot act, I fought back bitter tears; it was so unfair. As Steve walked away, he let me see the joyful smirk on his face.

We moved to Citrus Heights, a suburb of Sacramento, the next year. I gladly went to a new high school.

Yes, that's really me in high school

Chapter 3:
A Song for the Catholics

Pam was beautiful. More than that, she was elegant. The revealing styles of the late '70s got my instant attention, but the way Pam dressed intrigued me—captivated me. She always wore long dresses that accented her shapely figure. Her tasteful earrings framed her cute dimples. Her face glowed when she smiled. Pam and I sang in a madrigal choir together.

Music was a big part of my life. During one of my stints in a wheelchair, my father put a fifteen dollar guitar in my hand. I had nothing else to do, so I took lessons at school and practiced. I liked playing and got pretty good. At least good enough to badger my parents into buying me an electric guitar and amp so that I could jam with my friends. I learned to play the flute so that my band could play Jethro Tull songs. In the naive hope of youth, I was certain that I would be a rock star.

For a reason that eludes me now, I enrolled in choir as a freshman in high school. I had never sung before and didn't have any idea what to expect. I walked into a room that had twice as many girls as guys; this was a good start. The girls also seemed to be pretty excited that I was joining the choir, which I liked even more.

Mrs. Day, the choir director, asked me to talk so she could hear my voice. Before I said much at all, I was proclaimed a bass and directed to sit down with three or four other guys. I had played a little piano, so I knew something about rhythm and could read bass clef, but I was having a hard time with pitch. I kept trying.

One day we were rehearsing a Negro spiritual called, "Soon Ah Will Be Done With De Troubles of De World." At a key point in this song, the basses, all by themselves, had to sing out a bold new phrase—"I want to meet my Jesus." We had blown it many times. I remember the note. We were supposed to come in on A. That A perched on the top line of the bass clef like a predatory bird, ready to swoop down on us. But then came the magic moment—Mrs. Day cued the basses and I went for it, singing out, "I want to meet my Jesus," and I nailed the entrance, carrying the basses right along with me. When we finished the song, there was a burst of applause from the rest of the choir. Mrs. Day exclaimed, "Now, we have a bass section!" As we continued to rehearse the song, I was so primed to nail this part that I forgot to sing the rest.

I enjoyed singing and I even took private lessons for a time. While I didn't have much raw ability and showed little improvement, I had one thing in my favor: I was male. Teenage males don't do choir. Choir isn't cool. Many of the guys who did do choir still had their boy voices and were destined to be tenors. So even though I wasn't very good, I was male and I was a bass. Most of the time that was enough to get me into the best choirs. Being male got me into the madrigal choir.

Madrigal choirs are small—ours had twelve singers, three for each part: soprano, alto, tenor, and bass. This style of singing was popular in England in the 16th and early 17th centuries. Madrigal songs are quite secular, reveling in such themes as wine, tobacco, women, insects, and general partying. As such, these choirs filled the entertainment niche dominated, during my enlightened days of high school, by KISS. I still remember the words to one of the songs titled "Your Shining Eyes." It's in D minor, the saddest of keys, and goes like this: "Your shining eyes and golden hair/Your lily rosed lips most fair./Your other beauties that excel,/Men cannot choose but like them well."

While singing this song, I was often drawn to look secretly and in great detail at Pam. My research left me in full agreement with its sentiment.

There I was, long hair, overalls over a pudgy stomach, looking like I was touring with Lynyrd Skynyrd, becoming more and more infatuated with a smartly dressed, sharp, stunning young woman. We were only yards apart in our rehearsals, but I wasn't at all close to her.

As we prepared for our first concert, a ray of hope shone into my hopeless heart. My new director, Mr. Melton, intended to organize the couples by height. Right then, I knew where this would lead. At six feet, I was easily the tallest of the guys. Pam was also tall. We were assigned together. I was getting closer.

Some of the tenors in our group hung out at the local parish of the Catholic church. Because of this, we were invited to give a concert, and we were happy to do so. I washed my shoulder-length hair, put on my tuxedo, and slipped on my polished black shoes. As I checked myself out in the mirror, I thought that this was what I would look like when I got my first Grammy. I felt good.

When I got to the church, I felt a lot better. Standing there beside Pam was the first time I really appreciated the wonder and beauty of women. I could smell her. As she took my arm, I could feel the heat of her body. I felt powerful and handsome next to her.

At our director's cue, we lined up for our entrance, I blew a note out of a pitch pipe, and we began to sing "Follow Me" for our entrance. As we walked, I enjoyed the descending counterpoint of our song describing how a man wooed his lover to follow him to a secret place. As we walked, arms entwined, a small staircase leading nakedly to the stage came into view. This staircase didn't have a banister. I knew instantly that I would fall. Without calves, stairs are treacherous. I placed my foot on the first step and pushed, barely accomplishing the first step. I placed my foot on the second step, pushed off and fell. I didn't have the strength to walk up a few stairs. I've fallen a lot in my life, but I didn't want to fall then, with Pam. I wanted her to be proud of me and sense my strength. Just the opposite happened. Somehow, Mr. Melton showed up real fast and helped me up the stairs. We never stopped singing.

As I looked out on the audience, I met a number of strange looks. Some faces showed pity; they understood my embarrassment and empathized with me. Others showed confusion; they didn't know what had happened. Still others were angry. I didn't understand this. Then, like a flash, I understood. *They think I'm stoned.*

By this time in my life, I had performed enough to know how to put on a game face and get through—so that is what I did. I gave pitches from a pitch pipe and started the songs. As we left the stage, I took Pam's arm, but I could not meet her eyes. Mr. Melton met me on the way down and helped me so that I did not fall again. I was thankful for this. I didn't know what was going on with Pam. But when we entered the foyer, away from public view, she released my arm abruptly and walked away. She was embarrassed to be with me. I couldn't really blame her.

As vivid as this memory is for me, I can't remember a thing about what happened the rest of that night. Did I go out with some of my friends, like I usually did and watch a movie? Did I go home and cry? Did I get mad and start a fight?

I don't know. I don't remember much. Except this—I was very sad.

Chapter 4:
Rite of Passage

"Martin, before you graduate, you have to experience something very different." When my friend Don said this I was intrigued. But what did it mean? Would I be taken to an exotic brothel? Was this some kind of drug? With Don, you could never be really sure.

As freshmen, Don and I sat next to each other in math class. We were drawn together. We often talked long into the night, speaking of such things as art, drugs, religion, literature and education with the passion of youth. We listened to music all the time. We enjoyed variety and stacked records like Jethro Tull's "Aqualung," Gustav Mahler's "Second Symphony" and Dueling Banjos on our stereos. Don walked closer to the edge of life than I did. He took more chances. He was fiendishly handsome and, when he grew a mustache, looked a little like Clark Gable. He liked to wear hats.

I didn't know what sort of experience he had in mind until he gathered our friends John and Damon, loaded some backpacks, some trash bags and a shovel into my truck, and told me to drive to a small foothill nature preserve called Camp Far West Lake. Don wanted me to experience these hills while carrying a pack.

I parked the truck and Don filled black garbage bags with dirt. He placed the bags inside each pack to simulate the weight a backpacker carries. At this time, I had lived in the suburbs for three years, I had CMT and I was seriously overweight. But these frivolous details were lost on Don. He showed me how to put on a pack and how to adjust the straps. Then my friends just took off. There wasn't a trail. I tried to follow and immediately fell down. I got up, bloodied at the knees, and tried again. After a few steps I found a branch to use as a hiking staff. By now they were about 50 yards ahead and had stopped to wait. I slowly caught up to them and then, like deer bounding through an open meadow, they took off again. They got ahead. They waited. I caught up. They took off. Most of the day went like that.

At one point, deep within the shady canyon of a seasonal creek, we took a break. I shrugged off my pack and sat down, happy to be motionless. My feet hurt. But the guys were restless. They walked around in tight circles, like dogs searching for a place to rest. Finally Don looked up the steep side of the canyon and grinned at John, saying, "Race you to the top."

John feigned disinterest and then bolted. Don quickly followed and they scurried straight up that canyon wall on all fours leaving behind a cloud of dust and oak leaves. As I sat and witnessed such seemingly superhuman power at work, one thing was clear: *I do not belong here.*

Yet, despite this realization, I liked being there. The hills were beautiful. Cool breezes danced with bees and small streams filled every gully. For a few months, between February and April, the Sierran foothills were painted with the deep green of Johnson grass mixed with colorful splashes of wildflowers. All day California poppies had smiled at me; their golden bowls full of sunlight. During other rest breaks, I enjoyed the blue sky, tasted the fine air and watched the hills awaken to spring.

I walked no more than two miles that day. We camped by the truck that night and cooked steaks over a fire. I was hungry, but the steaks were cooked so badly, I didn't eat. My arms were covered with cuts and bruises from scraping against trees and crashing through bushes. My head hurt. When I took off my boots to go to bed, my socks were stained red with blood. My boots did not fit well, my toes jammed up, and unkept toenails gouged out the tender sides of neighboring toes. Blood—some fresh and some dirtied from numerous falls—covered my knees. I could not stand or walk. If I had muscles that could hurt, they did. I saw headlights guiding a truck out of the preserve on a nearby road. I longed to be in that truck, going home to normal food and my soft bed.

Don, however, had much more in mind than a day trip to Camp Far West Lake. He had planned a trip to go backpacking for twelve days in Yosemite National Park during the summer and wanted us all to go. Would we come along?

Part of me wanted to walk away from these hills and never see them again. I was humiliated, bruised, bleeding, and filthy. I felt out of place. Why, in heaven's name, would I willingly do this again? I'd experienced the hills; fine, let's go home.

Part of me wanted to explore. Something deep was planted that day; something that refused to die. I felt connected in the woods. I felt free among the trees. I felt challenged. I didn't feel these things in the suburbs. The pull of adventure was strong.

Of the many choices I've made in my life, few have been so evenly balanced. Perhaps if I'd fallen once more or walked another half mile, I'd have washed my hands of hiking and gone home. Or maybe if the sky hadn't been so painfully blue, I might have just let adventure go. Who knows? I do know that, as I stared into the fire, battles were waged. *Stay home! Go! Forget it! Take the chance!* Hours later, the scales tipped toward the high places—I would go to Yosemite.

Graduation came and went. During the weekends, I tried to walk a little along the shoreline trail at nearby Folsom Lake. I had to walk a mile or two to get past the beach party crowd, but after that I had the whole blue lake to myself. Sometimes I drove back to Camp Far West Lake. I began to sense the changing of seasons—green swaying grass gave way to brown crackling stalks.

Don's plan was to start high in the Sierra at Tuolumne Meadows and hike down toward Yosemite Valley, following the Merced River. Don took me to an army surplus store, where I bought my own pack and a sleeping bag. He picked up a new knife and cut himself almost immediately.

When the day for the trip came, eight of us, loaded with gear, crammed into an old family station wagon. Damon and John came along again. Damon was interested in photography. John played the saxophone in my rock band. John's father was our driver. Two of John's brothers and one sister came along for the ride. As we left the Sacramento area, we headed south on Highway 99, an unnaturally straight highway bisecting California's Great Central Valley. We sputtered past small towns with small names like Galt and Lodi, escorted by endless tracts of farmland.

With the Coast range to our right and the Sierra to our left, we turned east onto Highway 120 at Manteca. Just outside of this overgrown farming community, the foothills began, like the last surges of an ocean wave. I'd lived in the foothills, so this was familiar—the dry, brown grass straining in the wind. After driving by a man-made lake dotted with houseboats, we were confronted with the Priest Grade. Maybe it was named this because people felt like they needed a blessing before they started up or down. The Old Priest Grade was steep and thin. The New Priest Grade was a moderate ascent on a curvy road. Both offered stellar views of drop-offs of several hundred feet. John's father thought that prudence was best and opted for the New. But even being prudent didn't help us. Our old station wagon broke down half way up and we had to be towed to nearby Groveland. John's dad forked over 400 dollars to have an axle repaired. I spent my first night "backpacking" asleep in a junkyard behind a service station. A stray dog licked Damon's face as he slept.

We moved on the next day, and everything changed. Having gained a few thousand feet, the oaks gave way to pines, the air grew sweeter, and the sky a shade bluer. Now we were in the real mountains. Like a roller coaster, we drove up and down canyons and ridges, gaining altitude a bit at a time.

At a bend in the road, with no special view, we stopped to pay our entrance fee for Yosemite National Park. What I saw was making me really nervous. Rolling, pine-forested mountains gave way to thrusting, sharp granite peaks. Gently flowing creeks transformed into raging, churning torrents of water—spitting and fussing, like rabid dogs. Though it was summer, patches of snow still clung to the land. And still we climbed. My friends stared out of their windows, grinning with anticipation; I was terrified. There was no way I was going to walk through this. I almost quit right there, before I even got out of the car.

With a final short descent, we arrived in Tuolumne Meadows. One of the largest meadows in the Sierra, it is surrounded by countless peaks and domes, each sculpted by glaciers. The sparkling Tuolumne River meanders through the meadow in a slow, carefree way. We parked our wagon, got our packs out and said goodbye.

With staff in hand, pack on back, fear in mind, and anticipation in my heart, I took my first steps in Yosemite as a backpacker. We didn't get far the first day—maybe four or five miles. The drive from Groveland had taken some time. The thin air at 9,000 feet forced us to take plenty of breaks. And, of course, I was very slow. We camped a few miles before Tuolumne Pass by a small creeklet. Don, John, and Damon cooked and cleaned.

I was happy. I had walked for one day. My hike had been a feast of revelation. At every turn, some new flower popped into view. As ridges were climbed, whole new mountain ranges canvassed the skies. Small brooks and streams were everywhere—coursing over granite and lounging through meadows. Everything was so clear.

Sleeping arrangements were made and, last of all, our food was bear-bagged. Yes, there were bears here. To keep them from enjoying our tasty morsels, we counterbalanced two bags over a high tree branch.

I didn't sleep well that night. I woke up about fifteen times, gazing into the eerie blackness for bears, marauders, and whatever else I could imagine. At first light, I finally slept for a few hours without waking.

Morning was difficult. I was sore, and the pancakes didn't come out too well. I was not looking forward to walking.

Don shouted, "Hey, check this out!" I turned to see a black bear strolling into camp and I just freaked. The pain, the lack of sleep and the sheer terror of being ten yards away from an animal that could easily kill me surged up in an unstoppable wail—"Leave everything! Let's get out of here! I'm heading back to Tuolumne!"

The rest of the guys didn't pay attention to me. Damon took some pictures. They enjoyed watching the bear for a few moments and then grabbed some pots and pans. Using spoons as drumsticks, they beat the pans and howled like dogs to scare the bear away. This cacophony scared me and it certainly scared the bear. He left. I stayed.

Shortly afterward, my cronies took great delight in sharing this classic Boy Scout joke: "A bear comes into a camp with two campers. One camper hurries to put his tennis shoes on. The other camper says, 'What are you doing? You can't outrun a bear.' The first camper says, 'I'm not trying to outrun the bear; I'm trying to outrun you!'"

I was going to be bear-fodder. I knew it.

Our day's goal was Merced Lake. First, we had to finish Tuolumne Pass, the divide between the watersheds of Yosemite's two main rivers—the Tuolumne and the Merced. Tuolumne Pass is a pudgy sort of pass. Rain that falls on the top of this wide pass has to think for a while before deciding on a destiny. We oozed over the top rather than climbed it.

Second, we began the descent to Merced Lake. It is counterintuitive, but it is true that walking down is much more damaging than walking up. The only things you can really hurt going uphill are your muscles, which will come around after a break. But the jarring and pounding of walking downhill can cause blisters, toe-jamming, and injurious falls. I managed all of these on the granite staircases leading down to Merced Lake. The combined weight of my body and my pack rammed my toes into my boots with each descending step. My toes were being crushed.

By the time I got to camp, I was useless. I couldn't help with the chores. I just sat and watched, nursing my pain as night came to the mountains.

Due to sheer fatigue and no visits from any bears, I slept better.

The goal for Day 3 was the junction with the Half Dome trail above Little Yosemite Valley. I walked that day in a fog of pain and fatigue, probably making about one mile an hour.

But I could still feel and see a little through the ordeal. Our trail ran beside the Merced River. Her waters sprang out of Merced Lake like a sprinter at the sound of the gun. The Merced's full-throated song was strong and vibrant, loudly echoing through the canyon. The river ran white with foam as it churned over granite so clean and smooth it appeared mirror-like. Above the canyon rim, domes and peaks escorted the Merced downward with dignity and majesty. Though it was a pitched battle, Yosemite's beauty bested my pain.

At a forested trail junction, I laid my pack down to make camp in even worse shape than the night before—if that was possible. My feet were a composite of bleeding toes, broken blisters and moleskin. If a bear was going to eat me, he could start with my feet; they were already half-chewed anyway. I was happy to hear that Day 4 would be a rest day for me. The other guys were going to climb Half Dome. I had no desire to do so. Once again, too tired to help or talk long into the night by firelight, I slept.

Mr. Bruin came back with a vengeance. The sounds of breaking branches and scratching claws pulled me from a deep sleep. I found my glasses and through the gray moonlight saw a large, deeply black spot climbing the tree where our food stores were bagged. We banged pots and howled, but the tree was too far away and yelling didn't scare the bear. Finally, trusting in our bear bags, we tried to go back to sleep. But the bear's industry in trying to get to those bags was considerable. There were grunts, slashes, jumps and pops in annoying, irregular patterns. I was scared. I could not sleep. Then, after what seemed to be hours, the bear climbed down. I put my head down to sleep. But just before I let myself go, I checked camp once more. The bear had silently entered camp and was only a few feet away from me. He was sniffing my bag down by my feet. *He smells the blood!* I was too scared to cry out to my friends. So I kept as still as I could, while my heart went bonkers, pumping blood and energy throughout my body. He moved to check out my pack. He peered into each open pocket, hoping for a piece of candy. Then he came back and sniffed my feet. He stayed within a few yards of me for about ten minutes, grunting, searching. Then a strange thing happened. My nervous system couldn't keep up this accelerated state. My heart slowed down, my muscles relaxed. I got tired of being scared. Then, in an insane twist of logic, I reasoned: *I can't run; I can't fight; I'm totally exhausted; if he wants to eat me, he will; I might as well sleep.* So I took one more look at my omnivorous assailant and fell asleep.

The next morning, I still had my feet. The bags hung proudly from the bear tree, swaying in a gentle morning breeze. The score after three days: Humans 2, Bears 0.

I spent Day 4 practicing the art of stationary living. Before the guys took off for Half Dome, I filled my canteen, got a book, moved my pack to where I could reach it without standing and sat down to stay. I watched the sun move through its leisurely course and walked less than a few hundred feet. This was hard to do, but I managed. I shared the evening fire with my friends, who told me glorious tales of rock and sky and their ascent of Half Dome. Day 4 was a long but pleasant day.

Day 5 was not good. I shouldered my pack and began the final descent into Yosemite Valley. From our junction camp, the trail was soft, matted by pine needles on a bed of sand and loose dirt, and the hike went well as far as Little Yosemite Valley. Then, for a mile or so, the trail was flat as it worked its way closer to the Merced River. This gentle tread's whole personality then changed in a few yards. The trail broke out onto bare granite at a bridge over the Merced a few yards from Nevada Falls. Here, the trail needed three and a half miles of switchbacks to get down several thousand feet of elevation to

41

Yosemite's floor. This made the descent into Merced Lake look like a walk in the suburbs. To add insult to injury, the surface of the trail was paved. No longer was there a cushy blanket under my feet. Now there was unyielding, hot, black asphalt.

Somehow I stumbled down, taking strides so small I advanced by inches. I know wondrous views passed by me, but I don't remember them. I watched my feet. After passing Vernal Falls, a mere mile or so from the valley floor, more and more day hikers were on the trail. They looked with sad eyes at a young, overweight man, wincing with pain at every small step—a young man whose fatigue-filled eyes could not even see the beauty surrounding him.

We boarded a shuttle at the Happy Isles Trail Center—I didn't feel really happy just then. As we camped at the Muir Camp—an overflow campground for backcountry hikers—we discussed the rest of the trail. I knew that I couldn't go back into the woods for the second half of the trail. At daybreak, I called my father from Yosemite Village and asked him to come to get me. I had drunk the full cup of Don's graduation gift. They finished the trail without me.

The rest of the summer passed. Fall came and we all went back to school. I continued going to Folsom Lake and Camp Far West Lake as often as I could. That winter, for Christmas break, Don and I went camping at Yosemite. This trip was awful. Our plan to sleep in the truck with a ground cloth over us as a tent failed miserably. We spent one night sleeping in the public bathroom in order to get out of the snow. The smell was horrible, but it was warm.

One thing of note did happen. We stopped by Yosemite Village Visitor's Center to look at books—which was really an excuse to be warm and dry for a while. As Don browsed, he said, "This looks interesting." He took a book off the shelf to show me the cover. I saw a wild Sierran scene. Mountains shot for the sky; a lake snuggled beneath; a trail ran gracefully through it. The title was clear: *The Pacific Crest Trail: Volume 1, California*. In a moment, so much was understood—there was a trail that ran from Mexico to Oregon. And in the blink of an eye, as only friends can do, we both knew that we would walk this trail.

And so, after carrying a backpack for about six days, overweight and weakened by CMT, I decided to walk all the way through California. This made complete sense at the time.

Part 2:
First Ascent

Chapter 5:
Death and Dreams

Dreams percolate, slowly changing the color of life. My life certainly needed some changing. Many things had brought Don and me together. We shared an interest in the humanities—he was an artist, I was a musician. We shared a love for the wilderness. But what brought us together at this point was much darker: We both had deeply troubled mothers.

Don rarely talked about his mom. I learned in fragments that she was insane and was institutionalized somewhere. His parents divorced and his dad remarried and was living with his new wife in a nearby suburb. After he graduated from high school, Don came to live with me at my house.

My own mother does not appear much in my life. While I can remember hundreds of times when my dad played Monopoly, basketball, or ping-pong with me, I can't think of a single time when my mom did. She cleaned the house, cooked our meals, and washed our clothes, but she wasn't there. The few pictures that I have of my mom reveal sadness. I can remember her face, but I can't see her smile.

When we moved to Citrus Heights, her depression deepened with each passing year. She lost weight and her presence became almost spectral.

Nothing brought her joy. When my sister married a man who was head-over-heels in love with her, my mom didn't like the match. When my brother was accepted into West Point, she wished he was at a different school. She was annoyed that I played in a rock band. Then, she didn't even care about such things.

When my dad and I had about given up hope, she started to fight.

She cleaned the garage until the concrete gleamed and every spider web was banished. She took an unusual interest in the safety of our possessions and demanded that we park the truck in the garage at night and not out on the driveway. She changed the way we stored our stuff and moved some sleeping bags to the garage. Dad and I were encouraged.

She continued to rally. She even asked us to take her to the Ice Capades in downtown Sacramento. She never asked to go out. So even though Dad had just worked a graveyard shift, he cut short his sleep and gladly drove the three of us downtown to watch the show. A few times my mom tried to smile.

Mom talked about the show when we got home and since she rarely spoke, we stayed up and talked with her. When Dad went to sleep, he was dead tired. I slept soundly.

I awoke to my father's screaming voice:

"Ooohhhh nooooo . . . Martin, she's dead . . . come back . . . Nooo! . . . Martin, call the ambulance . . . now!" I have never heard such raw, overwhelming pain in a human voice.

My father's cries came through my bedroom window. I jumped up and looked out front. My lifeless mother was lying on the ground in my front lawn. My dad bent over her, wailing and stroking her hand, pleading for her to come back. I called for an ambulance and went to my father. I gently put my hand on his shoulder and said, "The ambulance is coming. Dad, she's dead."

The night before, she waited until we were both asleep. She left my father's side, walked past my room, and went to the garage. She started the truck, got out a sleeping bag and burrowed deep within it. She wrapped the opening of the bag around the exhaust pipe and went to sleep.

My mother's suicide had a strange effect on me. In life, my mother was barely present. She didn't take up much space. In death, she filled the house. Every time I started the truck—she was there. When I walked on the sidewalk across the front lawn—she was there. Once, late at night, after I had parked the truck in the garage, I heard something fall in the dark and fled in terror. I ran to Don's room and shrieked, "She's still in the garage!"

My friends and family thought that I handled her death well. They were wrong. I didn't handle it at all. I had no mentors to lead me in the ways of death. My brother and sister came home for a time, but they soon left. After a time, Dad remarried and moved in with his new wife. And so in this sad way, Don and I came to live together.

After such pain, Don and I needed to breathe clean air. I needed to leave the smell of death for the fragrance of life. As the summer of 1980 drew near, the call of Yosemite beckoned. We were ready for more—lots more. We planned a 30-day trip that would circle the entire park. I intended to be ready.

My feet had caused me a lot of pain. My left foot was almost two sizes bigger than my right. My ankles were really thin and my toes were really wide. Store-bought boots were not working for me. I always got really bad blisters in large quantities. I explained my problem to my doctor, who suggested a custom bootmaker. He made exotic boots, like rattlesnake skin boots with sequins for wealthy cowboys, as well as sturdy boots for hikers.

I drove to his shop in Fresno—more than three hours south of Sacramento. Photos of elaborately dressed cowboys, guitar players and singers covered the walls, each one featuring wildly extravagant boots. After I introduced myself and explained my situation, he got to work. As he measured both of my feet in every possible way, he asked me, "So, what do you want in a boot?"

I had thought about this for a long time. "I need a wide toe box. I get blisters really badly and I need space for my toes."

He nodded.

"I also want a lot of ankle support. I'm planning on some pretty hard hiking and want all the help I can get."

"Okay."

"I'm also going to hike in the snow. I'd like a boot that will keep my feet dry."

He got up from his measurements and said, "I make a boot for firefighters that is really sturdy. Made from the toughest materials. I'll widen the toe box and make the boot an inch higher for ankle support. I don't use a lot of pieces on this boot, so there is very little stitching. I'll seamseal the stitches and if you use boot wax and keep the leather supple, your feet should stay pretty dry. Of course, each boot will be form-fitted to the precise shape of your feet. I don't think you'll get blisters if you break them in."

Wow, that sounded good. Blisterless hiking. It also sounded

manly to have a boot that was designed for firefighters.

"Okay, how much?"

He thought for a moment, "Six hundred even."

After I picked my jaw off the floor—this was a ton of money to me—I agreed and made a date to pick them up in time to break them in before the hike.

We had hoped to reunite the group from out last hike, but my friend John, who was a Mormon, had left for St. Martin's Island on some mission. We thought John's summer plans were kind of quirky. Serving the Lord seemed to imply poverty and want, but John got to spend the year in the Caribbean—not bad! This left Don, Damon and me. In July, armed with my freshly waxed boots, we loaded everything into my truck to follow the same roads we did the year before—Sacramento to Yosemite. We parked at White Wolf, a small camp located about halfway between Yosemite Valley and Tuolumne Meadows.

First impressions were not good. Summer rain hardly ever graces the Sierra, but it was coming down in buckets. We sat on the porch of the White Wolf lodge and drank coffee to warm our insides. Around us, we could see patches of snow in the shade. The high trails would not be clear. Day 1 passed in the campground, close to the shelter of the lodge.

On Day 2, we walked south out of White Wolf, wet and cold, filled with dreams of high places and lush meadows. On Day 30, a month later, we walked into White Wolf, hot and tired, filled with memories of rock, air, and sun.

The last few miles into White Wolf follow a flat jeep trail through simple forest. The walking was easy, so I had time to reflect on the past month. *Why did I do this? Why did I go through so much pain and spend so much money for boots? Why did I go to places where mosquitoes constantly plagued me? Why did I want to sleep with bears?*

There were answers. Walking is very satisfying. Most of us don't feel like we really do anything from day to day. We go to work; we move some paper or lift a bale and then go to sleep. But do we *accomplish* anything? A day backpacking is a simple, beautiful thing—move from point A to point B. That's all. And when you ford the creeks, walk the miles, and finish your day at point B, there is satisfaction in knowing that you did something with your day.

Another reason that I backpacked was because I could. I couldn't run or do anything that required any real balance or grace. But backpacking is a lumbering sort of activity. I could lumber. Everyone walks slowly with a pack. Everyone feels a little gimpy when they get to camp. Whenever I was with a group of ten or so packers, there was always someone who had bad blisters or an ill-fitting pack who hobbled around worse than I did.

I craved the challenge. Nothing I had ever done before required more of me than backpacking. I had to give *everything* to hike. Every pass, every creek ford, every snow bank took every ounce of strength that I could force from my weakened body. I loved it.

But these things don't tell the real story. The real reason that I came to the Sierra was this—I had fallen in love. The symphony I heard in the meadows—the percussive "tick" of the blackbird, the lyrical call of the chickadee, woven together by the sound of rustling grass—was a sweeter sound than a Mahler adagio. The pure taste of water freed from a virgin snowbank satisfied more than the costliest bottled drink. The slow company of friends sharing an evening campfire was better than the rush of urban life.

I learned that my new lover was hard, but always good. She did not tease. If you pursued her, she would reveal her sweetest secrets and uncover her hidden places. Yes, she would grant those who came to her by car a measured beauty. There were wonderful things to be seen from the road. Her lesser suitors would jump out of their autos, snapping pictures, trying to save memories before having them, and hurry on. But what could be seen from a road is more enticing than revealing—like a shapely woman whose fleshly beauty cannot be hidden by modest garments but is made even more alluring. From the roadside her eyes would invite and challenge: "Will you pursue me?" I did. And though my pursuit cost me a lot—pain, humiliation, hunger and sleepless nights—she was good.

I had spent a whole morning strolling down the Yosemite Falls Trail in the constant company of the highest waterfall in the northern hemisphere. The waters of Yosemite Creek burst out over the walls of Yosemite Valley like a bull at a rodeo. And then they fall and fall and fall and fall until crashing into a series of swirling, cauldron-like cascades, only to be thrown once more over the Lower Falls. Here, as

49

if spent by the adventure, the waters slow into a mellow creek. At times I would grow weary in the descent, but then the wind would pull just right and her mists would caress my face. Refreshed, I went on.

I had spent a few days high in the Clark Range, well above the tree line. In this wild place, I first tasted the true High Sierra—a land of stark and wild contrast. Black, brooding mountains clothed with bright, white snow. Hard, jagged rock and dainty flowers—one of them called pussypaws because of its gentle form. Clear blue skies and dark, billowing thunderstorms. Piercing sunlight and star-filled nights. The Milky Way splashed across the star-stained sky.

I had probed well into northern Yosemite, going to places and over passes that only a few eyes see every year. I camped by Sawtooth Ridge and sat, entranced, as alpenglow set this fearsome ridge on fire.

And now I sat on the open tailgate of my truck. I had spent a month in the woods. Sure, there were many days when I only walked three or four miles. I took a lot of rest days. But walking the length of California was now a real possibility.

Dreams percolate. I went back to Sacramento, but I couldn't get back into the going-to-school-working-part-time groove. Most weekends I threw whatever food I could find into my pack, scrounged money for gas and set out for a fast backpacking trip to Yosemite or Point Reyes National Seashore.

My grades were falling.

My continued attempts to be a rock star failed dismally. My band was bad. Audiences didn't like us. My lead guitar solos sounded like Neil Young on a bad day.

I was working as a night cleaner at a fast-food place. I asked for more and more time off to hike. One morning, after working all night, I showed up for Music Theory II while still wearing my greasy uniform. I fell asleep in class. Did I snore in pitch? In this state of increasing disarray, Don once more changed my life with a simple sentence.

Chapter 6:
Moving to the Big Y

"I'm going to get a job in Yosemite and move there." Don's intention was simply to tell me his plan. I don't think he anticipated my response. My life was losing focus, and I needed vision. Don's plan sounded like a good one for me. I would not be a rock star, but I would walk through California. If I was going to hike 1,700 miles in one summer, I needed to train—and what better place to train than Yosemite?

So once again, I followed Don. Even though I was scheduled to work, and was taking courses in college, I got up at 4:30 the next morning, tossed some clothes in my backpack and started the three-and-a-half hour drive to Yosemite Valley. At the Employment Center, I was quickly hired as a roomskeeper. I was assigned a tent cabin in an employee tenttown and told to report to Housekeeping at the Ahwahnee Hotel. I dropped off my few possessions and made my way to the upper-crusty realm of the Ahwahnee, Yosemite's classiest, or at least most expensive, hotel.

I gave my employment verification to the assistant manager named Alan. He leaned back in his squeaky chair and looked at me through alcohol-dazed eyes. He had a butch haircut. Everything about him—from his cold stare to the strength oozing from his body—gave me chills. He crooned in an accent I couldn't quite place.

"Do you know what a roomskeeper is?"

At times my rapier wit saves the day. I said, "Someone who keeps rooms."

He didn't even smirk, not a muscle moved. He continued to hold my eyes with his own and said, "A roomskeeper is a maid. That's what you are. You're a maid."

51

Okay, I was a maid. But I was a maid who lived in Yosemite. Yosemite Valley is about six miles long and about a mile wide. The valley floor is flat and filled with a meandering river and many streams. Deer browse in meadows and raccoons are as common as dogs. Sheer, solid granite walls shoot up 4,000 feet from the valley. Thanks to Ansel Adams, images of Half Dome and El Capitan are known worldwide. Waterfalls of extraordinary beauty flow over these walls in a constant flurry of mist and cloud. Surrounding Yosemite Valley are hundreds of miles of trail winding through some of the most glorious wilderness on Planet Earth. This was home.

At this point, my tale gets hard to tell. I'd like to say that I discovered a wonder diet for CMT. I ate mountain trout every day, eyes and all, spiced with wild onion harvested from alpine meadows. I'd like to say that CMT was offset by drinking from Fern Spring, the same water that seemed to lengthen the life of Galen Clark, a Yosemite pioneer. He came to the valley to die of cancer and wound up living for many more years. Nothing like that happened. Like so many things in this life, my transformation was so gradual, I didn't even notice. I came to Yosemite in the fall of 1980, a barely average backpacker, and by spring 1982 I was ready to hike through California.

So what did I do? I walked. I walked a lot. I walked to work. I walked to the cafeteria. I walked everywhere. Weekend after weekend, I hit the trails. Slowly, imperceptibly, I earned my spot on the trail.

As I walked, I worked on a style of backpacking built on endurance and wisdom. Most young hikers can walk about three miles an hour, carry 50-pound packs and cover ten to fifteen miles a day without too much trouble. They can stay up late, get up even later, then pop onto the trail and make their camps with lightning speed. I could not do this. I realized that if I was going to cover big miles, I would have to walk for a long time each day. If I walked a rather slow two miles an hour, but walked for eight long hours, I could still cover a respectable sixteen miles. Yosemite was the perfect place to learn endurance.

An ancient Greek athlete wanted to compete with the discus. He heard that the record for the discus was something like 275 feet and that a discus was made of iron. So he made an iron discus of his own, marked off a field and began to train. His first throws fell woefully short of the record, but he kept trying. Finally, after years of training, he could beat the record and came to the games to compete. As he stepped forward to throw, the judges checked his discus and informed him that an official discus only had an iron edge and was mostly made of wood. His all-iron discus was much too heavy for competition. He received a regulation discus—a much lighter one—and proceeded to break every record with ease. Yosemite Valley was my all-iron discus.

There are flat trails on the valley floor, and they can be walked in a day or two. And then what? Every other major trail in the valley: The Yosemite Falls Trail, the Snow Creek Trail, the John Muir Trail, and the Four-Mile Trail all go straight up. So I went up—at first in small doses, but I kept going further and further every time. I started by just going to Vernal Falls on the John Muir Trail, a short two-mile round trip. Next, I explored the switchbacks leading up to Nevada Falls—a seven-mile round trip. Months later, I explored Little Yosemite Valley. I kept going further until I knocked off Half Dome as a day hike—a seventeen-mile round trip. In my last days at Yosemite, I walked all the way to the summit of Cloud's Rest and back—a 21-mile round trip. One thing worked greatly in my favor: Once you hike somewhere, it doesn't seem so far to hike there again. I began to think that a hike to Nevada Falls or Glacier Point was nothing; I'd been there many times.

I wondered what it would be like to walk 30 miles in one day. I got up early and walked the length of Yosemite Valley to the west and crossed the Merced on the Pohono Bridge. Then I turned around walked back and took the Tenaya Canyon trail as far as I could east. I retraced my steps in a few places and crisscrossed often, and managed to put down 30 miles by dark.

This gave me an idea. I went up to Tuolumne, spent the night at a fellow employee's tent, and set off at first light to walk in one day what had taken me five days on my first backpacking trip. The hike did, in fact, take all day, but it was fabulous. I hit Tuolumne Pass by breakfast and blew past the dreaded granite staircases of Merced Lake by lunch. It was dark when I got back to the valley, but what a way to spend a day!

In addition to these day hikes, I often went for overnight trips on my weekends off. This allowed me to go even farther and continue to develop endurance. At first, I brought up the rear of most of the groups I hiked with, but one pattern began to emerge. Other hikers, not as experienced in walking for ten or more miles a day, started out with great zeal and speed. About an hour or two later, I would catch them resting by the trail. I would stop a moment and say hi, then continue on at my leisurely pace. I had learned that the best speed is the speed you can walk all day. As I went farther and farther into the mountains, it got harder and harder to find partners. Don was assigned to the Yosemite Lodge, and we often had different days off. I began hiking alone. With nothing else to do but walk, I logged big miles.

I also wanted to walk smart. I looked for solutions to problems every time I hiked. Bear-bagging was a pain until I put a partially exposed screw on the bottom of my staff, enabling me to hitch the bag on my staff and gently lift it up.

Creek fords are hard for me. I cannot walk over log bridges, so I learned to crawl over them. When no bridge was available, I put on a pair of scuba booties, and stepped through uneven and sometimes rocky stream bottoms without a snag. I learned to take breaks after creek fords instead of before them. Whatever happened to get wet dried out while I took a break.

I couldn't walk unassisted on snowpack; I needed the "third leg" my staff provided. When I tried to use my staff in the snow, it just pushed right through like a straw through a milkshake. I knew I had to have a solution for this before the PCT. In a gear catalog, I saw an ice ax basket, a small circle of the same material used for snowshoes. When attached to the bottom of an ice ax, this small circle gave the climber far greater surface area on which real support could be found on the snow. I whittled down the bottom of my staff and secured the basket to the already existing screw. Thus empowered, I took my first wary steps on the snow.

I saw a belt pouch in a mountain store. I slid it on the belt strap of my pack and religiously carried three things inside: A cup for quick drinks; a candy supply for quick energy; and my map for quick reference. With this modification, I didn't have to stop and take off my pack to relieve a parched throat, feed a growling stomach or check on whether I was lost or not. I could just keep walking.

I talked to every hiker who would talk to me about the trails they had trodden. Was the bridge shown on the map still there? Were there any good campsites? How about bears? How was the scenery? And when people just looked at me and smiled, I walked there as soon as I could.

I went to ranger talks to learn about flowers, trees and geology. I read books on backpacking and mountaineering. In these pages, I read about the terrible things that can happen to you physically in mountains, like high altitude cardiac pulmonary edema, hypothermia, and hyperthermia. I spent so much time looking at topographic maps and comparing their bewildering lines with actual land forms, that I could "see" what the trail would be like, in fairly clear detail, by simply looking at a good map.

I started carrying less and less gear and walking more and more. The famous naturalist, John Muir had streaked across the Sierras carrying very little—a bedroll, black bread, a cup, and some matches. He even boiled pine needles to brew his tea. I imitated his style. My standard gear load for a weekend trip was this: a cup, a canteen, a sleeping bag, a poncho, a wool shirt and a loaf of peanut butter and jelly sandwiches. With this incredibly light load, the Sierra opened up to me like a flower.

Most of all, I learned from the wilderness. I listened to the sounds of trees as the winds sang through them. I watched as mountain passes came and went. I tasted the clear waters of the Sierras. I watched the skies and gained enough experience to know when to wait out a storm and when to keep going. I felt the wind and made camps so that breezes would help keep the mosquitoes away.

And I just kept walking. I kept one map of Yosemite as a record of my trails. The faint black line of a trail was made bold by a black marker when I had finished it. Gradually, I covered that map with lines until it looked like the face of an aged man.

By the summer of 1981, I was ready for a real test. Tentative plans had been set to start the PCT in spring 1982. I wanted to see how I was doing. I had heard that the southern Sierra along the John Muir Trail was even more glorious than Yosemite. Wanting to see for myself, I set out on a fourteen-day trip to walk from Tuolumne Meadows to Mt. Whitney. I couldn't find anyone who wanted to go so I went by myself. I thought that I would like to hike a long trail alone, since I did enjoy solo weekend trips, but this was not the case. After a few days alone, I found myself walking and camping with other groups—something I had never done before. Due to loneliness and a food shortage, I left the trail at Cedar Grove.

One event does stand out. I was somewhere south of Red's Meadow working my way up one of the Muir Trail's many passes. Way ahead, I spied a solitary man descending on granite switchbacks. Strange, shiny motions followed his gait; it looked like he was wearing aluminum pants. As we drew nearer, I saw that this shimmering came from his metal crutches. Our paths met. Both of his legs were shrunken and limp.

I said, "Hi."

"Hello."

"You have polio." This was not a question.

"Yes, I do."

"Where did you start from?"

"Mt. Whitney. I'll finish up in Yosemite Valley." He was soloing the whole John Muir Trail—a 210-mile trek through the highest, toughest mountains in the Sierra.

Looking at my lean calves, he said, "Something's up with your legs." This was not question.

"I have CMT." I briefly explained what CMT does.

"Hmmm, are you heading for Whitney?"

"Yes," I replied.

Our eyes met and locked. There was no pity or sympathy. There was no shared triumph. But in that moment, one thing was communicated: Despite our physical challenges, we belonged in the mountains.

Chapter 7:
The Battle on the Table

During the winter, Yosemite pretty much shuts down. The high country is blanketed by snow. The valley is transformed from a high-density tourist destination to a lazy, country resort. Employees are laid off; rooms go vacant; restaurants and stores close. One of the stores in Yosemite Village is set up as an employee recreation room. After work, employees could stop by for snacks and pop, play a little pool, read a good book, or play a real game, ping-pong.

While I was trucking around in a wheelchair, my dad looked for ways to keep me active. He bought a sanded piece of plywood and set it up on two sawhorses in our garage. Sometimes we used the space to set up a model racetrack. Most of the time, we played ping-pong. My wheelchair's armrests slid neatly under the board and I could return balls that were hit close to me. My father and brother spent hours hitting little lobs to me so that I could play. I appreciated their effort and I liked the game.

When I got out of my casts, my dad began to work on my defense. By increments, he hit the ball farther and farther away from me, pushing me to reach, pushing me to move so that I could return the ball. Because the field of play is small, I was able to cover most of the table by simply stretching my arms. Playing the edges and little taps right over the net was harder for me. But my father was patient. He kept extending my range, a little at a time. Over the years, I missed thousands of returns. But I got better. My dad also taught me that a lot of ping-pong is played in the head and not on the table.

I began to play against my brother more. It was not unusual for us to come home from school and play ten games before supper. Pat was more ruthless than Dad. He had vicious spins and played a faster game. I learned from Pat how to slam. I missed thousands of slams, but, as time passed, I started to land a few. And when I did, victory was sweet to my soul.

By high school, ping-pong was the only remotely athletic thing that I did. Anywhere I found a table, I played. I used my overweight, clumsy appearance to my benefit. I didn't look like a player, so I didn't strike fear into my opponents—I looked like a pushover. But when game time came, I was ready. So I was delighted to find a rec center with a table in Yosemite. In the winter, the sun goes down early in the valley, so most nights found me there, swinging my paddle.

I found stiffer competition here than I ever had anywhere else. Among the scores of people who played, there were four of us who challenged each other. Two of those guys I could beat when I really wanted to, but one of them I could not. His name was Kelly.

Kelly actually worked in the rec room. He opened the door, took money for snacks, swept the floor, and turned out the lights before locking up. When he didn't have something to do, which was often, he played ping-pong. We played quite a bit, and he won most of our games. The ones that I did win, I didn't think were clean—I thought that he was toying with me. This made me mad.

Our rivalry got a bit more intense when a tournament for all Yosemite employees was announced. I wanted to win that tournament. Those of us who are "challenged," who are "special," get used to losing. I lost in baseball because I couldn't run to first base even after a great hit. I lost in basketball because I couldn't keep up with the fast kids—or any kid for that matter. I lost in races, in fights, in Twister, and in Four Square. And by this time in my life—I WAS SICK OF LOSING! Losing gets into your head. You start to think that you *are* a loser. And even though I had come a long way against CMT, I still *felt* like a loser. If I was going to face a walk through California, I needed to feel like a winner.

To make matters worse, Kelly was arrogant. He disregarded me as an opponent. The little smirks on his face drove me nuts. He was Lord of the Ping-Pong Table. He strutted around the rec room like a rooster in a hen house. He was The Man. Oh, how I wanted to wipe that smirk from his face, but I couldn't figure out how to defeat him.

So I went back to square one and looked again for weaknesses. I went through all the combinations again. I tried a fast game—he hit my slams back, much to my dismay. I tried using a variety of spins—he blew right through them. I tried alternating speeds—no good. I tried deceptive moves to mask direction—he didn't bite. I kept losing, he kept winning, and the tournament kept getting closer.

We were playing a few days before the tournament and I was running out of options. I had a vicious serve. It was deep and fast. My serve was good for a point on most players, most of the time, especially to the backhand. Kelly returned my best stuff with precision and power. This so unnerved me that I hadn't experimented much with my serve. So I tried some things. First, a real hard shot to the forehand—he easily returned it. Second, a real hard shot to the backhand—no problem for Kelly. Then I began to serve more toward the middle of the table—he still got 'em. Then I served as hard as I could right at his belly button. He missed. That was interesting. I did some other things for a few points and then tried the belly serve again. He missed again. This was the exact spot on his body where he changed his paddle position from forehand to backhand or vice versa, and he didn't seem to be able to make returns—two tries, two misses. I didn't want him to figure out a way to return this serve before the tournament—I stopped.

Kelly ran the tournament, so he seeded the players. As an act of false humility, he placed me at the top and himself at the bottom of the chart that guided our battles. We played two-out-of-three game sets in a single elimination format. I worked the games that I played so that they were close, but I won every game. I wanted to get to the finals playing as few games as possible.

I worked my way down. Kelly worked his way up. I finished my semi-final round before Kelly, and the mind games began. I selected a seat that looked away from Kelly's game and pretended to read the paper. I didn't want to appear anxious to play Kelly; I wanted to project casual indifference, a laid-back attitude. I wanted to make Kelly come to me when he was finished. Having vanquished his opponent, Kelly strutted over and said, "Okay, McCorkle, let's get to it." I played the goof; "Oh wow, you made it this far?" Kelly smirked, "Whatever."

As we warmed up, I continued the goof routine, making stupid comments, dropping the ball and looking more unstable on my feet than I really was. Finally, the time came to rally for serve. I NEVER seek to win this rally. It is my way to be as casual as I can be until a game starts, not caring who serves first. Kelly knew this, and so we chitchatted as the gentle rally continued. Then he sent a shot I knew I could cream, and I smashed the ball back to him as hard as I could. The shot hit. Kelly looked surprised by my sudden slam. The ball bounced against the wall and came back to me. I picked it up, picked up my pace, put on my game face, and said, "I want to serve this time." I pointed at his stomach and said, "Every serve is going to come hard and fast right there."

A game of ping-pong is played to 21 points, with each player serving for five points before the serve is changed. Each of these five-point sections is like a mini-game—I sought to win three of the five points, leaving my opponent with only two. Or better yet, take four or five points. When I served, I had a much better chance of winning the first mini-game. I wanted to do that.

I kept my word and drilled five shots right at him. He missed all five. But the game was far from over. Kelly was really good and took four of his five serves, leaving me with a slim lead at 6-4. The game went on that way. I got all of my mini-games with the stomach serve, but Kelly came back on his serves. I feared that he would figure out a way to return the serve before I won. I wanted to start to mix and match serves and try to throw him off. But I didn't. Every serve—the same place, the same result. Toward the end of the game, he began to lose his cool. His anger got the best of him, and he lost control on his serves. I won the game going away.

Kelly grumbled something about needing to go to the john and he left. I sat back down in my chair and read the paper. When he walked up to me, the goof returned. "Did it all come out all right?" I said. He looked at me with utter amazement. His eyes betrayed his inner thoughts, *This idiot just beat me?* I chitchatted during our warm-ups; Kelly didn't say a word. Kelly tried to stay aggressive, but I was just playing around. In our tournament, the loser serves, so we didn't need to rally. Kelly did well on his first five. I continued the goof routine, while serving every serve hard and fast to Kelly's stomach. I praised his good shots. I made philosophical remarks about what a one-ounce ball must feel like as paddles beat it. Kelly was silent, trying to stay focused.

Halfway through the second game, he began to lose his

composure. His serves were wild and his returns spastic. I took the opportunity to begin mixing and matching my serves. After dozens of serves to the same place, I gave the same delivery and shot the ball to his backhand. He didn't even come close. Now I unleashed everything I had—deception, speed, direction—and Kelly became unhinged. I won game two by a sizable margin.

There were no cheers. No one was even watching the game.

Kelly ran outside the rec center to share his grief with the darkness.

I sat down to think.

Last summer, I'd hiked most of the John Muir Trail solo; I'd logged hundreds of miles and climbed quite a few peaks. This winter, I've won an athletic contest for the first time in my life. If there was ever a time to walk 1,700 miles through California, this was it. This was it.

Chapter 8:
Fever

Don and I had the fever. We were dangerously contagious. We began to talk about, plan, and work toward the PCT with an ever-increasing intensity. As the winter passed and the snows began to melt, our vision was infectious. People around us caught the excitement. Some just enjoyed talking with us about our dream, while others dreamed their own dreams of hiking, climbing, and adventure. A few decided to come along. What began as a dream for two young men had grown into an adventure for five people.

My brother signed on. Although he didn't have much experience backpacking, he had just finished his stint in the military and was in good shape. He is the most frugal person I have ever met and was attracted to the idea of such adventure at a great price. I was excited about the chance to hook up with my brother. When we were last at home, we still related as older and younger brothers and not as peers. I liked the idea of a new start.

Jennifer was a fellow employee in Yosemite. She had been a climbing partner with Don. The three of us had also hiked together a fair amount. She was motivated by the challenge of the trail, and her upbeat presence, ready smile, and thirst for adventure would be needed on the trail. She and Don had been lovers the previous year, but we thought we could handle it.

Completing our party of five was Sally. I had known Sally since high school. I met her one day while I was playing the piano in the music room. Her interest in me was intoxicating. She was so very *present*. Her eyes, her body, were so right there. She was captivating and powerfully attractive. Before she left for class, she wrote her address on my arm. I stopped by that address as soon as school was out. I had fallen in lust with Pam; I fell in love with Sally. She was the first woman to have my heart. As is the case in most of these situations, our relationship was as beautiful as it was scarring, as inspiring as it was depressing. In the years that followed—through high school, early college, and Yosemite—our relationship was a roller coaster. We became lovers. At times we seriously contemplated marriage. At other times, we broke up and went our separate ways. After a break-up several months before the trail, so quickly even a courtesan would blush, Don and Sally got together. People told us that this combination would cause problems, but we thought that we could forgive, forget and, quite literally, move on. For better or worse, this was our party.

We also gave thought to how far we wanted to walk. The PCT actually runs from the desert sands of Mexico to the alpine forests of Canada. We thought for a time about trying to walk through California, Oregon, and Washington. To do this, we would have to average about twenty trail miles a day. Only a handful of hikers, called tristaters, accomplish this every year. After much consideration, we decided to take a more leisurely approach and stick to the original plan—California only. With this goal, we only had to walk about ten trail miles a day. The trail through California was 1,700 miles, or 170 days. If we started in mid-April, while there was still water flowing in the desolate reaches of southern California, we could reach Oregon by the end of September, before the snows came.

At first glance, perhaps ten miles a day doesn't sound too adventurous. After all, even at a slow two miles an hour, I could be in camp after only five hours of walking. However, we are speaking here of ten *trail* miles. Trail miles are very different from walking miles. In a hypothetical ten-day stretch, we would plan to cover 100 miles of trail.

But what else happens in a ten-day hike? First of all, it's very easy to get lost on the PCT. Snow covers the trail for miles at a time, and logging operations tear through acres of route. At other times, through lack of use and maintenance, the trail just fades away. Whenever these kinds of things happen, we'd put down miles all over the place searching for the actual PCT. We'll say we needed to walk about five miles "exploring" for every 100 miles of trail. Because the PCT is designed as a crest route—a trail that seeks to ride the tops of the mountains—often there is no room to camp or no water available. So we'd have to hike off the crest for a place to stretch out our bags or get a drink. Add another five miles. Then, of course, we'd have to leave the route altogether to resupply in nearby towns. At times they're right along the way, but usually they are inconveniently located several miles off the trail—as much as ten miles. Lastly, due to injury, sheer exhaustion, or striking beauty, we'd just stop for a day to relax and enjoy the view. Plan to rest at least one day out of ten. We're now up to walking 120 miles in nine days, which is 13 1/3 miles a day. When we figured in the weight we would constantly carry on our backs, 13 1/3 miles was far enough. We wanted to smell the flowers.

And of course, our energies were directed toward food—a favorite subject among us backpackers. We realized right away that trying to feed five people for four and a half months was a huge undertaking. To supply our trail would take lots of money, lots of work, lots of packing, and lots of luck. Jennifer stepped up as trail food planner. For breakfast, she planned fine dishes like seed cereal and brown rice flour pancakes. For lunch, an endless variety of trail mixes and soups. For supper, such dishes as sunflower seed patties and chili sauce, rice curry and buckwheat groats would please our palates. There would be drinks aplenty and tasty desserts. We planned to supplement our supply with fresh vegetables and cheap wine from towns along the way, so she selected fondue mixes as well. She promised us that these recipes would create wonderful, filling meals, full of enticing smells, and, of course, would provide all necessary nutrients. We mapped out four and a half months of breakfasts, lunches, dinners, snacks, and drinks. From this schedule we made a master list of every ingredient needed to prepare these recipes. Armed with this huge and diverse list, we scoured the Sacramento area, purchasing grains by the bagful and Ziplocs by the case. One grocery store, annoyed by our massive wants, sent us to their wholesale supplier. From this wholesaler's bounty, we filled the bed of my truck with sacks of raw foods.

Our purchases came to well over $1,000. I had never written a four-figure check in my life. I had to write real small to make all those numbers and words fit. It was kind of cool. The owner looked at my old, beat-up truck, looked at the check, and said, "Is this a good check?" We had all pooled our money into a checking account for the purpose of buying food. We had the money. I looked straight into his eyes and said, "You bet." He believed me.

We scurried up to the Alpine Air backpacking food factory high in the mountains and bought freeze-dried shrimp and other meats by the pound. We didn't get much for our money—just a few small bags—but at least we had some meat.

We turned Sally's apartment into a factory for the production of backpacking food. We used plastic trash bins to store scores of pounds of oatmeal and other heavily used foodstuffs. Spices, freeze-dried meats and vegetables, grains, nuts, candies, cases of M&Ms, and bags of hot chocolate stacked in neat rows. Then the assembly line kicked in.

We had calculated the number of times each recipe was to be used. One person wrote the recipe name on a label and attached it to a Ziploc bag. Another person prepared the recipe, scooping the listed ingredients from sacks, bags, and cases all over the apartment. A final person sealed the bag and placed it in a neat row with the other recipes. When we were finished the next day, Ziplocs in tidy rows, looking like a culinary army marching to battle, stretched all the way down the driveway. Henry Ford would have been proud.

Finally, we packed boxes with exactly the recipes needed for a particular section of the trail and wrote post office addresses in big, black ink on each box. We put together a lot of food. We worked pretty hard, but, compared to buying conventional backpacking food, making our own saved us a ton of money.

I do, however, regret one thing. Jennifer divined that we needed more protein than her fruits, nuts, and flakes would provide. She solved this problem by purchasing a huge supply of brewer's yeast. Into each and every recipe, she studiously poured a few tablespoons. It didn't smell very good, but she promised that we wouldn't smell this yeast in the cooked recipes. She was badly mistaken. Every meal, from polenta cheese soup to apple crisp, reeked of brewer's yeast. Whatever nutritional benefit brewer's yeast may have, it stinks and it tastes bad. I know. I know *really* well.

Throughout the last month of our preparation, we were on our best behavior. We were overly civil and made sure that we laughed at every joke. We had so much to do—planning, baking, sorting, dehydrating, and eating—that we didn't talk about the things we needed to talk about—like how we were going to get along on the trail. We didn't have time, or chose not to make time, to talk. I often felt uneasy with the group and occasionally did not like the decisions we were making, but I didn't want to make anything a big deal. A casual visitor would have thought that we were fine friends—a great team for an adventure. A perceptive visitor would have been concerned.

The day we left to drive south to the trailhead, a storm made landfall on the California coast. I wearily watched as rain clouds sauntered westward toward the Sierra. The Sierra's foothills and mountains violently pushed these clouds upward and temperatures within them dropped below freezing. Snow fell. Winter had already left a heavy blanket of snow in the Sierra. And now, on our way to the trail, the snow continued to fall.

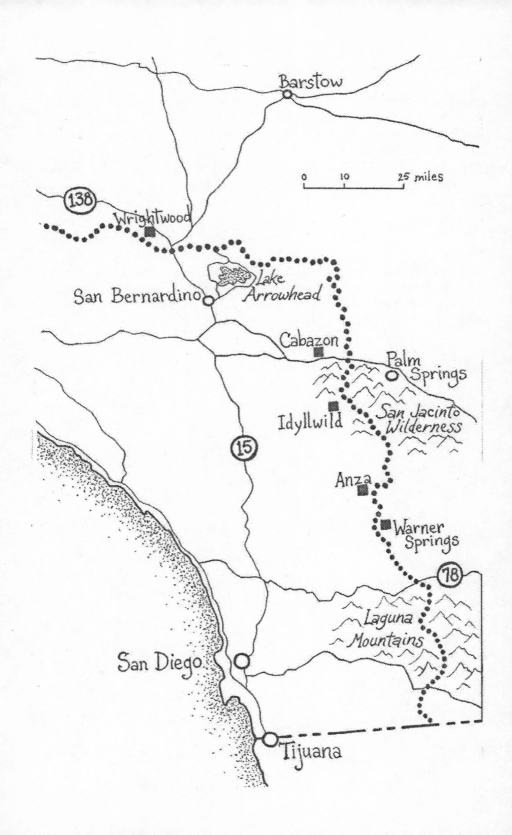

Chapter 9:
The PCT from Mexico to Wrightwood

Days 1-35
April 17—May 21, 1982

We took a group photo by the barbed-wire border fence. We looked clean and happy. A little afraid to start, we loitered at the fence, sneaking glances north. I remembered saying something stupid like "If you look really hard, you can see Oregon." There were groans. Walking was better than my jokes, so we shouldered our packs and took our first steps.

Day 1 was great—typical desert scenery. Lots of brush and small mountains. We had to walk most of the day on roads, but there was a nice breeze to coax us along.

Things started to go bad, though, on Day 2. Pat and I left camp in the cool of the morning and walked about 2.5 miles before we stopped to let the group catch up. Several hours passed. In order to pass the time, we made up a jingle called *Waiting for the Women* and sang it for a long time. Don, who was supposed to be bringing up the rear, showed up but Sally and Jennifer were nowhere in sight. We figured the ladies were lost, so we taught Don our jingle and waited. Finally, we spied Sally and Jennifer walking down the ridge. Jennifer took off her boots for a break and found a massive blister on her foot. When we got started again, Jennifer's painful blister slowed her pace. During the afternoon, Don struggled with the heat and almost passed out. Day 2 camp was much more sober. I washed my shirt in a cool stream.

As we began to ascend into the Laguna Mountains, poor Jennifer fought a constant battle with pain. We each carried a little of her gear in order to lighten her pack. But her blisters (they were now plural) were too much and on Day 5 she left the trail. After a short rest, she planned to join us again on Day 11 in Anza.

The group, now reduced to four, continued north.

The PCT through California is divided into eighteen sections. Each section has a supply point. This not only helps you plan for your supplies, it divides an enormously long hike into manageable bits. It's much easier to face a 76-mile hike from the Mexican border to Warner Springs, than a 1,700-mile one to Oregon. We hadn't even finished our first section before we lost Jennifer.

Don grew more accustomed to the heat each day and, with the help of an umbrella he attached to his pack, found his usual strength and endurance.

Pat proved to be a strong hiker. Taken as a whole, he was the least battered of us all. He did, however, have a tendency to get lost. He steadfastly refused to carry the weighty PCT trail guide. In lieu of this, he would study the next day's route out of my guide as part of his evening routine. Fortified with this knowledge, he simply walked, trusting his memory and the lay of the land to get him there. Even though he did make a lot of wrong turns, he always found camp. I really don't know how he did it.

Sally did really well on the trail—surprisingly so. She was, by far, the least experienced hiker. In fact, the PCT was her first overnight backpacking trip. This is not the recommended way to approach a multi-month backpacking trip. Yet from the start, she was resourceful and resilient.

On Day 6, we camped along a road at a California Highway Maintenance Center. It certainly wasn't glamorous, but it had running water and space enough to lay down sleeping bags. As I strolled into camp after a hot, dry day of walking, I said to Don, "Whoa, baby, I'm a thirsty pup!"

"Hey, there is plenty of water here, big dog."

I drank greedily straight from the spigot. The water was cool.

Pat walked up behind me, "We walked on roads a lot today. I thought this was the Pacific Crest *Trail?*" He wasn't complaining, he just wondered what the deal was.

I explained, "Well, wonder dog, either the property owners haven't given easements for the trail or they haven't built it yet. Until then, we've gotta pound the pavement."

Pat smirked slightly, "Hhhmph."

Sally chimed in, "Who's cooking tonight? I'm hungry."

Don grinned, "Oh, it's your turn."

Pat and I speedily agreed.

She laughed, "Oh well, I'll feed you, young pups. But dinner has to come out of my pack."

An acceptable deal for all.

Why we spoke in this canine theme, I haven't a clue.

We arrived at Warner Springs and were underwhelmed. There wasn't a small grocery to buy snacks. The post office wasn't much more than an oversized closet. There was some kind of pricey sensitivity camp for seniors in Warner Springs. Busloads of elderly people showed up wearing shirts that announced, "I'm 100 percent satisfied!" The camp's young workers ran around like cheerleaders, jumping and waving their hands with mock joy. We were uncomfortable being there and there was no reason to stay. We got our supplies and moved on in the night.

Along the way to Anza, the walking was easy. Horned toads were common, but rattlers were not. Pat and I were working on tree identification and, with the help of my field guide, identified the Coulter Pine. Because of the wet winter, we found water in every seasonal creek. We even came across springs and creeklets that were not on the maps.

On Day 10, we descended from a small mountain range into barren, arid Terwilliger Valley. People didn't seem too friendly here: There were NO TRESPASSING signs everywhere. We saw another sign indicating the Bailey Valley Store and turned. This store was no more than a hut in the middle of nowhere. As soon as we walked in, a plump woman dressed in cowgirl attire smiled and said, "Hey boys, how are you doing? Welcome to Terwilliger Valley! I'm Prudence."

Well, at least we were welcome here.

Pat and I bought a bunch of junk food. As we purchased our stuff, Prudence said, "You boys look thirsty. Go grab a beer. I'll throw it in for free."

We were thirsty and accepted her gracious offer.

She continued, "Yep, Terwilliger Valley, this is where it's at—this place is better than Disneyland."

"Oh yeah, why do you like it so much?" I asked.

"Because it looks like Oklahoma!"

Don didn't miss a beat, "Well, if this is what Oklahoma looks like, I don't want to go there."

Prudence slapped her knee and laughed.

Before we all left, she recommended Camp Anza just down the road. The rates were cheap and there were showers. We thanked her for the beer and made for Camp Anza.

We had intended to take a rest day at Warner Springs. But Warner Springs did not have the amenities necessary to warrant a rest day. We decided to spend our first rest day at Camp Anza.

Something happened to me on Day 10.

I had been so busy for the last several weeks. There were all the preparations; then we actually had to walk. There were things around to keep my attention off of Don and Sally. But at Camp Anza, I sat most of the day in the shade of a small tree, watching them. Without things to do, I could not control my heart.

Hatred for Don welled up. My thoughts ran wild: *How could he have done this to me? Is there any honor among us? I don't trust him at all. Was he waiting for me to screw up? How could he go after Sally when he knew we had this trail planned? Didn't he think about what that would do?*

Then I thought about Sally: *Boy, she really must have loved me. She waited all of several days before she started running with Scott. I must have left quite an impression. I'm such an idiot; I still love her. But she makes me so mad. I want her back, but could I ever trust her? Should I fight for her?*

My heart boiled under the desert sun. I turned this stuff over and over in my mind all day, watching them.

During the darkest moments of this day, I wanted to kill them. I actually looked at my trail maps for cliffs that I could push them off of and pretend it was an accident.

But I didn't want to feel this way. I was horrified by the hatred in my heart. In other moments of almost-sanity, I was annoyed with myself because I was so annoyed. After all, Sally and I were not together when Don made his move. So what was my problem? Sometimes I wanted to forgive them. But there was not grace in my heart to do so.

With all of California surrounding me, all I wanted to do was get away from Don and Sally. This was not what I imagined the PCT would be like.

On Day 11, Sally and I walked alone together for the first time on the trail. My heart had broken through; I had to say something:

"I still love you."

"I still love you too."

"But what about Don?"

"I can't deny what's happened between me and Don. I love him too."

"Will you come back to me?"

"No."

At camp that night, I was watching Sally move through her chores. Her beauty and presence overwhelmed me, and I whistled a loud, primal whistle in praise of her. She thought it was Don.

Jennifer rejoined us that day. Her blisters weren't healed and her boots still didn't fit. She tried to enjoy the walk through her constant agony. We were walking on the Desert Divide—a high, desolate, but beautiful ridge—when, through her pain, she smiled one of her full and spontaneous smiles and said, "There is no place on earth I would rather be than right here, right now."

On Day 12 we began to climb into southern California's first real mountains, the San Jacintos. Mt. San Jacinto itself stands at 10,804 feet. On ominous Day 13 we ran into trailside snow for the first time. By Day 14 we were lost in it. Don and Sally were in front that day. I was third. There were patches of snow, but it wasn't too bad until the trail made a sharp west turn into a trail-less blanket of white. Marty the Route-Finder kicked into action.

At the edge of the snow, I took off my pack, got out my guidebook and spent several minutes poring over the topographical maps. I looked for ridges and took note of the flow of streams. *Is there anything on this map that could guide me?* Then I gazed over the lay of the land. *Which direction were the ridges tending? That small mound I saw on the map, could I see it? If not, where would it be?* I thought about how the trail had been routed so far. Some trail builders tend toward steep, more aggressive trails; others toward mild, less direct routes. I sensed direction. I only used my compass three or four times along the whole trail. I seemed to know which way was north and when I wasn't sure, my brother had a compass needle in his brain and could unfailingly point the way. When I felt I had taken in all that could be absorbed, I put my pack back on and walked off of the trail and onto the snow.

Just because the snow covers the trail does not mean that there aren't any other ways to "see" the way. Sometimes there are brightly colored PCT medallions nailed onto trees by the trail, though these were rare. More often there were blazes cut into trees with axes. Sometimes there were piles of rocks, called cairns, that could still be visible through the snow. I was never sure these nonspecific signs marked the PCT, however. When a tree falls over a trail, chain saws are used to cut it up and clear the way. The obvious cut of a tree peering through the white was sign of trail. People ahead of you sometimes leave footprints. Footprints are tricky. They're only as reliable as the heads that guide them. I didn't take footprints very seriously. I walked slowly, constantly reviewing all of these factors. I stayed a little higher than my intuition guided me. It was easier to see trailsign from above and easier to get to it when I found it. I was a good route-finder. But Don was the best route-finder I have ever seen. He had an uncanny way of finding the trail—as if he could smell it. I learned nearly everything I knew about finding routes from watching Don.

I found Don and Sally waiting on a rock. Pat and Jennifer were forever in catching up. I figured Pat was lost and Jennifer was slowed by her feet. I got cold sitting around so long and took off. The extra time that I needed to scout the trail allowed everyone to catch up. I finally found a signed trail junction to the Devil's Slide Trail that led to Idyllwild, our next supply point. I pulled the group close to the ridge as we searched for the trail.

This is usually a good idea. Because the edge of a ridge is more exposed, there is often less snow. But this ridge was very steep and very challenging. We were tired and a little cranky because of the snow. We weren't being as careful as we should have been. Just ahead of me, Sally stepped on a branch right on the edge of a severe drop-off. The branch gave way and Sally fell. She grabbed at some bushes with her hands and was able to find her footing again. She probably avoided a deathfall by about two inches.

I was relieved that she was still alive. I was relieved that I was relieved.

After we found the Devil's Slide Trail we made great time to Idyllwild and went straight to the post office. We kibitzed with other PCT hikers, worked through our supply shipment, read letters and wrote replies and wandered back to a small city park to make camp.

After we settled in, I said to Pat, "Hey, let's go to a restaurant and get a real meal. I want something with meat. This vegetarian drivel is getting to me."

"Sounds good."

I felt uneasy leaving camp. Money had become an issue. While we had pooled our money to buy our shared supplies, only Pat and I had brought a little of our own money for personal use on the trail. We did share what we had often enough, but the others seemed a bit annoyed when we would go off on our own and spend our money. None of this was spoken, but they thought we were selfish for spending our own money and we thought they were slackers for not having their own.

Screw 'em, I thought as Pat and I walked to Jan's Red Kettle. I had top sirloin, baked potatoes, soup, veggies, iced tea and finished off with several cups of real coffee. I enjoyed my brother's easy company. We talked when we had something to say. Otherwise, we were content with silence.

It was night when we got back to camp.

Don shared some bad news: "Jennifer wants to take a rest day tomorrow. She's pulled some muscles and thinks she'll be better after a break."

Not good. I knew Jennifer was not going to make it on the PCT. Her boots didn't fit. Her feet were bruised and battered. Her body could not take the daily demands of backpacking. Waiting again would not help. Sharing her pack weight would not help. I knew that Don also knew this. Furthermore, I did not want to take another rest day. The rest day at Camp Anza was enough for me. Pat and I had talked about climbing Mt. San Jacinto.

"Well, we just had a rest day at Camp Anza. How about this? Pat and I will leave tomorrow and climb San Jacinto. You guys can stay here tomorrow with Jennifer and we'll meet on the trail the next day."

Don was silent for a minute. "If that's what you want to do, go ahead." He walked away in disgust.

The next morning, Pat and I woke early, showered, and ate breakfast. We left a tense camp. For the first time, our group was officially split up.

We began our ascent back up San Jacinto and snow met us all too quickly. We abandoned hope of finding the trail under the snow and followed the lay of the land. We knew we needed to reach the top of

Fuller Ridge, so with each snowy step, we worked our way up. After several hours of this tiresome labor, Pat looked at me and said, "I feel like I'm in a Russian movie."

In a small clearing free of snow, we made a cold camp.

The next day, Mt. San Jacinto repelled our attempt at her summit. The brush around the peak was too thick and was painful to walk through. There would be other mountains. I set up my hammock between two small pines on the crest of Fuller Ridge and took a nap as we waited for the others to catch up.

When I awoke, the sun had moved considerably west and there were dark thunderheads in the sky.

I looked at Pat, who was quietly sitting against a tree, "Have you seen the others?"

"Nope."

"I wonder where they are?"

"I don't know."

"Maybe they got lost in the snow. I wonder how Jennifer is."

"Hhmph."

We each thought for a while.

I said, "We've got to get off this ridge. There's no shelter up here. If those thunderheads let go, we'll get soaked."

"Uh huh."

The trail had been visible for a time. It was exposed on the afternoon side of the ridge. Shortly after we started again, the trail moved to the morning side of Fuller Ridge and was lost in deep drifts of snow. I tried to stay close to the trail route, but I got sick of the snow and pulled down the ridge a bit. By accident, we ran into a deserted YMCA camp. This was good. The camp was on the map. We knew where we were. The YMCA camp became our home for the night.

The next morning, after a small breakfast, we worked up a plan.

"We've got to get back to the actual PCT," I asserted.

"Are we lost?"

"No, we're in California!"

"So, where's the trail?"

"It's up on that ridge, under the snow."

"So why go to the trail?"

I thought about that. It really didn't make much sense to climb up to the trail when it was covered with snow. Maybe it would be better to stay low on the ridge and just contour over until the snow went away. Maybe I shouldn't worry so much about staying so close to the trail.

"Okay, we'll contour the ridge however we can and find the trail after it comes down a bit,"

"Sounds good. I'm going to take a leak and then after I'm back we'll get going," my brother said. Or at least that's what I thought he said.

I filled my canteens at a nearby creek and returned to camp to wait for Pat. Time passed. At first I figured he was having one of those constipated moments on the trail. But he didn't come back. Finally, after fifteen minutes or so, I knew he had taken off without me.

I was concerned. Pat tended to walk behind me. He didn't have the trail guide, how would he know where to go? With each step I took, I feared that we were getting farther and farther apart.

After about three miles, I came to a three-way junction and opted to take the jeep road ascending the ridge. It began to curve the wrong way and I retraced my steps. There, standing in the junction, was my brother. We were lucky, very lucky, to have met in such a place.

We continued on together until we found the actual PCT and came to a trail junction. The guide told us that the trail along Dutch Creek, which was the shorter route, had been trashed but was now repaired. No choice there. Follow the shorter route.

After a few miles, weeds began to invade the trail tread. We came to a sign that read: 'Trail becomes hard to follow beyond this point.' Pat and I laughed, "When was this trail ever easy to follow?" From where we stood, atop a 1,500-foot ridge, I could see the jeep trail we were trying to get to about 1.5 miles away. I thought that even if we lost the trail, so what? We hadn't really followed the trail through the snow and we were often unsure of our exact location. I can see the road, right there. What's the worst that can happen? We lose the trail? No problem. Just walk to the jeep road.

"Well, let's just go for it."

"Okay."

We lost the trail almost immediately. It faded to a game trail and then just disappeared. We began our descent straight down the ridge through sparse desert brush. The first 500 feet of our descent went rather well. Plenty of room between bushes; good footing. The second 500 feet of our descent got a little tight. There wasn't much room between the branches and our packs were starting to get caught by clawing thorns. But we still could, with patience and care, maneuver downward. The last 500 feet of descent was horrible. We met a wall of dense, high, tough, sharp desert brush. At times we made like squirrels, working beneath the brush canopy, contorting through branches and crawling on all fours. At other times, when all else failed, we just pushed through, like bulldozers, as desert thorns two inches long punctured my exposed calves. I began to bleed in several places. And it didn't let up. We fought for inches. We paid in pain. And there was no relief.

An entire afternoon passed in this way.

When we finally emerged from our torture chamber, we were spent. We drank from our canteens, set out our ground cloths, pulled out our bags and went to sleep, yearning for the healing touch of night.

I awoke to the gentle patter of rainfall. I couldn't see a single star. The sky was covered with clouds. Both of us were still wasted. Pat yanked a circular piece of plastic called a tube tent from his pack. There weren't trees around to provide tie-offs for the tent rope. We just crawled inside the plastic and tried to sleep. The rainfall increased and the sound of it against the plastic so close to my ear was deafening. My bag was getting wet. I was so tired, I fell asleep anyway.

We didn't look so good the next morning. My arms, legs and face—any part of me that was exposed—was cut and oozed blood. The continuing rainfall streaked our dusty bodies. Our clothes were torn.

Wearily, I got ready to walk and said, "We only need to get to Cabazon. It's not that far. We can rest and regroup there."

Our pace was slow, but resolute. We would walk until we got to Cabazon. The jeep trail was easy to follow and, though we almost made another wrong turn, soon we were switchbacking down the ridge with civilization in view.

But then the trail began to fade. When it was all but gone, Pat looked down at Cabazon and smirked, "Hey, let's just head straight for it. Forget the trail. I mean, we can see Cabazon right there."

I was not amused.

Fortunately, the trail came back and we soon arrived at a city park in Cabazon as the thunderheads marched away from the San Jacintos. But where were the others?

As I sat on the park bench table, a truck drove up with two hikers in the back. The truck stopped and Don and Sally hopped out, grabbed their packs and moved toward the park. They had taken a ride.

I realized in that moment that I had a different vision for the PCT than Don and Sally. I wanted to *walk* the PCT. They wanted to *travel* the PCT. It was very important to me to walk every step of my northbound route to Oregon. I didn't mind taking a ride to a supply stop so long as I came right back to the place I had left. I was kind of compulsive about this. When I took rides I touched things like stop signs and fence posts, so that when I came back I could touch them again and know that I walked every step. It didn't matter to me that certain stretches of trail were ugly or followed roads. That was part of California. With every northbound step I took, I knew I had left custom-made boot prints all the way from Mexico. When I got to Oregon, I wanted to look at a map of California and say, "Been there, done that."

But Don and Sally wanted to *travel* the PCT, only walking the sections that were interesting to them. If they were offered a ride through a boring, hot stretch they would take it. If a ride could make up some lost time, take it. This is an acceptable way to approach hiking the PCT. Most tristaters take rides through snowy mountains and/or uninspiring sections. There are advantages to this approach—more human interaction, more enjoyment of the cities along the way. Even though I knew this, I despised them for not walking.

That night, camp was tense. Don told me that Jennifer had dropped out for good. She would meet us later on at her family's cabin so that we could rest there as a group. But she wouldn't try to hike with us anymore.

I had seen it coming, but I was sad. I missed Jennifer.

We moved on as a foursome. The hiking was easy and the few days I had spent alone with my brother had calmed me some. During this section we saw our first rattlesnake, came across a photographer shooting a beautiful model in the heart of the desert and had two dogs run into our city park camp at Big Bear in the middle of the night. Pat

79

and I identified the Western Tanager. Although Don and Sally bothered me, things weren't too bad. Besides, we were working toward our first real break—two days of rest and relaxation at Jennifer's family cabin by Lake Arrowhead, just off of the PCT. I was anxious to wash my clothes, eat some home cooking, and not move. I was ready now for a rest day. Two, in fact.

On Day 30, we left the PCT, met some of Jennifer's relatives and gladly accepted a ride to their cabin. While my body was ready to rest, my heart was not prepared for the cabin.

From the start, it was awful. Don and Sally had walked ahead and were already there. They greeted us when we arrived. They had moved into the "master" bedroom. Pat and I got to sleep in the "kids" bedroom. They had already arranged the meals. We got to come to dinner when they called. I felt like one of their children.

One afternoon I sat in the family room while Don and Sally enjoyed making supper together. I tried to think about my future plans regarding college, finances and employment, but that's not what I thought about. Their voices intertwined with my thoughts.

"You can't cook chicken like that," Sally said.

"Oh yeah, you're going to love it. Taste this."

"Mmmmm, that's good."

You know, they make a better couple than we did. I don't like that kitchen stuff and Don loves it . . . Man, I blew it. I lost. That's rather obvious now, isn't it? She sleeps with him.

"Pass me that wooden spoon."

I guess most guys blow it on their first loves. But when it's over, it's over and you can go on. I get to be reminded every day of what I lost. I get to be reminded every day of who took my lover. I get reminded every night—Don and Sally kissy-kissy in the next bedroom. This is worse than all that stuff with Mom. At least when she died, it was over. Puff! This never ends.

"Hey, watch it." There was laughter.

Why am I here? What is keeping this group together? I can't do this all the way to Oregon.

"When do you think you'll be ready?"

"Me? I'm ready anytime!" There was a slap. More laughter. "Oh, you mean supper! In about fifteen minutes."

"I'll round everybody up."

I've got to get beyond this. I have to move on. This is my past. I have a future. There is a woman for me. I'll find her. Focus on the future.

I spent as much time as I could playing with kids outside. I didn't rest. I didn't feel better when we left.

I said goodbye to Jennifer and took another ride back to the trailhead. I never saw her again.

It was good to hike. I needed to burn some energy. It wasn't good for me to sit around. And Deep Canyon was wooing its way into my heart. Unique plants, trees, snakes and rocks were everywhere. Deep Canyon was the only place in all of the PCT so far that warranted a second visit. The beauty of the cascading creek, the gentle breeze and the swaying, brilliant flowers moved me. This was why I was on the PCT.

The next day, as Deep Canyon was coming to an end, I was entranced by the views and trail. I heard the joyful laughs of people splashing in the creek. At first I was delighted by the sounds of such sheer human joy. But then I recognized their voices. My serenity was violated by the childlike play of Don and Sally skinny-dipping. I was mad. I was hurt yet again. Yet at the same time, I was frustrated with myself. Why shouldn't they have any fun?

I was a mess.

Camp was disappointing. We were supposed to find a campground at the end of Deep Canyon. But there wasn't a campground. Just desert bushes, a small creeklet and, well, that was it.

We threw our bags out on our ground cloths and tried to sleep. Sleep evaded me. My insides were wrapped as tight as could be. I had had enough of Don and Sally. They were ten yards away, bags next to each other, speaking in the low, hushed voices of pillow talk. I was so lonely. They lost me, but got each other. I lost them both—my best friend and first lover in one ironic shot. I was sick of the pain, sick of the struggle, sick of the tension.

Then it hit me: *You don't have to stay. You and Pat made it through the San Jacintos. You can do it together. Why stay in this group? Why torture yourself? It would be better for them too. It can't be much fun to have me around.*

But what about the Sierra? You can't do the Sierra without Don. Sure Pat is a strong hiker, but he's never done any mountaineering. He's never used

81

an ice ax. What we went through back in the San Jacintos was nothing compared to the Sierra.

Okay, we'll just split up until the Sierra. That's about a 30-day break.

Maybe I'll be able to handle this better by then.

Now, when should I split up the group?

Our next supply point is Wrightwood. Do it there.

The next three days took us through desert country. I found a lot of peace in my walks. I knew that a change was coming—a change that needed to be made.

At the Wrightwood post office, we got our supply shipment, read and wrote letters and signed the PCT register. Sally noticed a note on the bulletin board. "Hey, the Small family will come and get PCT hikers and give them a place to stay for the night. There's a phone number here. Do you guys want to call?"

No question. Showers, home-cooked meals, maybe a stereo for some tunes. And a neutral environment for a difficult conversation. We called them and they took us to their Wrightwood home.

We were all uneasy. Perhaps Don and Sally noticed a change in me and were anxious. Finally, I called the group together into the family room—Pat and I sat on one side, Don and Sally on the other.

I started, "This isn't working. I would like to split the group up until the Sierra."

Sally jabbed, "What isn't working? What don't you like?"

I knew this wouldn't be easy. "I like to hike with Pat. It'll just be easier for everybody."

Sally punctured, "Why is it easier to hike with . . ."

Don interrupted, "How will we handle supplies?"

"We'll arrange a time to meet at the post offices to divide the shipment. But between post offices, we can hike as two groups."

Don looked at me. "So you want to give up on the group?"

"Yes."

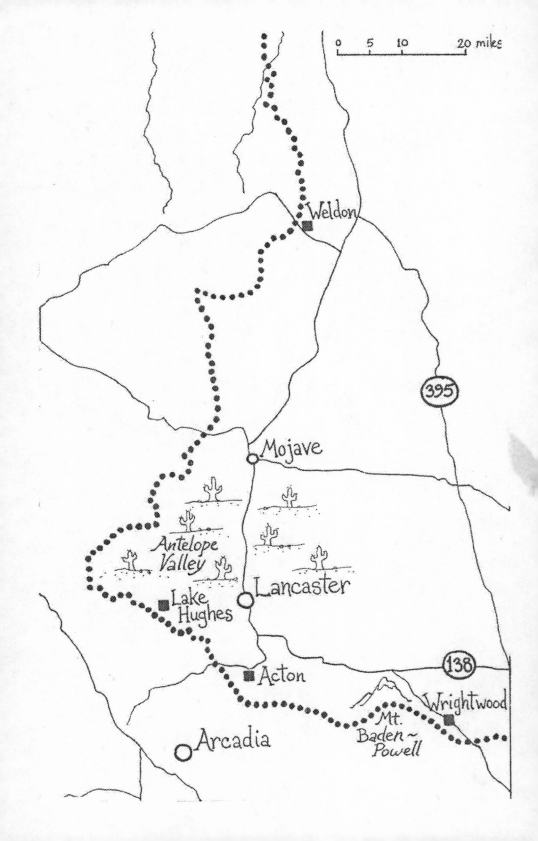

Chapter 10:
The PCT from Wrightwood to Weldon

Days 36-59
May 22—June 12, 1982

Although this was a hard decision, splitting up was the right move. Pat and I, after being fed a massive breakfast by the Smalls, accepted a ride to the trailhead and started again. We were now the MBET (the McCorkle Brothers Expeditionary Team). We quickly worked up the spur trail leading back to the PCT, then strolled half a mile to Guffy Campground and stopped. Reveling in our newfound freedom, we decided to call it a day.

We drank cool spring water and, sitting lazily in the shade, reviewed the 46 Latin genus and species names we had learned for trees. Why speak of a normal incense cedar when you can extol the virtues of the *libocedrus decurrens*? We played chess on a backpacker's chessboard that when rolled up looked liked a big Tootsie Roll. Tension flowed out of me with each breath. I filled my eyes with visions of sweeping pines and dancing wildflowers.

Hiking with my quiet, contemplative brother was a balm to my soul. On days when the heat did not demand an early start, we stayed in our bags well into the morning. We hiked separately, his pace being quicker than my own. Yet, after a time, we knew when to expect each other. We were good partners.

We still came across Don and Sally on the trail. We were, after all, going to the same place in the same amount of time and there are only so many places to camp. But the pressure to interact was gone.

On Day 38, we came to snow-covered Mt. Baden-Powell, named after the founder of the Boy Scouts. As I slipped, fell and crawled my way up the mountain, my thoughts dwelled on the Sierra: *I can barely make it up this little mountain. How am I going to get through the Sierra? Maybe I should avoid the Sierra. Maybe I should walk on Highway 395. Maybe I should wait a few more weeks. Maybe, maybe, maybe! What am I going to do? I can't walk through miles and miles of snow over those high passes. It's just not possible.*

At the snowy summit, a guy we met hiking up the mountain shared his flask of Amaretto. We toasted the memory of Lord Baden-Powell. Another snowy ascent was behind me.

Our next goal was the desert town of Acton. We had plenty of food and plenty of time. We played several games of chess every day. Because we were making our camps with little effort, we started to climb more peaks. The views weren't that great. To the west lay the usually smogged over Los Angeles basin. To the east lay the barren and dusty desert. But it's always fun to be on top of a mountain.

As I walked, certain songs and melodies would catch in my mind and provide rhythm for walking. One day, Simon and Garfunkel's "America," the next "The Muppet Show Theme" and the next, "At the Ball from Berlioz's Symphony Fantastique."

In this tuneful way, we arrived at Acton on Day 45 for our first resupply after the break up. The last few miles had taken us along hot, arid roads and we were steaming when we got to a small grocery.

"Hey, let's eat a half-gallon of ice cream," my brother suggested.

"Mmmm. That's pretty good, a quarter-gallon a piece."

"No, you misunderstand! Let's *each* eat a half-gallon."

"Wow. Now that is a worthy goal!"

The selection of ice cream was minimal. I wound up buying a carton of strawberry from a local producer. After Pat made his choice, we got out our spoons and attacked our frozen adversaries.

Somewhere during the battle, a dairy truck pulled up to make a delivery. As he went about his business, the deliveryman watched us work steadily toward our goal.

The last quarter-gallon was pretty tough. I had brain freeze bad and my throat hurt. I shivered joyfully in the desert sun. But I prevailed and finished, able to eat no more.

"Done," I exclaimed in triumph.

"Done," answered Pat.

The deliveryman looked at us in amazement, "You guys ate all that at one time?"

We nodded.

"Do you want some more?"

I couldn't eat another bite. Pat piped up, "Sure!"

The deliveryman threw a pint of gourmet ice cream to Pat, "Here ya go."

Pat ate it. Five pints of ice cream in one sitting.

There were six hikers at the post office. Don and Sally had arrived and things were pretty civil. Larry, who had shared his flask of Amaretto with us on Baden-Powell was there. A new hiker I'd never met before named Cindy was talking with Sally. There aren't many women on the trail and they tend to stay together.

Don's Uncle Jerry, who lived nearby, had left a message for Don on the post office bulletin board. He wanted Don to call him so that the group could rest at his house that night.

As we divided up the shipment, Don called his uncle and arranged for him to come and get the group.

"Cool. We're going to stay with my Uncle Jerry tonight. Larry and Cindy, you're welcome to come along."

Larry said, "Thanks. I'll take that offer."

Cindy seemed surprised by the invite but accepted anyway.

Then, out of nowhere, I asked Don, "Hey, can Pat and I come along?"

Don looked at me in confusion and asked me, "I thought you wanted to split up the group. Why do you want to come with us?"

"I don't know. A shower. Some good food." I really didn't know.

Don struggled, weighing his thoughts. "Okay. Whatever."

When Jerry showed up, we threw all our packs into the back of his truck and climbed in. He didn't live far away and soon we were kicking back in an eccentric Southern California bachelor home. It was a mess. Baby chicks pecked around in cardboard boxes under sun lamps in the living room. Cartons of snacks were strewn everywhere, half full. Jerry himself was a likable, overweight, cowboy-hat-wearing, content man. He loved horses and led groups of equestrians into Yosemite in the summer.

We spent a large part of the afternoon in his Jacuzzi, which periodically doubled as a spa for his horses.

The tension wasn't too bad. I felt that Cindy already didn't like Pat and me, probably because she had only heard Sally 's side of what had happened. I didn't worry about it; there were other people around.

Some more of Don's relatives—Uncle Glenn and his wife and children—joined the group that evening. They were so *happy*. Glenn loved his wife and his kids. His eyes followed them with glee. Somehow, we got to talking about money and family life. They didn't have a lot of money, but they had something much deeper.

"You don't need a lot of money to have a family," Glenn said. "People who wait to have kids because they don't have enough money are stupid. You never have enough money!"

I kind of felt that waiting to have a little money made sense.

He continued, "You know, being poor is a challenge. You have to be creative. You have to find alternatives. It really is fun."

He spoke with conviction. He believed every word. His joyful family proved his point.

The next morning, Jerry took us all to Bonnie's Home Cooking for breakfast. He was on a first name basis with everyone there. Rested and now full, he drove us back to the Acton post office.

Pat and I left the group for the four-day walk to Lake Hughes, a small town south of Antelope Valley. We saw a few more rattlesnakes and felt the desert heat intensify. I had asked my dad to send my flute to Acton. Every night I spent an hour or so playing songs from memory or making up tunes. I tried to imitate the birds and capture the mystery of the desert. Music was a great comfort.

On Day 49, Pat and I strolled into Lake Hughes late in the day. We went straight to the post office and worked through the supply. We sent a package of unneeded supplies on to Mojave. We didn't need a lot of our mountain gear for the next section of trail. We made camp behind a gas station in great anticipation of the next day. Our sister, April, and her husband, Paul, were to stop by and say hello.

Lake Hughes Community Center held a pancake breakfast the next morning. I was confident that Lake Hughes would feed us. As the morning dragged on, I was about to give up hope, when an old man, reeking from alcohol and obviously feeling it, pulled up and said carefully, "Hey, you guys want some breakfast?"

"Sure!" we eagerly replied.

"Let's go."

We got into his ancient car and hoped that he wasn't so smashed that he couldn't drive. "Here, ya want a beer?"

He handed us a brew. So much for the open container law.

At the community center, he paid for our breakfasts. We all got our food and sat down. No one seemed to know this man. It was sad.

"I was in the war."

"Oh yeah, what was that like?" We felt obliged to speak; after all, he had paid.

He sat for a few minutes confused. Then he ate. So did we.

"I was in the war."

"Hhhmmm."

"Oh yeah?"

Back to eating.

After breakfast, he took us back to the gas station. "Here, you guys want another beer?"

"No, we're fine. Thanks for breakfast." We meant it. He drove slowly away.

Before long, April and Paul pulled up in their car. April got out, threw her arms in the air and exclaimed, "Oh my goodness! You don't look like my brothers at all. Martin, you have a beard and Pat, you're so skinny! We're going to have to feed you." She hugged us.

Paul joined in, "Yeah, there were two other hikers down the road that look more like you than you do."

April and Paul are a one-in-a-million couple. They are average-looking people at best. My sister has long brown hair, a pug nose and is pudgy. Paul is losing his hair at about the same rate he is gaining weight. What makes them extraordinary is their relationship. We've all heard of such things as soul mates and matches made in heaven. Every word of this is true in their case. They love each other. They are passionate about each other. Whenever I'm with them, I feel like I'm interrupting something. They only have eyes for each other. They still hold hands and enjoy every second. That this relationship thrived on this tired globe always gave me hope.

We jumped into the car and went out for pizza. After we ate, Paul and April sat quietly talking in a booth, while Pat and I played an Asteroids video game. Pat creamed me.

We were not in a hurry to get back on the trail. The PCT leaves Lake Hughes and marches due north about twelve miles on 180th

89

Street West through Antelope Valley. Here the route meets the covered California aqueduct and follows it to Mojave. This section is a hot, boring, shadeless, relentless stretch of route—it is not a trail. Pat and I figured we would walk the road at night to avoid the heat.

April and Paul walked a bit with us as we pulled out of Lake Hughes, but they were in horrible shape and quit after a few hundred yards.

"You guys be careful!"

"Yes, April," we said in practiced reply.

We hugged again. Paul and April, hand in hand, turned and walked back.

As the sun set, Pat and I crested a small ridge and could see our road. The muted browns and reds of the desert mixed with the unyielding black of asphalt. We could not see the end. Our route faded into haze and mirage. The other side of Antelope Valley looked far away. It was.

We walked two abreast, right down the middle of the road. Sunset climaxed and faded. As was my custom, I watched for Polaris, the North Star, to appear in the sky. The Big Dipper's last two stars pointed the way. When darkness was thick enough, I found Polaris, lined up right above our road. We had been attentive to the moon cycles and knew that our night walk would be witnessed by a full moon. Before our eyes were even fully adjusted to darkness, the moon rose, cold and bright over the quiet desert.

Many miles passed in this way. Pat and I talked aimlessly and we worried about stepping on the elusive Mojave green rattlesnake—a snake with a particularly nasty venom. Blacktop is hard to walk on and our feet started hurting, but we kept going.

At some point along the way, things got a little weird. Maybe I was fatigued, or the beer I had for breakfast freaked me, or maybe the moon glow caused a form of temporary lunacy; I don't know. But we started to see things. I kept seeing a goat's head popping up from behind the creosote bushes that lined the road. I knew I was only imagining this, but the goats got to me; it was weird. Pat was getting a little goofy too.

We just kept walking. What else was there to do? Sit on the road and wait for the Mojave greens to get us? If they didn't, those goats surely would. I have never experienced such a long twelve miles.

90

There was nothing to draw us; no beauty to compel us; no rest awaiting us.

Our road did not take us to Polaris, but eventually we did arrive at the aqueduct. All we did was confirm to each other that we were in fact on the aqueduct and then we both pulled our bags out and fell instantly to sleep.

The first task of our new day was to figure out how to get water out of the aqueduct. The irony was thick. We only needed a little water. Millions of gallons were rushing past just underneath our feet, but we weren't sure we could get any. Thankfully, the aqueduct cover had periodic vents. Pat's ingenuity saved the day. He found a way to get his canteen down there, into the life-giving flow, and pull it back, full of water. The aqueduct's water was heavily chlorinated, but we drank it thankfully anyway.

Our second task of the day was to do nothing. We would, once again, rest while the sun ruled the day and walk at dusk into the dark. I planted myself under a Joshua tree and made like a sundial all day long—moving my body slowly to stay in the tree's slim shadow. At Lake Hughes, in a fit of insanity, I had purchased a watermelon to carry into the desert. I figured if I had to carry water, why not take it in a delicious form? That melon had been a ghastly weight to me the previous night. Pat and I ate the whole thing, licentiously enjoying the heart and sucking every drop of precious water out of the rind. I sometimes wonder if there is a patch of wild watermelon thriving somewhere in Antelope Valley, fed by the aqueduct, planted by yours truly.

During these long days and lonely nights, I felt the power of the desert. The desert reduced me. The dry winds and harsh sun stripped me of all but the most essential elements of life. First, I needed water. Water was everything. I always thought about water. Second, I needed shade. I had to get out from under from the relentless stare of the sun. Third, I needed food. And that was it. So reduced, I felt power in the land, power in the sky. I was aware of energy all around me. My flute solos, supported by an enormous lung capacity, featured long, long notes that drifted across the desert wastes.

On Day 53, we walked into the desert town of Mojave. With the efficiency born of experience, we attacked the post office, working through the shipment and the mail in short order. I wasn't bothered much by the others. In fact, the four of us often hiked together over the next section. I was too scared to be bothered. The snowy Sierra Nevada was only days away. Things were coming to a head. If I was going to leave the trail and follow Highway 395 on the eastern Sierra, the town of Weldon was the place to make the break. Every northbound step caused my worry to deepen. Sure, we had come through some tough snow. But Southern California was nothing compared to the Sierra. I knew what the passes were like in the Sierra without snow. They were steep and they were plentiful. All you do in the Sierra is go up a pass, go down a pass, and then go up the next one, gaining and losing as much as 5,000 feet in elevation every time.

When sober minded, I thought I was crazy to hike directly into the wintry teeth of that snowpack. But the alternatives weren't that great either. I could hike along Highway 395. Sure, there wasn't any snow. The view wouldn't be bad for a road. But I had walked on enough roads. I was sick of walking on roads. I wanted to walk on a trail. This was, after all, the Pacific Crest *Trail*. I could hitchhike up to Tuolumne Meadows and spend a month hanging out in Yosemite. By the gentle shores of the Tuolumne River, I could watch the snows melt away from the mountains—waiting, until the rest of the party slushed into the meadow. But I didn't want to spend a month sitting around. I wanted to hike. I had motion in my blood.

I was also afraid of hiking without Don. Hiking through southern California was one thing. But I felt pretty scared when I thought about Pat and myself alone in those mountains.

And what I learned from other hikers wasn't helping. Most tristaters had decided to take 395 at least a portion of the way. There was too much snow to average the kind of miles they needed to make it to Canada. As we talked to hikers along the way, we learned of an aerial survey of the PCT conducted by the forest service. This survey revealed only a few impassable places in the Sierra. Only a few! That's just great!

Even as I walked into Weldon on Day 59, I still didn't know what I wanted to do. Don and I sat down to talk.

He asked, "Well, what are you going to do?"

"I don't know."

"Uh huh." He thought for a minute. "I've talked with Sally. We think that splitting up the group permanently is the best way to go."

"Okay, good luck."

"You, too." And that was that.

I was venting my indecision to Pat that day, as the pines of the Sierra were visible above us. Should I be stupid and take my CMT-ridden body into the heart of the High Sierra while she was covered with a solid mantle of snow? Or should I be more reasonable and subject my feet to a road-pound or an enforced rest-break? Pat just listened. I had to make the choice. If I was going to leave the trail, I had to make my move; there weren't many places left where I could leave. Finally, after months of worry, consideration and discussion, I looked at Pat and said, "Oh, let's just go. If I don't make it—so what? At least I'll have better stories to tell."

That night we were camped by a meadow several miles north of Weldon. Just as sleep was taking me, I heard shouting. I was annoyed. This is the wilderness, people. Shut up! The shouting continued. Two words were repeated over and over. But I couldn't make them out.

I asked Pat, "Can you understand that?"

"No."

It continued. We heard something like: MMMMMMM . . . . . . aaaaahhhhhh.

We waited until we heard it clearly; someone was yelling *Martin* and *Pat*.

We yelled back, "We're over here!"

Within a few minutes, Cindy walked up to our camp. "Can I hike with you guys to Cedar Grove?"

Pat and I looked at each other a little surprised, "Sure."

We said no more. I thought this odd. What a great time to sit around and talk about what we didn't like about Don and Sally. Something had obviously gone wrong between them and Cindy. But Don and Sally were now behind us. All that mattered was what was ahead. The Sierra Nevada.

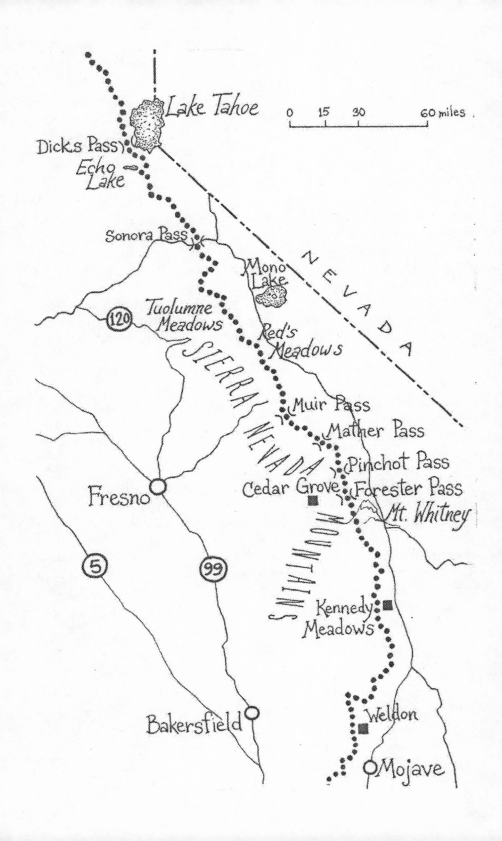

Lake Tahoe

Dicks Pass
Echo Lake

Sonora Pass

Mono Lake

NEVADA

120 Tuolumne Meadows

SIERRA NEVADA

Red's Meadows

Muir Pass

Mather Pass

Pinchot Pass

Cedar Grove

Forester Pass

Mt. Whitney

Fresno

MOUNTAINS

5

99

Kennedy Meadows

Bakersfield

Weldon

Mojave

0   15   30   60 miles

Chapter 11:
The PCT from Weldon to Dick's Pass

Days 60-110
June 13—August 1, 1982

The Sierra Nevada is a hiker's paradise. For two months I'd told my brother stories about the Sierra, raving about beauty and wonder. Now we were there and my brother loved it. We walked through green, lush meadows bursting with wild flowers. Streams and creeks were everywhere, providing us with cool, clear water and refreshing places for breaks. Familiar granite domes soared over the pine-blessed landscape. Cindy folded into our group and brought with her some wonderful snacks. Her recipe for trail fudge was one part peanut butter, one part honey and one part protein powder. We savored each priceless bite.

The MBET would not work as a name for our group anymore, so we renamed our band the SET (The Sierran Expeditionary Team) and moved on toward Cedar Grove.

On Day 61, we hiked up to Siretta Pass at 9,350 feet. Along the climb, there were only small patches of snow. At the pass itself, we stared at a sweeping view of the High Sierra: It was covered in white.

The group tried to make light of the situation.

"Doesn't look too bad."

"We won't be to those mountains for a long time."

"No problem."

Yeah, right.

We strolled into Kennedy Meadows, a tiny mountain resort, a few days later, expecting to find our food shipment and our extra mountain gear at the post office. Our food and mail was there, but our ice axes were not. And because it was Saturday, we would have to wait until Monday to get them. I tried to call Dad to confirm the shipping of our axes, but he wasn't home. So we sat around the river, made camp and watched the snow melt.

The next day, we all went to watch the old Jimmy Stewart flick, *Mr. Smith Goes to Washington*, at the Kennedy Meadows outdoor theater. The best part of the deal was that the entire SET got in for one dollar.

We sat around some more. I tried to finish *Zen and the Art of Motorcycle Maintenance* before I had to carry it into the Sierra. I sent back my flute. And we waited.

Finally, on Day 66, the axes came through and packing for the leg to Cedar Grove got serious. I had an enormous pack that had never even been close to being full. But as Pat handed me package after package of food, it got stuffed. Anxiety crept back into my soul. *I can't carry this pack. It's too heavy.*

Pat kept handing me food to carry. "It's a long way to Cedar Grove . . . and we should have extra for this section."

That sounds good, but this is too much.

Pat still gave me more and more food. I looked at my stuffed pack in disgust. "Stop giving me food. I can't take anymore food."

"Yes, you can. We're going to need this food. And here, pack this rope as well."

I got mad at my brother for the first and only time on the PCT.

I had to do something to burn some energy. I looked around and saw a huge boulder several hundreds of yards away. I walked swiftly to it, climbed it and sat on the top. The debate began again.

You can't go into those mountains. Take the road down to 395 and walk the highway.

But I've come so far.

Hey. You're a good backpacker—better than average—but the High Sierra will require mountaineering skills, and you are not a mountaineer.

I'm not so bad. I got through the San Jacintos.

Have you ever used an ice ax?

Yes, I've walked with one. I've worked with cutting steps.

But have you ever self-arrested?

I know what I'm supposed to do.

But you've never done it.

No, I haven't.

And if you go, you'll have to do this without Don.

I thought about the scores of times Don had helped me through tough situations. I remembered how he talked me into jumping off of a pinnacle on the summit of Johnson Peak. Jumping was the only way I was going to get down and I didn't want to do it. Don got me to jump. On another trip, he literally pulled me up the last several yards to the summit of Mt. Clark. He had been incredibly wise in teaching me about the woods. He had always been there. And now he was gone.

Pat and I can do this. The only thing against Pat is lack of experience and he'll get that soon enough.

Come on, Martin, the tristaters are going around the Sierra. The strongest hikers in the country are choosing to avoid this section and you think you can walk through it!

I don't know.

You can die out there. If you get hurt between those passes it'll be days, if not weeks, before Pat could get out and get help.

That's true.

But you're going to go anyway.

Yes, I am.

You're a fool. You know that.

Yes, I do.

I told myself to shut up.

I walked back to camp, apologized to my brother for being a jerk and finished packing my pack. I could barely lift it when I was done. It had to be at least 70 pounds. I said goodbye to Don and Sally, got into my bag and went to sleep. The next morning, we left early. No roads would cross our trail for several hundred miles. I was to see Don and Sally for only a few tension-filled hours for the rest of the summer.

The focus of our expedition was Forester Pass. Although it would be several days before we came to this barrier, it was always before me. Each day we climbed further into the Sierra, propelled by the wonder and majesty of snow-covered mountains and stalled by raging creeks and rivers. Very few hikers shared the trail and the longing of solitude mixed with unceasing, outrageous beauty intoxicated my spirit. I loved every step.

On Day 71, we came to the Big Horn Plateau, a flat expanse surrounded by huge mountains. Everywhere I looked, peaks soared and granite gleamed. The crest of the Sierra stood proud to the east and the Great Western Divide, a row of towering snowcapped monuments, marched off to the west. Forester Pass was a day away.

Tyndale Creek, which drained the Forester Pass watershed, foamed and frothed as the summer snowmelt swelled its banks.

"This ford is not going to be easy," I said.

"Well, we have our rope," Pat replied.

"I'll have to keep my boots on. My scuba booties won't give me enough support. I won't be able to focus on the ford if I'm thinking about my feet."

"Your boots will get wet and probably freeze tonight."

"True, but at least I'll be on the other side."

Pat just nodded.

Creek fords are hard. The uneven, rocky bottoms of creeks scared me and my scuba booties did not provide ankle support. My balance, which is horrible to begin with, was constantly challenged by the pulsating demands of flowing water. I've fallen into a great many creeks. And here was the mother of all creek fords—a deep, long, raging, cold, rocky creek ford. Falling here, though, was a bad idea. Before I could even scream, I would be 20 yards down the flow.

With rope secured, I took each wary step toward the other side, steadying myself against the current. The creek was not only fast, it was deep. Toward the middle of the ford, I was in over my waist. The pull created by the force of water was enormous; I could barely move. My body was shivering. The noise of the crashing water around me assaulted my ears. *Think inches, Martin. Think inches.*

I slushed out of Tyndale creek with most of my body covered with water. Fatigue was starting to set in and I was very cold. We gathered on the far shore.

"Let's walk until the snowpack takes over, then we'll hit Forester in the morning," I suggested.

Right after the ford, patches of snow graced the trail and it wasn't long before the PCT was permanently lost under a white blanket. We made a hasty camp on the last dry patch of earth.

As I happily slid myself into my warm mummy bag, I set my mental alarm clock. At first light, I wanted to awaken. Day 73: Forester Pass was our goal and I needed to be ready.

Awakened by light, I freed myself from my bag and found my

boots frozen solid. After a few minutes of pulling and tugging, they painfully covered my cold feet. I tied the laces of each boot and stood up.

We made our way up the pass and managed, by rope and prayer, to traverse a death-fall ice chute. After the pass, the way down was marked by several lengthy falls all too close to a frozen lake. And finally, a summer snowstorm capped a long and trying day.

It was still gently snowing the next morning. Fog still surrounded us. We were not pleased. But Cedar Grove was just down that trail and we were ready for a break.

After walking for several wet and snowy miles, Cindy and I took a break on some granite rocks. I got out some trail mix and she pulled a lettuce head out of her pack. She looked hungrily at my lunch and said, "Trade ya' for some of that trail mix."

"Trade for trail mix? You don't have anything I like."

She turned her lettuce head seductively, "How about half of this?"

"You know I don't like stuff like that."

"Have you tried it? Do you really know?"

I looked at the lettuce. I don't like salads, but that lettuce looked good all of a sudden.

"Okay, I'll trade you."

Cindy got out a knife and cut the head in half and I handed her the trail mix bag.

From the first crunch, I came to culinary heaven. The texture caressed my mouth and teeth. The juices from this fresh vegetable enlivened my tired taste buds. My body, obviously craving some of the nutrients held within, welcomed the well-chewed lettuce to my stomach.

I devoured that lettuce.

So empowered, the SET made our descent into Cedar Grove.

Even though California had been my home for 22 years, I hadn't seen a thing that I recognized since Mexico. On the last switchbacks into Cedar Grove, my eyes gazed upon land where I had walked before and I started to cry. This surprised me. Perhaps I was just happy to see familiar places. Perhaps in that moment I dared to hope that I would walk through the Sierra. I don't know.

Cedar Grove was not one of our scheduled stops. Cindy wanted to leave the trail at this point. She had friends there and wanted us to meet them. Pat and I had intended to hike 155 miles from Kennedy Meadows all the way to Florence Lake. This was a loony plan when there was no snow on the route—the distance was too great on one supply. With the snow still holding the mountains firmly in its grasp, getting to Florence Lake from Kennedy Meadows on one supply was impossible. So we all decided to go out. We'd called Dad, our trusty supplier, from Kennedy Meadows and asked him to send us a supply package to Cedar Grove. But, when we asked for general delivery packages for the McCorkles, there was no package at the post office. For some weird reason, Dad couldn't get a package into the park. This was bad: We had no money and no food, and we were hungry. We were ten days away from Florence Lake, where Dad would drive our supply package up to us.

Pat wrote a check to one of Cindy's friends to get a little money. At the general store, we purchased a meager supply. As we packed up outside the store, we met a team of packers who had left their trail early due to the same bizarre weather that had plagued us on Forester. When they heard of our situation, they gladly gave us the rest of their food. For this generosity, we were very thankful. Our meager supply was a little bigger.

Now we had another choice. Did we wait around a day or two for Dad to bring us a package, or did we set out for Florence Lake, a ten-day trek, with what we had? Polaris beckoned us, and we decided again to walk.

Early the next day, we said our goodbyes to Cindy during a feast of chicken, cheeseburgers, and chocolate sundaes. Someone offered us a ride to the trailhead, and we happily accepted. Signs, rangers, and hikers all told us that the passes were closed and that no one was getting through. We'd heard this all before. We didn't even pay attention. Our ascent of Forester gave us a little attitude. We had conquered the highest, snowiest pass; what could be worse than that?

On our way up to Paradise Valley, the Mist Falls of the South Fork of the Kern River soaked us. The Sierran runoff was in full swing. We camped in Paradise Valley, a noted bear hangout, in order to see a few bears, but none visited us. The next day, we moved up trail toward Pinchot Pass until the snow claimed the land.

As Day 78 started, a day when we would walk on snowless terra firma for only about one fourth of a mile, Pat and I weren't even sure which of the many passes around us was Pinchot. It's kind of important to get the right pass. A lot of work goes into climbing a pass and we didn't want to be wrong. So only after a vigorous discussion of landmarks, topo maps, and direction did we finally pick up our packs and start on our way.

First impressions were not good. The snow looked really steep, but as we drew near, kicking in one step at a time, we found solid routes and reasonably safe passage. Toward the top, we had to move over to a rock face and do a little climbing, but handholds and footholds were plentiful and sure.

Just after the pass, we ran into a guy coming up from the other side. He had a nametag on a green shirt. He briskly walked to us and introduced himself, "Hi, I'm Dario. I'm a backcountry ranger and I haven't seen anyone for ten days!"

Poor Dario, he was starved for company. Even though I was shivering on the pass and I wanted to keep moving before the snow got any slushier, we sat and chitchatted with Dario for a while.

"Nobody for ten days! Where is everybody?" I asked.

"These passes are keeping everybody out. I crossed Mather Pass several days ago. Once you cross over, no one's going to follow."

He pointed out Mather Pass in the distance. Mather looked steep and was covered with snow. Was this ever going to stop?

After sharing the milk of human companionship, Pat and I walked through the snow and didn't even bother to find the trail. The concept of "following the trail" had little meaning here. We would follow the water shed down Pinchot until it merged with the waters draining the Mather Pass region and then follow these waters up until they were lost under a great white blanket. If the trail was available and clear, great! We walked on it. But most of the time, we wandered through the Sierra by river and by pass, as free as anyone who had ever walked here.

The way to Mather Pass led through the unearthly Upper Basin. This was a wide, open expanse, dotted with tarns, lakes, and streams—a harsh land that spoke of desolation. Nothing much grew here. The wind howled; the coyotes did not. The thunderous mountains around this waste stood guard—black, tall, and ragged. Pat and I walked toward Mather Pass through this basin in silence. Human speech did not fit.

Finally, as we neared Mather Pass, we had to talk. Like Pinchot, the snowfields up the pass looked steep. Unlike Pinchot, they really were. The open rock faces gave us a better shot, so we started to climb on rock. We did all right for a while, but the rock got steeper and the climb more technical. In a sort of desperation move, we took to an ice cave for about fifteen feet in order to get to more manageable rock. Although beautiful inside—a tube of gleaming ice—our desperation move did not lead to an easier route. We finally decided that the only way to climb the pass was to traverse a long, steep snowbank to a patch of climbable rock leading to the pass. Pat didn't need to use his ice ax. The snow was slushy and he made good steps by kicking his feet directly into the steep bank. I followed these steps across the field, using my ax as an anchor in the snow.

Things went great until the halfway point. I planted my feet in one of Pat's kick-ins and as I moved my other foot around, my foot slipped out. I couldn't regain my footing. I held onto my ice ax with great determination, praying that it would hold. If my ax came out, I would slide for hundreds, if not thousands of feet. But I couldn't get my footing back. I tried kicking new steps that would lead me up to Pat's old ones, but I kept sliding out of them. And every time I moved, my ax gave way in the snow. I could not hold on for much longer. Somehow, I don't remember how, I got back up to Pat's steps. With a sigh, I started again, only to fall again five steps later. Now I was really scared. I cried out to Pat. I prayed for strength as I hung on to Mather Pass. I was tired. I didn't know what to do. Pat came down and helped me get back in the steps. He stayed close to me as we moved forward, kicking in the old steps until they were deep and sure. One step at a time and soon I stood on solid rock.

From the rock, we had an easy climb to the pass. Mather was our last pass over 12,000 feet. It was the Fourth of July.

The mountains expanded me. Standing on a snow-covered passes gazing over wilderness as far as I could see, I felt powerful. Walking through forest without a trail to guide me left me confident and able. Sitting by creeks and rivers as they fussed and spat made me aware of energy flowing everywhere in the mountains: In the clouds, in the rocks, in the trees and in the earth. I could feel this mighty power in the quiet.

The next day, food began to be an issue. I was hungry all day, yet there wasn't enough food. We still had to walk a long way. I studied the labels of everything I ate and discovered that I had consumed around 1,100 calories while walking through twelve miles of Sierra wilderness carrying a backpack. Hikers on the PCT have put down as much as 4,000 calories a day and still lost weight. 1,100 calories weren't nearly enough. I was always hungry and always irritable. There wasn't a McDonald's nearby.

We walked in a weary, zombie-like way up to the Muir Hut on Muir Pass. At 11,955 feet, the Muir Hut was our highest camp on the trail. The landscape from this hut in the sky was stunning. Thunderheads dissipated over the dark colors of the Goddard Divide. Sunlight from a setting sun danced on the snow. But hunger held our minds and hearts. We made a big helping of cheese casserole. But that dinner did little to fill the yawning void that was my stomach.

From here, we had to walk five days, mostly downhill, to Florence Lake. The creek fords were outrageous. Evolution Creek went up to my waist, daring to engulf my backpack and me. Once in a while, hikers, who we were starting to run into a bit more often, gave us a small amount of food. We must have looked like sticks! On Day 84, my journal entry is brief: "Hungry, starving, lazy—can't wait for the 11th—two days to go."

We walked and we were hungry. When I settled into camp, I fantasized about food. I conjured up visions of feasts where voluptuous waitresses carried platters filled with glistening meats, grilled vegetables, full cups, and aromatic breads in endless quantities. I remembered Thanksgiving meals and cranberry sauce. I sat and thought about what I would order at the next restaurant—grilled steak with onions and shrimp with cocktail sauce, two baked potatoes with heaps of butter and sour cream, broccoli in cheese sauce, steaming bread hot out of the oven, red wine and, to finish off the feast, two pieces of cheesecake with fresh coffee and cream and sugar. Oh, I wanted to eat, eat, EAT!

As we neared Florence Lake, we ran into a man on a horse who looked every part the cowboy. He took off his hat and said, "Hello boys. My name is Fred Ross. How are you? You look a little trailworn."

Pat answered, "We're PCTers. We've just come over the passes from Cedar Grove and we're really hungry."

He considered this. "Not too many PCTers this year. You do look hungry. Listen, I'm the owner of the Lost Valley Packing Company. We have a cabin along the trail. When you get there, tell my daughter-in-law I said to feed you. I think you need it."

Such hospitality was eagerly accepted. We had eggs with cheese, English muffins with peanut butter and jelly, and Coke. We ate a lot. We were very happy.

Dad showed up the next day with the supply. And, in addition to this bounty, he brought along Kentucky Fried Chicken, peaches, and some of Grandma's cookies. We ate everything, right down the hatch. I doubt the Colonel has ever seen chicken bones picked so clean.

I learned from Dad that Don and Sally had called him from Cedar Grove. The food package never arrived so Dad had to drive all the way to Kings Canyon to deliver a special package to them. Although he didn't seem to mind, I was irritated. *Pat and I figured out a way to get through without putting my dad under that kind of pressure. Why couldn't Don and Sally? Why did they have to rely so much on my dad? Didn't they have parents?* I stuffed these bitter thoughts into the back of my mind and geared up for the next section of the Sierra.

In preparing the food for our trail, Jennifer baked a fruitcake for each supply box. They were good, but they were heavy. We also got a shade tired of fruitcake after a while. Pat and I began to give away the fruitcakes to people who helped us along the way. Even though conventional wisdom holds that friends don't give friends fruitcakes, we enjoyed spreading them around. As we left Florence Lake, rested and full, we ceremoniously placed the Fruitcake Award on the Ross' porch, but alas, no one was home.

Although there were many high passes to climb, the highest of the Sierra lay south of us. Along the way north, I walked with a porcupine for about five minutes on Seldon Pass. He wobbled around aimlessly on the snow, completely secure that his impressive armor of quills would keep him safe from me.

Pat and I also worked on faster ways to get down passes. He started to ski on his boots. With so much opportunity for practice, he got to where he could make sharp turns and handle some fairly rough snow. I didn't have the balance for that, but I could sit on my butt and use my staff like an oar in a sea of snow and "row" down mountains.

We started to look forward to downhill snowbanks for the sheer entertainment of "boot and butt skiing."

At one such spot, we couldn't see the end of the snowbank. I was game to plunge downward. But Pat was more cautious. We walked down a bit only to find that the snowbank ended abruptly at a small cliff—but large enough to kill or maim us. From then on, we only slid down on what we could see. Good plan.

There was still a lot of snow. We still didn't have enough food. The supply package was not at Red's Meadow when we showed up. I was really annoyed by this. We had looked forward so much to all that food and a little money. And it wasn't there. What was my dad doing? I called him on the phone and he wasn't home. My brother and I sat hungry and poor outside of the general store. How to get food? I began to think about how Don and Sally had bugged my dad into bringing food to them. This gave me an idea. We had given Sally's parents a box of food for emergencies when my dad might not be available. I figured Don and Sally were a day behind us. I called her parents on the phone.

"Hello, Tim. This is Martin. How are you?"

"I'm fine. Where you are?"

"Pat and I are at Red's Meadow. Don and Sally should pull in here tomorrow. We're in kind of a jam here. The food shipment didn't come in. Could you drive that emergency box up here tomorrow?"

"We'd like to see Sally. Are you sure she'll be out tomorrow?"

"Oh yeah. She'll be here."

"Okay."

I gave him directions to Red's Meadow.

The next day they showed up with the food, but Don and Sally were nowhere to be found.

"Where are they?" They were more than a little perturbed.

"I'm not sure. I thought they would be here."

"So you really don't know."

"No, I don't. But I think they'll be here tomorrow."

They gave disgusted looks to each other and Tim said, "Okay. We'll get a room tonight and stop by again tomorrow." *And they better be here* was also implied.

They weren't. I felt like a total idiot. Finally, Sally's parents left Red's Meadow without seeing their daughter. I felt very bad about this. It was the last time I saw Sally's parents.

After receiving a monster breakfast from a family in the campground—I believe I ate fourteen pancakes—we made for Tuolumne Meadows in Yosemite National Park. I took a day off and hitched down to the valley, where I ate as many meals as possible with old friends. I ran into Sally in Yosemite Village and she read me the riot act for the stunt I pulled with her parents. She was right, I deserved the tongue-lashing. But I didn't let her know that. After nightfall, I watched the Benny Hill show with Damon and slept a deep sleep in the valley. I thoroughly enjoyed the much-needed rest.

I hitched back up to Pat in two rides. The first was a bus driver from Yosemite, who failed to recognize me as a former tour guide and also failed in trying to recruit me into the Klan. I was happy to leave his company. The second ride was with a charming Italian couple. We didn't understand each other much, but we enjoyed the ride. By the time I got to the Meadows, Pat had worked out the food. All I had to do was load up my pack and go. It was a little late, so we didn't get very far, about seven miles. I was pretty tired from my visit to the valley and didn't bring much energy to the camp. I went to hang the food after supper and did a shoddy job of bear-bagging on a short tree. Good bagging starts with a good tree. Sometimes I looked around for a while before I found a tree tall enough, with a branch that was strong enough to hold the bags, but not a bear. I didn't want to look around. I knew they weren't high enough, but I was tired and didn't care.

Pat and I were in our sleeping bags before dark. We woke up a few minutes later to the unmistakable sounds of a bear snorting and breaking branches. In the last light of day, I looked up at the bags and saw a bear on his hind legs, clutching our food bag in his paws, pulling it to the ground. All of our precious food was in those bags. We needed those bags. We were tired of being hungry. We wanted to go north, not back to Tuolumne.

My brother was the first to act. He got out of his sleeping bag, bare naked, and began to pound his sierra cup with a spoon and scream at the bear. A rather primal scene presented itself to me: My naked brother challenging a bear for food. He moved in small steps closer and closer to the bear, screaming the whole time. I got up and joined in the drama. We pounded and howled the best we could, but by now, the bear had our bags on the ground and was rooting through them with his snout. Things didn't look good.

I don't recommend the following approach, nor do I think that I myself would repeat it, but we wanted that food and we were going to get that food. Seeing that mere clanging and screaming wasn't working, we began to throw rocks around the bear, getting closer and closer to his black mass. We were about ten feet away, pounding, screaming, throwing, jumping, when he retreated about ten yards.

Pat's command of the situation was complete. "Shove the food into our packs. Let's load up and get back to the bear cables at Glen Aulin." Glen Aulin was a High Sierra camp about a mile back. When we grabbed our food bags, we found them coated with bear slobber. Most unpleasant. But we could hear our black adversary snorting and moving in the pines only a few yards away; a little bear slobber was not going to stop us.

We moved away from the bear and began to walk back to Glen Aulin, when a second bear appeared to the side of the trail. We kind of lost control. We started screaming, pounding our staves against rocks, and stumbled in the darkness toward Glen Aulin, where the cables would save us from this madness.

We lurched into camp, warning the newly retired hikers that we had two bears on our tail. They were excited. We were exhausted. The food was securely bagged and we were in our sleeping bags, asleep, in five minutes. The bears never came.

My brother Pat, a poet in his spare time, penned this remembrance:

Encounter with a Bear

A branch cracks in the twilight.
A thud.
The rustle of tearing fabric.
A moving shadow silhouetted
against a standing stone.

I leap naked from my sleeping bag,
Banging my cup
Like the Rangers tell you.

107

A low growl.
A snort of ursine disdain.
He returns to his fresh picked dinner.
Food I'd hung out of his reach.

There I stand, twentieth century man,
Ten barless steps from five hundred pounds
Of tooth and claw.
Yelling and dancing in the cold.

As for me, this is one of my favorite stories. And besides, thanks to my brother's naked challenge, I got to see three "bares."

Although the riot and glory of the High Sierra had passed, there was beauty and wonder along our way. We left Yosemite National Park through mosquito-infested Grace Meadow and gently inclined, snow-free Dorothy Lake Pass. I didn't expect much from the Sierra north of Yosemite, but I was pleasantly surprised. Periodically, the granite of the Sierra would yield to volcanic rock so red I felt like I was on Mars. Reynolds Peak added to the Martian theme with sharp pinnacles and harsh tones. Further north, we were blessed with views of big, beautiful, and blue Lake Tahoe.

These were the halcyon days of the PCT. The trails were clear of snow while the high peaks were still dressed in white. Pat and I managed our ten miles a day without too much stress and pain. My back hurt and I was weary, but the beauty of the trail inspired us. We developed a style of camping titled "horizontal/vertical camping." As soon as we got to camp, we did everything that required a "vertical" stance—we got water, went to the bathroom, stuff like that. Then, space permitting, we laid down our ground cloths beside each other with about a foot of space between them. We got out our bags and stove so that we could cook, clean up and go to bed while staying horizontal.

My clothing was suffering from months of extreme use. The trail was so dusty that every bit of moisture had leached out of my boots. They got so hard and dry that I had to sleep with them on one night for fear that I wouldn't be able to get them back on in the morning. A little bit of boot wax from a nearby town took care of that. The seat of my shorts, much abused by the harsh granite that I often sat on, wore completely out. I walked for several days with my brown underwear prominently visible to those unfortunate few who had to walk behind me. My dad brought me a new pair at Sonora Pass.

At a stop near Lake Tahoe called Echo Lake, we heard from local hikers about major snow on the north side of Dick's Pass. I didn't want to hear about snow. But I kept hearing the same report and I began to feel tired and frustrated. I was SICK of snow. With a heavy heart I left Echo Lake to work my way toward this last snowy test. We heard more tales of snow. The south-facing ascent was clear, but the descent was where the problem lay.

The summit of Dick's Pass was a revelation. Compared to Forester, Pinchot, Mather, and Muir, the snow found there was not worth even a footnote. White did cover the trail at times, but I followed the trail all the way down. This was a relief. I wouldn't worry about snow again.

But the pass also revealed to us where we were going. Instead of endless snowy peaks and passes chasing the horizon, we looked, uninspired, at the gently rolling northern Sierras. There were no distinct peaks, calling for climbers to scale them. There were no intriguing valleys, inviting hikers to explore. There was nothing to draw us. I heard no song. In some ways, this was a problem worse than snow and ice.

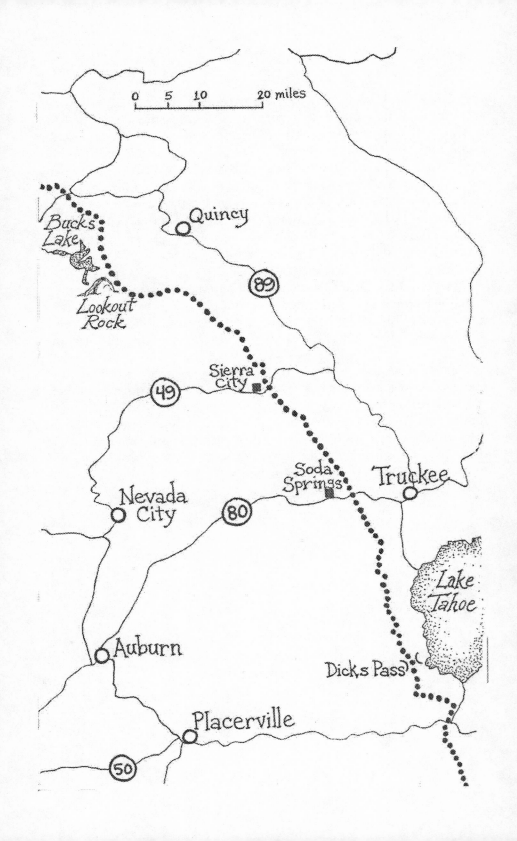

0   5   10   20 miles

Bucks Lake

Quincy

89

Lookout Rock

Sierra City

49

Soda Springs

Truckee

Nevada City

80

Lake Tahoe

Auburn

Dicks Pass

Placerville

50

Chapter 12:
The PCT from Dick's Pass to Lookout Rock

Days 111-124
August 2-15, 1982

Humans are not pack animals. We aren't designed to carry large amounts of weight for long periods of time. Even strong, young men are slowly worn down by the incremental challenges of the PCT. Now I am a man, but I am *not* strong.

The trail rarely rises up to thwart hikers. The PCT rarely goes for a fatal blow. Rather, the endless days of hiking just plain wore me out. How many blisters could I put up with? Two? Three? Twenty? How much could my back scream in awful misery before I quit? How many small nicks, cuts, scrapes and sores would I ignore before I started to feel the agony? How long would I avoid the obvious problems with my stomach before I wised up and went to a doctor?

My body was falling apart.

My journals started to read more like medical charts than adventure stories. I wrote like a hypochondriac gone berserk. I was having terrible gastrointestinal problems. I had thunderous gas. My bowel movements were painful and irregular. My right leg had become practically useless, more like a wooden appendage that I dragged along—a pirate's peg leg—rather than a part of my living body. My belly strap, which didn't fit, chafed my sore hips until open sores appeared. My back began to hurt—not when I carried my pack, but when I took it off. That scared me.

Nor was my spirit in the best of shape. The High Sierras had been challenging, drawing me through windswept passes and rapturous views. But the High Sierra was gone. There were no more snowbound passes daring to stay our progress while beckoning us by their beauty. Instead, there were jeep trails and forested saddles. There was no vision to call me beyond my pain. And my pain, so long suppressed, would not be suppressed any longer.

From Dick's Pass we made our way north. As I read my journal entries from these days, I can't close my eyes and imagine the camps I describe. Perhaps I just was full of mountain memory and didn't have the space to remember any more. But more likely, the land did not leave an impression on my mind. I walked through this country; I wrote about meadows and streams, but I do not remember them.

We held a feast on day 111. On this day, we passed the 1,000-mile mark. A full spaghetti dinner was prepared and consumed. Apple crisp aplenty capped the feast. Camping at the 1,000-mile mark was a deeply satisfying moment. One thousand miles is a long way. If I drove from the urban environs of Chicago, linked up with highway 80 and went west, I'd pass through Illinois and the Quad Cities, I'd continue west through the lilting hills of Iowa and the flat, heartland of Nebraska into Colorado and come up about 40 miles short of Denver before I logged 1,000 miles. But I didn't drive; I walked on my own two feet. Every step. Carrying everything that I needed to live right on my back.

The next day, however, was just another day in a seemingly endless string of days. We labored north, working our way through Soda Springs and Sierra City. I started to lose focus. I kept thinking about arriving in Oregon and not on the next day's camp. Walking was no longer joyful; backpacking was more like work. I "punched in" to walk and "punched out" to camp.

Pat and I rarely spoke anymore. There was no need. In the long hours of past camps, we had already talked about everything there was to talk about. We didn't need to speak about who would cook or clean, we just did it. Our economy of motion in "horizontal/vertical camping" was imitated in economy of speech—we used as few words as possible. People overhearing our conversations wouldn't have been able to understand our sparse communications. A typical evening's chat with translation in italics follows:

"Middle Velma Lake, " I said. *Middle Velma Lake looks like a good camp for tomorrow.*

"Water?" *Is there water along the way?*

"Yep. Gilmore Lake Outlet?" *Yes, there's plenty of water along the way. How about lunch at Gilmore Lake Outlet?*

Pat would take the PCT guide; look at it for a few minutes and nod. *That sounds good to me.*

And that was it.

The end was coming. Don and Sally had dropped out in Sierra City, having completed about 75 percent of the trail through California. Even though I didn't like them and couldn't stand to spend more than a few minutes with them, I was sad when they left the trail. I wanted them to walk all the way to the Shakespeare Festival in Ashland, Oregon. Other hikers we had followed in the post office PCT registers were disappearing. The combination of deep-set fatigue and lack of beauty and challenge was taking a toll on a lot of hikers. We felt abandoned on the trail.

Day 120 was the beginning of the end. We were camped just off the PCT at the headwaters of the Feather River. For supper, both the patties and the cake we made were raw and barely edible. We didn't have enough oil to fry them properly. By the time I went to bed, my stomach felt like a drum. I could slap my belly button like a tympani. It had pitch—B flat, I think. Gastrointestinal battles were raging within. I couldn't sleep. I defecated five times that night in a vain attempt to rid my body of pain. I lost track of where I had buried my feces. As I moved about in the darkness, searching to make yet another hole in the ground, I feared that my bare feet would step into a warm, soft mass.

Finally I slept, but I wasn't much better in the morning. Pat and I decided to take a rest day right there, hoping that a 24-hour break would repair four months of stress.

During the day, the man who lived in the Pilot Peak Fire Lookout Station visited our camp. He brought along his two dogs: Zeke and Calhoun. I played fetch with the dogs for a while. Their playfulness was good for my downtrodden spirit. He got some water from the infant Feather River and invited us up to his home the next day.

Day 122 was a long day. We did visit our friend in the sky, and the station was kind of cool. Glimpses of Mt. Lassen and even Mt. Shasta, California's northernmost major peak, were inspiring, but our host was rather hard to talk to and seemed uncomfortable sharing his space—what other kind of person could live alone and look for fires all day?

The trail wasn't any better. Almost immediately after we left the fire lookout, the tread got difficult to follow, and Pat and I were separated most of the day. I wasn't sure whether he was ahead or behind and, by nightfall, I was getting concerned. I had seen a rattlesnake that day—the first sighting in a long time—and I imagined Pat somewhere on the route alone and bitten. I didn't know what to do.

I scribbled some notes on blank pages torn from my journal and left them for Pat if he was behind. I didn't know what to do if he was ahead. As night fell, I left a note at a saddle where I left the PCT to find water. I found a small creek about 200 yards off the route and settled in to spend my first night totally alone on the PCT.

As long as there was light, I continued to look for Pat. I grabbed my journal and walked back to the trail and wrote as I waited for his familiar gait to appear in the twilight. It was here, waiting for Pat, that I finally got honest with my situation. My back hurt really badly, and the pain was getting worse fast. I simply didn't know if I could go 45 more days. If I could, I worried that I might do permanent damage to my back. It was here that I finally admitted that I might have to leave the trail.

Just as last light flickered out, Pat showed up. I don't know how he did it. He didn't have the guide or a map, but he got to camp. Just like he always did. I was so relieved to have him around. We talked about my back and decided to switch packs and see if that helped.

The next morning, I was pretty depressed. The idea of walking with the kind of pain my back was in was not motivating at all. Pat sensed my depression. We had the laziest morning we could possibly have—and that was something since most of our mornings were pretty laid back. But finally, I had to put Pat's pack on and walk. At first walking wasn't bad; I pounded down the switchbacks to the Middle Fork of the Feather River and swam in her warm waters. Then we walked across an impressive bridge and began to climb out of the canyon. This climb was agonizing. Shards of pain shot through my back in wild and electric bursts. I couldn't escape the pain, no matter how I walked—no matter what pack I wore. I wanted so much to stop and rest—to experience relief from this torture. But when I arrived at camp, my back only got worse. I sat down with my back straight as a rod against the sides of a bridge and found some comfort. But after I got settled, I couldn't move. Movement of any kind was misery. Pat cooked supper and did the chores. I tried to write in my journal, but on this day, I ran out of ink. I couldn't write anymore.

As I lay down in my bag, I couldn't straighten my legs. My back was flat against the ground, but my legs were bent at the knees. This wasn't restful, but it wasn't painful either. In slow, agonizing increments, I slid my legs down. Hours passed before my legs were flat on the ground. Every quarter-inch was a battle against pain. Sometime late that night, under the disinterested stars of a black sky, I made my choice. I had walked enough. Leaving the trail was not a matter of convenience; it was a matter of wisdom. I couldn't walk to Oregon. Even if I wanted to risk permanent injury, I just couldn't hike another day. It was ironic. I'd always thought my feet or my legs would fail me—I hadn't even thought about my back! Life is a strange thing. But after this decision was made and my legs were relaxed, I slept well. I knew what I would do.

Pat completely understood. He saw my pain. We had done everything we could. Now we had to get me to a road. So once more, I shouldered my pack during the 1982 PCT. I walked, step after step, out of the Feather River Canyon, limping to Buck's Lake, where there was a road. I've never been so motivated to get to a road. I came to a point called Lookout Rock. From here, I was rewarded with a commanding view of the Middle Fork Valley to the south and forested valleys to the east. I stopped there for my last trailside view.

A jeep trail skirts the PCT right after Lookout Rock; I flagged down a forest ranger who, after hearing about the PCT and my back, rather begrudgingly gave me a ride to the Buck's Lake campground. Pat walked into camp that night and we switched our gear around so that he could keep going. He intended to finish the route. I called back to Sacramento and asked for a ride home. I was finished. Don would come the next day.

That last night under the stars was hard. My back was thanking me for leaving my pack behind. But I was sad. I wanted to finish. Sure, 1,200 miles was a long way, but I wanted to walk to Oregon. I didn't want to stop at Buck's Lake. What is that? In a deep place, buried in my heart, I hid a promise. I would come back to Lookout Rock. I would hike every step to Oregon.

115

The next day, Pat walked north, carrying the PCT guide for the first time. He, alone out of the five who began, walked to Oregon as planned.

As for me, Don picked me up. I tried not to wince in pain every time the car took a corner or hit a bump. I tried to talk to Don. I failed in both pursuits. In the space of a few uncomfortable hours, we were back in Sacramento.

Chapter 13:
Convergence

At first, my life continued to fall apart. Dad had rented out the house in Citrus Heights, so I wound up living with him and his new wife. This was an okay place to stop by for a while, but it wasn't my home. I didn't feel comfortable there. Long before my back was healed—after two or three weeks—I shaved off my beard and left.

And that was only the physical part of my situation. I was a young man without a vision. I had worked toward the PCT for about three years. Now the trail was over. It was done. I had nothing to do, nothing to dream about, nothing to strive for. I had no reason to get out of bed. So I went back to Yosemite—not because I wanted to go, not because I wanted to explore, not because the move was part of a dream—I went to Yosemite because I didn't have anywhere else to go.

The pickings for jobs were thin at the end of the summer, so I got hired as a lobby porter, a janitor for the public areas at the Ahwahnee Hotel.

I lived a strange sort of life there. While at work, I pretended that I was fine; but I wasn't. My back was in constant pain. There were times when every push of the broom sent a shock of misery through my spine, but I didn't wince; I didn't let on. I didn't want to lose my job. I didn't have anywhere to go if I did. I fought through the pain every day.

When I got home, I didn't do anything. If you've had back pain, you know what I mean. Back pain takes energy away like nothing else. I was always tired; I was always craving immobility. I worked and I rested and that was about all I could handle.

To make things worse, I was developing some rather serious

misanthropic attitudes. The other employees annoyed me—they didn't appreciate the mountains the way I did. I was bothered by tourists; their short, picture-taking trips to the valley were a sort of sacrilege to the park. I was still hurt by Don and Sally.

I asked a few girls out, but our dates were strained and uncomfortable. After spending so much time alone on the trail, I was less annoyed when I was by myself, so I lived a basically solitary life. I was becoming less and less connected with humanity. I was becoming less and less connected to myself.

As the months went by, my back got better slowly—oh so slowly. But my heart stayed cold. As soon as I was able, I started to walk again. Mostly I took late afternoon walks by the Merced River. There I was soothed by the gentle, flowing waters.

Then, the strands of my life began to converge.

One afternoon, I was sitting on a washing machine in the employee laundromat reading *The Brothers Karamazov*, when an attractive young woman began to talk with me. I thought she was trying to pick me up, so I put my book down and focused on the possibilities. Shortly into the conversation, she asked me if I wanted to go to a Bible study. I grinned. So this was the deal—she didn't want to sleep with me; she wanted to convert me. She was nice and I didn't want to be rude, but I didn't want to go to a Bible study, so I said, "Thanks, but I've done the church thing before; I'm really not interested." I thought she would take off after that, but she didn't. We chatted some more; I finished my laundry and took off.

As a young kid, getting up on Sunday morning and going to church was automatic. I never had strong feelings one way or the other about religion. My overriding sense of the whole thing was boredom. Playing in rock bands and climbing mountains were much more challenging and rewarding pursuits than church. As Mom's depression deepened, we went less and less. I was troubled that her faith did not help her. What good was Christ if he couldn't help my mom?

In high school, Don and I sometimes went to the Wherehouse. The Wherehouse was an old warehouse where Christian performers and rock groups gave free concerts for young people. I liked watching the bands. Some of them were good. I liked the price even better. There was more to this experience than free music, something deeper. But

I didn't want to deal with God; I was having too much fun elsewhere.

I even took a Bible on one of my first backpacking trips. I was looking for a light book to carry and found a paperback New Testament lying around. I started reading the Gospel of Matthew and got to where the soldiers began to mock Christ and beat him. I stopped reading—I couldn't handle the evil way the soldiers treated him.

There weren't that many employees at Yosemite, so I often ran into Marsha, my religious friend, during my walks and errands. She was always nice, genuinely interested and kind. This was disarming. I wanted her to be uptight, petty and self-righteous—that would have made disregarding her religion much easier. But she wasn't any of these things.

I was already in bed one Wednesday night when she dropped by my tent and asked me if I wanted to come to a Bible study. For reasons that I can't really explain, I decided to go. Marsha waited outside as I threw some clothes on. We walked a few hundred yards to the home of Larry, one of Yosemite's store managers.

When the Bible study got started, Larry began to explain the basics of Christianity. God loves us, but we have sinned and messed up our relationship with God so that we can't enjoy God or receive his salvation. I had heard this gospel hundreds of times in the Baptist churches I'd attended and the Wherehouse concerts I'd enjoyed. But my recent experiences clarified this message. Over the course of my four and a half months of walking in solitude and silence through unrelenting natural beauty, I had become increasingly aware of some sort of power undergirding creation. Life was so mysterious and complex that I couldn't believe anymore that our universe was some cosmic accident. I sometimes thought of this power as the Force of *Star Wars*. At other times, I thought of this power in a more eastern way as I read *Zen and Art of Motorcycle Maintenance*. I didn't think of this "undergirding power" as "God," but I was okay with thinking of it, or Him, in other ways.

The sin stuff made lots of sense too. I knew that there was something deeply wrong with me. I felt like I was bent. I wanted to forgive people, but I couldn't. I wanted to feel a deeper love, but I was powerless. I had lots of beefs with people, but in the end, I knew that my own anger was the real problem. Until that moment, I had not thought of these things as "sin." No one else I was talking to or anything I was reading was dealing with this deep sense of "bentness" like Larry was during our Bible study. He showed me that Jesus, the Son of God, had died for my sins, to pay for them so that I could be fully and justly forgiven. Even though I had heard this many times before, I was riveted by every word Larry said.

At the end of the study, he challenged me to receive Christ by faith. I knew right then that Christ was my savior and that what I heard that night was true, but I couldn't make this jump. Becoming a Christian was just too weird — too soon. Larry gave me a couple of books about Christianity and I left, much to my relief.

I got back to my tent, but I couldn't stop thinking about our conversation. I picked up one of the books he had given me called *Evidence That Demands a Verdict*. I read page after page about textual transmission, personal testimonies of changed lives, evidences for the resurrection and so much more. I read for hours.

Sometime very late that night, I felt the power of God around me. I was not alone. At the Wherehouse I had felt something. There in my tent, I felt someone. I knew in my head and my heart that this "gospel" was the truth. I really had no choice. I had to believe or I would destroy myself. There was nothing left but the truth. I closed my eyes and said, "Okay." That was all; that was my confession. I yielded my life to God. I fell into a deep sleep.

The next morning I was different. My heart felt warmer and people weren't so irritating. As a matter of fact, I kind of liked some of them. Soon afterward, I found grace in my heart to forgive Don and Sally for whatever I thought they had done. I met a lot of other great people who walked in the faith. They were fun people and I started to enjoy my life again.

One of these new friends was Pastor Bill, the leader of a small church of about 35 people in El Portal, a town just outside of Yosemite. I went down to El Portal to work with Bill on Monday mornings before I had to be at the Ahwahnee. We talked together, split wood for some of the church's widows, visited hurting people and helped out in all kinds of practical ways. This active, physical service was a balm to my soul. I was living and feeling again.

Through this work with Bill, I began to sense that I should become a pastor. I enjoyed the social part of our work. Sitting around drinking coffee and sharing a fresh pastry with an elderly widow was interesting. Elderly people have such great stories to tell. I liked the scholastic side of pastoral work. I led a few Bible studies, and people seemed to like my teaching. What a hoot! Me, the prince of misanthropes, lover of solitude and avoider of humanity, a pastor! There was certainly a great deal of cosmic humor in this.

A few months later, I was playing my guitar under a tree in the Lower Yosemite Falls parking lot. A group of us was waiting to meet some new employees and go off to Devil's Elbow, a picnic ground along the Merced River, for a barbecue. A truck pulled up and a bunch of people hopped out. One of them, in particular, caught my eye.

She jumped out of the back of the truck, and I was intrigued right away. Her eyes flashed with intelligence. She was catching and assimilating everything *really* fast. Her whole body seemed to radiate life. Her skin did not appear substantive enough to contain the energy she generated. Her face was beautiful, glowing with vitality and joy. Her inviting smile was enhanced by earrings that flashed in the sunlight. At the barbecue, we got to talking. She was a musician, a piano major. She was interested in hiking. Her name was Rebecca.

We took long walks under the pines of Yosemite Valley. We often rode our bikes up to Inspiration Point and sped back down the highway, laughing as the wind's fingers tussled our hair. We took picnic baskets to the tops of waterfalls, where we shared clear mountain water, cheese and our sweet lips. We spoke of dreams.

Things were moving along quite well. But something was troubling me. We sat down on a concrete bench, a place of rest that was hard as rock. I needed her to know some things about me. I explained that I had CMT and what it could do to me in the future. She might have to take care of me. I also shared my vision for adoption. I'd thought about this since I was about thirteen. I didn't know all that I needed to know, but I was almost certain that I would pass on CMT in some genetic form to all of my children and grandchildren. I didn't want to do this. I could see my sons unable to play Little League, slowly limping to first base. I could see my daughters, stumbling through their lives. I was not so selfish that I had to have carbon copies of me as my children. I wanted to adopt. I needed to marry a woman who could share my vision for adoption. If having children naturally was important to Rebecca, I needed to know that up front. Rebecca received this with such grace that I was blown away. She understood the situation and, of course, agreed that adoption was the way to build a family.

I was used to women who left when things got tough. Pam, my mom, and Sally didn't stick with me when life got hard. At first, I hadn't wanted to talk to Rebecca about CMT and adoption. I thought she would do the same thing—leave. But Rebecca stayed. After this conversation, her eyes welcomed me and said, "Well Martin, what's next?" I could build a life with this woman.

After I had known her for about four months, I asked Rebecca to marry me while we were visiting the California Coast. She accepted. She asked if I had talked with her father about my proposal. This was news to me; I wasn't planning to marry her father. But I called him anyway. His faith must have been great. I had been a Christian for about a year. I was a college dropout. I was living in Yosemite, working as a janitor. I didn't have a car, but I was careful with Rebecca's red Renault Alliance. I was going to be a pastor. Would you let this man marry your daughter? Well, he did. Thanks, Dad.

We planned to be wed the following summer, on July 14, 1984.

During the summer of 1983, my hiking days entered a golden age. My back was fully recovered. I went hiking almost every weekend and became an unofficial tour guide for the backcountry. Even though we had different days off, Rebecca and I managed to visit Ten Lakes and climb Mt. Dana and Mammoth Peak. On other weekends, I put out the word that I was planning a trip to places like Cloud's Rest or Mt. Hoffman, and employees from all over the park would join me, some of whom I didn't even know. Weekend after weekend I scoured the park always taking along a new bunch to share the wonder.

My new spiritual awareness iced the cake. The mountains glowed for me in a fresh way. I found God in the heights. Trees praised him. Streams sang his song. Flowers lifted their petals to the heavens. No one has said it better than John Muir: "No temple made with human hands can compare with Yosemite. Every rock in its walls seems to glow with life."

Before I left the Sierra, I had one place that I still desired to see. I needed to go to the highest place.

Chapter 14:
The Highest Place

I put out the word that I wanted to drive south and climb Mt. Whitney. I knew my days in Yosemite were coming to a close, and I wanted to bag Whitney—the highest mountain in the contiguous United States. Although I'd planned to finish off my John Muir Trail trek at this mountain, loneliness and lack of food had forced me out at Cedar Grove, well short of Whitney. On the PCT, there was way too much snow and Forester Pass was enough excitement at the time. I wanted to try again.

Tom and Diane, two very casual acquaintances, signed on. Diane had some wheels, so we set out bright and early to make the long drive south to Whitney Portal. I thought that was the coolest name for a place to start a trail—not trailhead or campground, but portal—a window to a new world.

The three of us arrived at a packed parking lot, got our wilderness permit, shouldered our packs and got going. While it was only 11.5 miles to the top of Whitney, we would climb from 8,500 feet to 14,496 feet—an elevation gain of 6,000 feet. I set a purposeful pace, one that would get us there about sundown.

At our only break, we started up a conversation with a guy named Fred. Fred was preparing some tea beside a serene lake. He had a relaxing demeanor and offered to share his warm drink. Fred didn't know whether or not he wanted to climb to the summit that night.

"I've got lots of food and lots of fuel. I don't need to be in a hurry."

"Yeah, but think of the view up there," I replied. "I want to spend the night up there. Can you imagine what the stars on the summit must be like? Besides, we have to get back to work, we have to climb the summit today."

We chatted some more, and Fred decided to join us. This was good. I would need Fred.

We continued to climb, mostly walking on switchbacks and rarely on level ground. Trees gave way to rock. Granite overruled the ground. And still we climbed. I pushed the group hard. Time was passing, and the summit of Whitney was still far away.

We came to a very long and very exposed section of switchbacks blasted right out of a granite wall. These switchbacks led up to the crest of the Sierra. Our party was alone. Those who had planned to camp on the summit were already there. Those who had planned to finish the summit tomorrow had already laid down their packs.

I would not let the group rest. With a sigh, we came to the crest of the Sierra Nevada. We were now only 1.8 miles from the summit. The sun was low in the horizon so we hurried on. I was in the best shape of my life, but I began to feel a little lightheaded at about 13,500 feet. I needed more air. I slowed my pace a little. The others were pretty happy about that.

During the whole day, not a single hiker or group passed us, while we overtook scores of hikers. But on these barren heights, I heard the sound of music and was passed by a huge man with a gigantic pack singing *Ghost Riders in the Sky*. I was having trouble just walking and he was singing! He grinned as he swept by us.

Finally, after gaining all that elevation and walking 11.5 miles while only taking a single break, we came to the summit of Mt. Whitney. The sun's full circle still held its place in the sky, but sunset was near.

I looked over the camps on the summit. There were only a few places on this barren granite summit where a party could camp. Over the years hikers had picked the small rocks out of the dirt and left small clearings—about the size of a two-man tent—all over the summit. They looked like nests. There were five of these nests on the summit.

As my eyes panned over the camps, I saw a man sitting on a boulder, staring into the wind, his mouth wide open. He wore a yellow windbreaker over bare skin. I walked up to him and said, "How are you doing?"

"Ahh haf fins." He weakly pointed down the mountain.

I got closer to him, touched his shoulder and said more

emphatically, "Hey, how are you doing?"

He looked at me with vacant eyes and repeated his enigmatic phrase, "Ahh haf fins" and pointed.

I looked to where he was pointing and saw another man come over the ledge. He was stumbling. I walked over to him and tried to learn more, but he couldn't even speak. He sat down and wouldn't move. Three more men crawled over the ledge. They were dressed in tee shirts and shorts. They didn't have any packs. Only the last man up could talk.

"Hey, what's up with you guys?"

"We're camped down at the base of Whitney by the lake. We took the mountaineer's route up to the summit. It was a lot harder than we thought. I didn't think it would take this long."

I looked over his group. I had read about hypothermia many times. I thought that I'd had a touch here or there myself. But as I looked over these four men, I saw real hypothermia for the first time—slurred speech, loss of muscle control, and impaired decision-making ability. They were in serious shape. People die from hypothermia.

"All right, all you guys get in the shelter."

Their leader resisted. "No, we're going to take the trail down and get back to our camp."

I held his eyes with my own and said, "Four men in your group have hypothermia. You don't have any food. You don't have a stove to make hot drinks. You don't have any clothes. You don't even have a flashlight. If you start down that trail with these guys, it'll be pitch black by the time you're done with the first mile. The switchbacks off the ridge are dangerous. If you don't fall off, you'll just stop somewhere to rest, fall asleep, and die. Now, get…in…the…shelter."

We stood glaring at each other, like two mountain goats ready to butt heads. He thought for a minute, and then his shoulders sagged as he agreed. He seemed glad to pass his group off to me.

I got the group to the shelter and found that it was full of snow and smelled awful. The shelter doubled as a bathroom. I looked around inside and spied an open space behind the snow. I crammed them in. "Stay close to each other. Hug each other. Share what warmth you have. I'll be right back." The sun set in a distant bank of clouds.

I went over to Fred. "We've got a problem. We've got five guys who need to get warm fast." I gave him my stove. "Use my stove to heat up water for drinks. Fred, if you've got extra food and fuel, I need you to share." Fred set up a little kitchen and got cooking.

I went to each camp and explained the situation. I needed hot drinks, any available food and extra items of clothing, ASAP! This was tough. Hikers only take what they need, especially up to Mt. Whitney! But in a pinch, hikers are always willing to share. I met the huge singer—his name was Joe. He wanted to help out, so I assigned him to shuttle the hot drinks to the men. A woman went around gathering clothes.

A half hour later, the late arrivals had used up all that we had to offer. The hot drinks helped, but the clothing was not adequate. As I looked them over where they huddled next to a pile of snow, I didn't think the few scarves, hats, shirts, and gloves we'd scrounged would keep them warm against the cold night. I walked over to our tent and grabbed my sleeping bag.

Back at the shelter I covered the men with my bag. "Okay, huddle up and keep this bag over you. Do not separate. Stay together. Keep this bag as tight as you can over your group. I'll see you guys in the morning".

I looked them over once more and was still uneasy. I wasn't sure they would be alive tomorrow. When I left the shelter, stars spilled across the dark sky. I worked my way back to the tent and quickly zipped it up.

Tom said, "Man, where's your bag?"

"I used it to cover the guys."

"You did what? How are you going to stay warm? We're up here . . . "

"I'll be fine. Our body heat will warm the tent. You and Diane can lean over me on both sides and I'll make it. Did you leave me any dinner?"

"Yeah, it's right here."

I devoured my cold dinner in a few gulps.

I laid down and pulled Tom and Diane over me. I reviewed the evening. Funny, I'd never even looked at the scenery. That was okay; I'd do that in the morning. Before I slept, I prayed a simple prayer. "Keep them alive."

That night, the winds raged. Cold often drew me from sleep, and

I had to pull my companions' sleeping bags over me again to stay somewhat warm. It was a long night.

At first light, I opened the tent and my face was slapped by passionate winds and driving snow. Black clouds attacked Mt. Whitney and screamed over the top. Visibility was down to about five yards. *Why did it always snow when I came to the southern Sierra?* As I walked to the shelter, I felt an overwhelming sense of dread. *Time for the body count.*

I tentatively said, "Hey, guys, how is it going?" Nothing. I grabbed my bag and shook it a little, "Hey, guys, how is it going?"

"What? Is it morning?"

Another voice, "I'm cold."

I was never so glad to hear complaining.

The whole group was fine. They were cold, and that was good. Serious hypothermia victims don't feel cold. I went to each camp and woke them up. I wanted us to move out together in thirty minutes. Again, whatever hot drinks could be sent to the shelter were welcome.

As we gathered together for our descent, I saw that most of the hikers were scared. They had never experienced snow in the summer before. Our group huddled together. I was the coach.

"Thanks for your help with the guys. They're fine. Now, we need to get off this mountain. Joe, I want you to walk in front. Set a slow pace. We need to stay together. No one is to pass Joe. If you pass Joe, he is authorized to tackle you." The group loosened up a bit, and there were a few more smiles.

"Behind Joe, I want our guests to follow. Behind them, the rest of you follow. Stay close, only a few feet apart. Know who is behind you and who is in front. Keep the line tight. I'll take up the rear. We won't stop until we make it to the junction."

We got the mountaineers out of the shelter and made an orderly descent. No one passed Joe.

At the junction, some of the hikers headed west to continue the John Muir Trail. How I envied them! What glory awaited them! The mountaineers were revitalized by the nearness of their camp. They stripped off the last of their borrowed clothing and took off, without a word of thanks. The storm's strength dissipated as soon as the clouds passed the crest. As I looked to the east, blue sky reigned. I began my own descent.

Back in Yosemite, the summer waned. Rebecca and I would soon move to the Midwest. I had selected a seminary in Deerfield, Illinois. We were anxious to begin our new life, so we left Yosemite Valley after I finished work, late in the night. Our cumulative possessions fit easily in the trunk.

Rebecca has a tough time staying awake at night when she is driving, so this duty was passed to me. That was okay; I was happy to drive. I wanted to remember in solitude. Driving through Yosemite under a clear night sky, I passed the turn off to White Wolf and reminisced about the trip I'd taken after high school. I savored each pass and each panorama I could pull from the gallery of my mind. Each trailhead led to memories stored lovingly in my heart. Even though I couldn't see them, I felt the Clark Range Mountains to the south. My, what times I'd had there. The place where I crossed the road on the PCT went under my tires. Then, I passed where Rebecca and I had begun our walk up to Mammoth Peak. Finally, I came to Tioga Pass. There was no one there. It was the darkest hour of night. I rolled down my window and took a deep breath of chilled, high air. The massive shoulder of Mt. Dana to my right filled the sky, blocking out any gentle starlight. With a contented sigh, I pressed slightly on the accelerator and began to descend. I left Yosemite National Park.

First light was beginning to break as I drove silently off the sheer face of the Eastern Sierra. The desert stretched, unending, before me. A few miles east of Lee Vining, I pulled off the road, stopped the car, and got out. As I gazed west, the morning rays of the sun bathed the Sierra in pure light. My heart was filled with thanksgiving and joy. In those mountains, I had grown from a fat, weak, CMT-ridden boy to a man. I had walked well over 2,000 miles of trails—1,200 in one stretch. I had climbed more than 20 peaks, domes, and points, including Mt. Conness and Mt. Clark. I had met God in those mountains. I had met my wife. I was sad to leave. I would miss the high places.

Around me, the desert insects were awakening. The bushes nearby pulsed with life. There were things flying, singing, chewing and jumping. An endless song of life—a song that went on whether I was there or not—surrounded me. Somehow, this comforted me.

With a final, purposeful gaze, I looked at my Sierras, willing their essence to be forever stored in my heart and mind. But I didn't stay long. I had to move on. I got back in the car and looked at the serene form of my sleeping wife. I cranked the key and began the long drive east. A new kind of life and a new vision compelled me. Looking into my rearview mirror, I saw the Sierra Nevada—a majestic mountain range framed in a two-by-six inch rectangular mirror. It faded.

Part 3:
Descent

Chapter 15:
A New Life

The next seventeen years were the best in my life from a CMT point of view. Two things worked to make it so. For starters, my chosen direction wasn't very challenging from a physical standpoint. As a student, my gluteus maximus was a more taxed feature than my calves. In the past, I spent my spare time wandering over hills and dales. In seminary, I spent my time sitting in a library puzzling over Greek verb forms and scribbling Hebrew. I could do that. No one ever said that a pastor's life was a physically strenuous one. There were frustrations, but CMT wasn't one of them.

My attitude helped me as well. Although I didn't finish the PCT, I was proud of how far I had walked. I felt strong. I felt physically competent. I might struggle here or there with a stairway. I might fear that I would fall down during a baptism in Lake Michigan. But I didn't *feel* weak. If I struggled physically, struggle was the exception, not the rule. The rule was that I was 1,000+-mile hiker. I was strong. The need to feel strong is important in any battle. I felt the strength of the PCT enlivening my body for seventeen years.

There were things, however, that were working against me. I left one of the most beautiful places on earth, Yosemite Valley, and moved to Chicago. Now, there is much to be said in praise of Chicago and the Midwest. Chicago is a great city. The cultural scene is phenomenal. The pizza is astounding. People in Chicago are politically thoughtful and committed. As one of the city's slogans says, "Vote early, vote often." The Midwest is the heartland of America. Sustenance for millions of people is grown here. Folks work hard.

Many of these folks even find the Midwest a beautiful place. The vast, open fields and the crisp, cold, clear winter nights speak to them. But this land did not speak to me. I was not attuned to hear her song. Some of my friends gloried in the beauty of Lake Michigan, nestled against Chicago. But whenever I thought of a beautiful city by the water, San Francisco won hands down.

Even though I knew that searching for wonder was probably a lost cause, I tried to find wilderness in the Midwest; I tried to feel the magic. I tried pretty hard. The first problem was that Midwestern trails don't go anywhere. I'd start a hike in a forest preserve or a state park and walk all day and still be seeing the same trees and the same plants. Boring. Perhaps I was too impatient. Maybe there was a deeper song. But the song evaded me.

There were other problems. In California, there were mountains to climb with open, sweeping views. Most "mountains" in the Midwest are mere lumps with trees on top. After paying the price to reach a summit, I was routinely disappointed. Midwestern trails did not draw me. Like unimaginative lovers, they revealed all they had in the first five minutes.

To add insult to injury, the trail builders in the Midwest prefer steeper grades. I love switchbacks! A well-graded trail is a joy to my soul. My scrawny calves don't like steep trails. But that's what I got a whole lot of—steep trails right up the sides of small mountains that didn't have good views.

Part of the glory of hiking is following streams and rivers. I've walked beside watercourses from their beginnings high in the mountains, when you can cross them with a simple step and followed them down until they grew to become raging torrents scores of yards wide. Such a walk is a pristine pleasure. Rivers in the Midwest don't sing, they slurp.

I remember trying to enjoy the Midwest wilderness on our honeymoon. We explored the Upper Peninsula of Michigan, which I was told was great country. Tahquamenon Falls State Park was recommended to us, and we went to check it out. We stepped out of the car for a day hike in mid-July and were greeted by the Midwest's notorious humidity. We felt like we were walking in a shower. And the flies—I couldn't believe it—there were tons of them. Their bites were painful and plentiful. Our hike through a field was short.

But I wasn't so easily turned away from trying to find some good spots to hike. I spent twelve hours driving up to the Porcupine Mountains of Upper Michigan for a two-night trip with some friends. My study of this area's topographical maps led me to hope that we could find real wilderness. Some trails ran right by scenic Lake Superior. There were some decent mountains and the actual trail started out pretty well. There were stunning views of Lake of the Clouds along the Escarpment Trail. I didn't hear the song, but things were definitely tuning up. Then the trail dropped into a nondescript forest and never came out; we camped by a nondescript creek. Could this get much worse? "It might be raining." And indeed, during the night our camp was deluged. Morning brought no relief. I opened the flap of my tent to see one of my friends standing under a tree totally drenched by water—it dripped from every part of his body. His expression was laden with disgust. His eyes met mine, and I saw the question they held, "Do you think this is fun?" No, I didn't. We walked straight out and skipped our second night. We had driven 24 hours round-trip to be soaking wet and walk in a forest. I didn't go back.

I hiked sections of the Ice Age Trail in Wisconsin. Maybe it was just a freak year; I don't know. But there were ticks everywhere. I had hiked over a thousand miles in California and only one or two ticks hitched a ride on my leg. But here, I could sit on a log and see them moving around on the ground. This vigorous display was disgusting. My partner, Mike, and I spent a great part of the night pulling them off of each other. We looked like apes out in the woods picking bugs off of each other. Unlike apes, however, we were denied the pleasure of eating them. Even after we were home for a day, Mike found one on his back.

I kept trying. Part of the North Country Trail in Michigan went under my feet, and I checked out Starved Rock in Illinois. I really tried to hear the song again, but I couldn't hear it. There was nothing here to draw me, challenge me, or woo me. I went out less and less.

At last I came to a sort of peace with the Midwest. There was no reason to lug around a backpack. There weren't any places that required backpacking. So I hung up my pack. The summer of 1987 was the first summer in many years that I didn't carry a pack. I became a day hiker.

I joke with my Midwestern friends that, while the Midwest is

135

llenged, it is beautiful in the fall, between
)ctober 2. This is true. For a blessed week or so, the
ɔine with crisp, clear skies and make for good
ɔn, the insects and humidity, which can be
ʒ the summer, are all but gone. So I not only became
a day hiker, ᵕᵕ⸺ day hiker with a very short hiking season.

Finally, my passion ebbed. I had such a fulfilling life as a husband
and pastor that I didn't need the woods. I had other challenges, other
pursuits. So when I set out to type my journals from the PCT, I titled
it *The Fire and Light Both Fade*. The phrase is taken from Day 82, as I was
camped by Evolution Creek, watching the campfire burn down and
the sunlight weaken. But as the title of my journal, I meant these
words to reflect that my fire and passion for wilderness had faded.

My life was also changing in other ways. After seminary, I got
involved in starting a church in Evanston, the first suburb north of
Chicago. Evanston is home to Northwestern University (Go,
Wildcats!) and a rich variety of people. Shortly thereafter, in 1990, we
adopted our first son, Maxwell Patrick McCorkle. Most parents I've
talked with agree that marriage is not as life-changing as having your
first child. After all, the people we marry are, hopefully, adults. At
least for Rebecca and me, we continued to stay pretty active once we
were married. I often went on short packing trips. That all changed
with the advent of Max. Please don't misunderstand, I love Max and
gladly sacrifice for him. And then Andrew Dalton and Grant Elliot
came along. Any time I had for something as frivolous as hiking in a
place like the Midwest was immediately absorbed by the onslaught
of changing diapers, figuring out how to snap up Onesies, and
buckling up car seats.

My family and my church needed me. I needed to be there for
them. To the best of my ability, I was. The strength that my PCT
journey gave me, both physically and mentally, enabled me to do the
things I needed and wanted to do.

But CMT is a patient, insidious thing. I didn't feel different from
day to day or month to month or even year to year. But, make no
mistake, slow, methodical decay crept through my frame. Nerve
endings were destroyed and muscles lay dying, bored from lack of
stimulation. No matter what I did, whether I was hiking or changing
diapers, CMT continued its creeping assault.

I had periodic awakenings that things were
the muscles in my legs just shut off, like a switc...
the ground. I quit doing baptisms in Lake Michigan ...
that I would fall. One day, I couldn't stand up on my ...
pedaled my bike.

But I didn't want to hear these warnings. I wanted to feel strong
and competent. I put them off. I still felt that I was the mountain man,
the overcomer, the 1000+-mile hiker. I was not a gimp.

I have mentioned before that, in hiking, going up is easier than
coming down. When you hike uphill, only your muscles are being
taxed, and they'll be fine after a short break. But when you go down,
that's when you get blisters, take bad falls, and suffer the most
damage. This is also true here. There was joy and challenge in my
pursuit of the PCT. My first ascent was fun and energizing. The
descent off of such competence, though, was bitter and painful. In my
PCT journal I once wrote, "I pay on descents." Indeed, I do.

Chapter 16:
Red Deficit

Years passed by. I hiked a little here and there. Nothing too taxing. I finally answered the call to go back to Yosemite in the summer of 1992, ten years after the PCT. Two of my good friends, Mike and Rich, had backpacked with me a little in the Midwest. They were intrigued by my constant praise of Yosemite and wanted to see for themselves.

Somebody somewhere along the way suggested that we all go out to Yosemite and see some of this blessed land. We worked out our schedules and arrangements. In addition to Mike and Rich, Rebecca and Mike's new wife, Katie, decided to come along. Once again, a team of five would seek the tidings of the mountains.

I set to work on selecting a trail. I took out my old Yosemite map and dreamed of places that I had never been. One place stood out— Red Peak Pass in the Clark Range. Although I had hiked the Clarks quite a few times and bagged Mt. Clark and Grey Peak, I still hadn't conquered Red Peak Pass. I selected the trailhead near Chiquito Pass in southern Yosemite—a trailhead far off any main road.

We all left bright and early on the day we traveled west. Gone were the days when I could walk out of my tent and start a hike. We flew out of Midway Airport in Chicago and took all sorts of stops on the way to California. Rebecca, who signed on to the trip late, took our two young sons to their Aunt Sue's in Salt Lake City and had to take a different plane. Somehow, we all descended from the sky into Sacramento, where my father picked us up for the drive south.

We left Highway 41 just outside of Oakhurst and began our winding ascent into the Sierra proper. It had been dark for many hours when we left the pavement for jeep trails that cut through the pine forests in narrow veins. I tried to guide my father through a maze of old and new dirt roads, some of which were on my map and some of which were not. I pretended that I knew exactly where I was, but I wasn't at all sure. I was greatly relieved when I saw an old sign indicating the trailhead. The car's glowing clock indicated that 2:00 a.m. had come and gone. We threw our packs out of the car, got out our sleeping bags, said goodbye to Dad and went to sleep.

I woke at sunrise and walked out of a small grove of pine trees to an open mountainside. I met the dawn as light gently awakened an endless forest of green. The trees stretched toward this heavenly, pure light. There was not a cloud in the sky and the blue of the morning was deeper than any ocean. The sun's rays touched my face, warming my cold skin. John Muir was right to name these hills the Range of Light. Everything glows. I set up my stove and worked up some tea while the sun's rays warmed up my urban soul. I smelled familiar pine smells. I sensed familiar morning breezes. I still knew this land.

The others were slow, *really* slow, to wake up. Sunrise comes early in the summer. We'd probably gotten only a few hours of sleep. But I wanted to get going. I'd waited a long time and come a long way to get here. I didn't want to waste time doing something as mundane as sleeping. I could sleep in Chicago.

Day 1 wasn't much to write home about. We walked several miles through lots of trees, although a few joyful meadows graced our path. I wanted to get as close to the Clarks as I could. At day's end, Rebecca spotted a most excellent camp overlooking Upper Merced Pass Lake.

I did notice, however, one thing: I never pulled away from the group. They were always right on my heels. I had expected to show more speed and endurance than my urban friends. But this didn't happen. I didn't think too much about my pace. I needed to get my legs back and I would be The Hiker again.

Day 2 was much more provocative—for a lot of reasons. From Upper Merced Pass Lake, the ascent into the Clarks got serious. We had walked through a lot of red fir forest on Day 1. Red firs are tall and majestic trees. They grow close together and dominate the land. There are no panoramic views or even regular sunlight in the red fir belt. As we continued to climb, red firs gave way to lodgepole pines. Lodgepoles are ugly trees. They are bruised and crushed by deep winter snows and grow in hideous shapes. Higher up, these trees begin to diminish in size and dominance. And here, high in the mountains, nothing replaces them but sheer granite and open sky. The lodgepoles were thinning as our upward trail arrived at Lower Ottoway Lake. The majesty of the mountains was fully revealed. Oh, I heard the song BIG TIME! The Clark Range is just the best! The peaks! The lakes! The glaciers! The birds! And the memories. I was right there twelve years ago with Don and Damon. The snow stopped us that year—it covered these mountains like wool on sheep. Snow wasn't going to stop me this time.

I was pumped. I was psyched. After a break, we continued up the trail into the heart of the Clarks. Upper Ottoway Lake opened up to our right—a circular pool of deep blue water nestled under a black mountain. This was high country—bare, shining granite, blue lakes, and sapphire skies. With each turn of the trail, I was becoming more entranced.

The group, however, was getting tired. They began to pester me with questions about the pass.

"Where is it?"

"How far?"

When the pass finally came into view, I pointed out the high notch above a lengthy section of switchbacks. They all started groaning and whining. I was stunned. Some even suggested going back. What was that! I snapped at them, "You guys have calves and you're whining. I don't have any calves and I'm going up the pass!" I took off and left the group trudging behind me. This ascent would be the last time, for the rest of my life, that I would walk in front of healthy hikers.

I smelled that pass, I wanted that pass, and I was going to have that pass. Switchback after switchback went under my feet. I was in the zone. I increased my lead. I was The Hiker once again. Then, in a final burst of power, Red Peak Pass was mine. Feeling tired, but satisfied, I took off my pack and surveyed a part of Yosemite I had never seen before. The basin under the shadow of Red Peak was a swirling collection of tarns, lakes and streams. The watercourses were lovely. The view was satisfying. The song was enough.

The others joined me at the pass. We ate the view together.

Mike, my younger friend, looked to the left and felt the pull of Red Peak. He wanted to bag the summit. He asked if anyone wanted to climb the peak with him. The top was, after all, only about a mile from the pass and we didn't have that much elevation to gain.

I've made thousands of decisions about when to push and when to stop in the mountains. I'd made good decisions most of the time. If I hadn't, I'd probably be dead. I haven't finished some summits and I didn't complete a lot of trails. But this decision was one of the worst— I decided to go, not because I really wanted to bag Red Peak, but because I still wanted to be The Man.

Rich and Rebecca were smarter; they decided to go down the pass to a trailside lake and make camp.

Mike took off into the pinnacles around the pass while Katie and I followed. Mike had a ton of energy, but he did not pick great routes, and because he was in front, we wound up gaining and losing a lot more elevation than we needed to. But I couldn't stay in front. I wasn't picking the route. I was getting tired. When the pinnacles didn't work out, we had to drop way down in order to get around them. This took a lot of time, and, when we finally stood on the summit of Red Peak, the sun was setting. A day, a season had passed. Because sound carries so well in the mountains, we were able to yell down our accomplishment to the others in camp as our shadows made us into giants against the far mountain walls.

The descent was terrible. I was spent. We decided to move farther down the mountain to avoid the pinnacles, and then come around, and pick up the trail to the pass. This sounded good. The ground along the way, however, was not good. Instead of brown, solid earth or steady, unyielding granite, the slopes of Red Peak are made of scree—small ballbearing-like granules of granite. With every step down, I dislodged boulders and sent small avalanches down the mountain. We began to spread out so that no one would get knocked over by someone else's mini-avalanche.

As I worked downhill, plowing through this scree, boulders around me started to move. A large one, about two by three feet, rested precariously above my head. I loosened this mass by my stumbling descent, and it came toward me. I fell, and the boulder slammed onto me, completely covering my right leg. I smelled the metallic odor of granite slammed into granite. Thoughts sprang through my mind with the swiftness of crisis. My life was over. I would die right there. I had a compound fracture; there was no other possible result. Mike was our fastest hiker, but sunset had come and gone. He couldn't make it out for at least two or three days. I would stay right there, watching the stars take their leisurely course, and breathe my last earthly breath into the dark, chilled night.

I couldn't lift the rock by myself—it was too heavy and I really didn't want to see what had happened to my leg. I didn't feel any pain. I was already moving into shock. Mike and Katie ran over and lifted the boulder off. My bent leg was inserted neatly and precisely between other granite rocks. These rocks formed a perfect cast, protecting my leg from the boulder with no more than a half-inch or so of slack. These rocks absorbed all the impact of the fallen boulder. My skin was not even touched. We marveled at this for a moment. A half an inch one way or another and I was dead.

I was *really* tired now. We made slow progress over to the trail, where, once again, I had to tackle Red Peak Pass. Unlike the first time, this ascent was pure will. I just wanted to be done and climb into my bag; I was tapped out.

Darkness ruled by the time we made the pass for the second time. We all agreed that we couldn't walk another step, so we yelled down to the others that we were okay and pulled out our bags to sleep right there on the pass.

As we settled in, Mike, ever the inquisitive soul, asked me without a trace of sarcasm, "So, Martin, what did you learn about God today?"

I thought for a moment and said, "I guess I still have some things to do. If God was done with me, I'd be dead."

I slept the deep sleep of the weary.

We had planned on Day 3 to follow the high trail toward Mt. Lyell's watershed, but this wasn't going to happen. I got up and started walking down to the others. I was stiff and slow, but who wouldn't be after the day we had just experienced? We joined up, shared our tales, and got back to the business of walking. The others were always waiting for me—I couldn't keep a steady stride. I couldn't stay on my feet for any length of time. I tried everything I knew to try. I took smaller strides. I rested more often. I stopped for a quick breath every ten steps. I ate different snacks. I sang snappy songs. But I couldn't shake this feeling of exhaustion that had seized me at Red Peak. Finally, disgusted with myself, I talked to the group about shortening the hike. We would take the low trail to Merced Lake and go over Vogelsang Pass to Tuolumne Meadows. We camped that night, after a difficult day of walking, by Triple Peak Fork, well short of our planned Day 3 camp. I hoped that a good night's sleep would help.

It didn't. Day 4 was more of the same. Every step was sheer will. Walking seemed more like torture than leisure. Even though the country was incredible, I couldn't enjoy the scenery. On this day, I named my condition "Red Deficit." I was in debt to Red Peak. Red Peak was going to make me pay, with interest. We camped above Merced Lake by Lewis Creek—a camp with no brown, soft soil, only hard granite. We had two days to get to Tuolumne.

On Day 5, my bad decision-making got much worse. Rich had taken a shorter trail to Tuolumne in order to arrive at the lodge a day early for a hot, homestyle meal and a warm cabin. We wished him well. As for me, I plodded along as best as I could up toward Vogelsang Pass, thankful that I had two full days to reach Tuolumne. We started to see scads of hikers along the way. A little joy came to me at the top of this pass; it was gently downhill all the way to Tuolumne. Mike wanted to climb Vogelsang Peak just off of the pass, and we happily waited for him to do so. My pride was in shambles now. I was content to watch.

Mike came back and we started toward the Meadows. The skies began to cloud up a bit, and rain became a real possibility. We only had a tube tent to keep us dry. The others didn't want to sleep in a tube tent, so we just kept walking. I was beat, but I had to keep walking. At some point along the way, someone suggested that we walk all the way out to Tuolumne. Trail's end wasn't that far now, and we could share a room with Rich. I should have stopped that plan right there. I knew that Tuolumne was still a long hike—for anybody, and especially for me. I knew that I was in no shape to walk out that day, but we just kept walking, and the momentum of the idea pushed me forward. At one point, about three miles from the meadows, the clouds threatened so much that we set up our shelter against the storm. When the others saw what a meager shelter a tube tent was, they became more determined to finish that day. They took off, and I lurched behind them.

Those last few miles were horrible. By sheer will, for I had no power, I forced myself to walk out of those mountains. I ceased to feel, to think, or to respond to the glory around me. I did not smell the pines or sing. I didn't hear a thing—birds were not relevant. I was in pure-walk mode. Every ounce of energy I had was solely given to one goal—take this one step, and then every ounce I had was again focused—take this next step. In this trance, I walked out of the mountains; I walked through the car campground; I walked by the Tuolumne Grill and sat down on a nearby bench.

Words fail me. I wasn't tired or exhausted. I wasn't tapped out or weary. I wasn't sore or achy. These words do not come near to describing my state. I'll simply say this: I have never been so completely empty. Never. Not after that crazy day at Camp Far West Lake. Not on the PCT. Never. My body felt beyond pain or fatigue in a way that I hope to never experience again. I sat on the bench and my entire body shivered uncontrollably, even though I was not cold. I could not have moved more than a few feet to save my life.

I was too spent to search for Rich or hike to the backpacker's portion of the campground. We moved a few yards into the night and slept in the woods between the store and the gas station.

My father picked us up the next day. My body spent weeks paying off Red Deficit. This trail showed me that, while I still had the will of a hiker, I no longer had the legs to match. CMT had leached a great deal of strength from my legs and I hadn't even noticed. Unfortunately, I was to keep learning new things from trails.

Chapter 17:
Flight from Phantom Ranch

Some hikes are bad from the start. I don't remember whose idea this hike was. I don't think it was mine, but maybe that is just me trying to clean up the mess a bit after everything went south.

The destination was fine—even excellent: The Grand Canyon. We would day hike down the Kaibab Trail 9.3 miles to Phantom Ranch, where we would spend the night and spend the next day in a leisurely exploration of the depths of the canyon. Then, with a family-style breakfast under our belts, we would take the moderately graded Bright Angel Trail 12.5 miles back to the top. So much for plans.

I took a strange group to the Canyon—my sister April and my father. I had some serious reservations about this. April was not in good shape, and my father was getting old. As we talked on the phone, they tried to reassure me that they were walking and getting in shape for the hike. I urged them to do more, explaining that a mile walk in the city was nothing compared to a mile in the Grand Canyon. They seemed to understand. At least, I wanted to hope that they did.

So, once again, I boarded a flight and went west, but took a heavy left at Nebraska and headed for the Valley of the Sun. I met up with Dad and April in Phoenix, and we sped away in April's car.

We drove a long time. I liked Arizona. The land was spacious, beautiful, and mysterious. The roadside businesses cracked me up— all sorts of little jewelry shops run by Indians (or so they said) were housed in shacks along the way. Big Chief Red Rock advertised that he loved the white man! Come on by and see him! Strange world.

By the time we checked into our hotel on the rim, sunset had come and gone. I sensed a chasm, but the darkness hid it. My sleep was sweet, filled with visions of exploration and wonder.

Sunlight woke us. I moved back the curtains and got my first look at this landmark. I didn't have a great view, but what I could see was enough. I was pumped and ready to go.

The first sign that all was not well came shortly thereafter. April had forgotten her boots and would have to walk down in her rather old tennis shoes. This was not good. Having had my share of problems with shoes, I could only imagine what kind of shape her feet would be in after the relentless pressure of downhill hiking assaulted them. It wouldn't be pretty.

I ate quickly; I wanted to get going. We walked a short distance along the rim to the Kaibab trailhead. I stopped here for a good, long look. Big Canyon just doesn't cut it. Large Canyon doesn't either. She is well named—she is the *Grand* Canyon. I had hiked in the desert a fair amount on the PCT; I knew a little of the desert song, and I liked these rhythms and melodies. This was not a desolate, lifeless place, oh no! Morning clouds promising afternoon thundershowers strolled at a royal pace across a clear, blue sky. Shadows shifted. Bright reds were muted and glowing yellows were tempered only to be strengthened again as the endless procession of clouds passed and burning light returned. There were small birds living in the trees along the rim. They took holy delight in diving into the canyon with daring speed. I was happy just to watch them.

From my vantage point, I saw our hike in three stages. The first stage took us steeply down the canyon wall. Then the trail met the Tonto Plateau—a relatively flat section. I could see where the trail cut across this plateau miles ahead. Our path looked like an incision cut into the flesh of the earth. Stage three was the inner gorge—a steep downhill section leading directly to the Colorado River.

Signs around us, in astonishing number, warned hikers of extreme temperatures and the need to carry lots of water. Summer was still a few months off, so I wasn't worried much about the heat, and we had lots of water. Although the walls of the inner gorge blocked my gaze, I looked again to where Phantom Ranch would be. It didn't look that far, but I knew better.

We had nothing left to do but go down. So down we went. I was delighted to be on my own two feet and not riding on one of those mules. Mule trains are constantly running up and down the canyon. I got to see a lot of mules, and I noticed something: Those mules loved to walk right on the edge of the trail. I imagined being seven or eight feet in the air atop a mule and having that stubborn animal take every step at the razor edge of a trail with hundreds, if not thousands, of feet of air right next to me. I couldn't dream of doing that all the way down. No thanks. I'll stick to my own feet.

I noticed a bunch of hikers with their cameras out and, knowing what this usually means, I walked over to see what I could see and there, a few yards away, was the most relaxed mountain goat you could conjure up. He munched desert bushes and remained completely indifferent to the clicking sounds of shutters and the advancing of film. We took a break and just watched him. We all munched together. In all my miles of hiking, I had never seen a mountain goat until then.

The previous year's hike in the Clarks had left me uneasy. As I mulled over my Red Deficit disaster, I came to this conclusion: I needed to listen to my body more. I was going to have to rest when I was tired and drink when I was thirsty and camp when I was through for the day. I could no longer just push myself and expect to bounce back. Red Deficit was bad, and I didn't want to put my body in debt again.

As the trail continued down, I constantly checked in with my body. I thought endlessly about my feet—*Was I getting any blisters? Was there bad chafing at any point? Were my socks getting too wet? Did I need to put on a fresh pair?* I thought about my intake of fluids—*Was I getting enough? Was I drinking at every break, even when I didn't feel thirsty? Was I drinking at a rate that would use most of what I had before Phantom Ranch?* I thought about my pace—*Could I walk this fast all day? Are my legs getting too tired?* I was not going to burn out a second time.

The Tonto Plateau was the neatest part of the day's walk. After the steep drop off the canyon wall, walking on fairly flat ground was a joy. An eerie feeling pervaded the Tonto Plateau. In the midst of all this harsh, jagged, and steep land, there was a plateau—an oasis from the vertical. As I walked through this easy section, I checked in with myself. Things were looking good.

By early afternoon, we sat at the top of the inner gorge. We weren't going fast, but we were getting there. We would surely get to Phantom Ranch in time for supper without too much trouble.

Everything changes in the inner gorge. The color of the rock changes. A purplish color dominates, as if it has been bludgeoned. Hard things have happened in the earth. Hard things happen to people in the heat and fatigue of the inner gorge. It is a bruised place.

April and Dad were slowing down, and, about two-thirds of the way to the river, they just stopped. They couldn't walk any more. I sat with them and rested. April got sicker and threw up. Dad got more and more distant. They weren't getting better; they were getting worse.

I finally asked them, "How much have you guys been drinking?"

"Not very much," they both replied. They thought they were supposed to be saving as much as they could. They didn't want to drink their water too fast.

I checked their supply. They had walked most of the day in the Grand Canyon and drunk less than half a quart. I had put down two quarts by this time and was working on my third. April had exacerbated her dehydration by throwing up. They were both in bad shape.

I was annoyed with myself. I had been thinking so much about myself that I was not paying attention to my party. *How could I have let this happen?* I knew we needed to drink. We had enough water, but I was too worried about my body to notice they weren't drinking enough. Stupid.

I had them begin to drink in small sips and tried to think about what to do. Neither of them looked like they could walk. The ranch was about two miles away. I could hurry over in less than an hour and bring help; I was about to leave when a ranger showed up.

She assessed the situation quickly and correctly: They were dehydrated. She prepared a mix of Gatorade and had them drink it to replace their electrolytes. Her competence and demeanor were so comforting that I began to feel better—and, soon, so did April and Dad.

After about half an hour, we were able to get on our feet and wind down the last few switchbacks to the river. At a snail's pace, we crossed an impressive bridge and stumbled into Phantom Ranch. I was very happy to be there.

Dad, however, continued to decline. He couldn't walk twelve miles back up to the top. He had trouble walking to the bathroom. I feared for him; I thought something pretty serious might be wrong. I went to the ranger station and explained the situation. Another ranger looked Dad over, agreed that he could not walk out, and offered to fly him out in a helicopter. Dad was eager to accept.

During the next day, we rested in the bottom of the canyon. Unlike mountains, where summits are full of freedom, air, and space, canyon bottoms feel weighty, oppressive, and dark. Here, it seemed like time and rock leaned over me, willing me to stay down—like the restless waters of the Colorado, always clawing lower and lower.

I stayed close to the ranch and close to Dad. I did take a few short hikes out to the bridge over the river and to the edge of Phantom Creek, where I heard rocks underneath the water tumbling and grinding their way down canyon, pushed by the relentless tide of runoff.

I was helping Dad to the dining room for supper. We were quite a pair—the blind leading the blind. I did Okay until we got to the stairs leading up to the dining hall. Once again, I was undone by stairs. I couldn't hold onto Dad and get enough power from my legs to move us up. I wanted to be there for my dad, but I couldn't help him. I felt like such a failure. I blew it with the water and now I couldn't help him get up a few stairs to dinner.

A man with a military bearing appeared next to us, and, with a firm voice, asked, "May I help you?" We were happy to have him help us. He grabbed my father's arm high by the shoulder. I felt his strength radiate through my father's whole body as he lifted him upward. He did this with such grace that it seemed we were the ones helping him.

We talked a lot about the helicopter ride. The Park Service discouraged any unnecessary passengers on these medical flights. For April to ride with Dad and for me to walk out of the canyon alone seemed like the best plan. I didn't want to leave my dad, but that was the way the cards went down.

I woke before April and Dad and, after a quick breakfast, began the long, solitary hike up the Bright Angel Trail. It was 5:45 a.m. when I pulled out of Phantom Ranch. Two things compelled me. I didn't want to have to finish the hike in the heat of afternoon. After walking ten miles uphill, I didn't like the idea of hiking two more miles straight up switchbacks with the high sun pounding on my back, but more important to me was the condition of my father. I wanted to know how he was doing and I had to get to the top in order to find out.

I walked along the Colorado River, following a trail cut out of the side of a steep wall, until the route turned and began to ascend. I powered over the first long set of switchbacks, named the Devil's Corkscrew, before the sun's rays touched the land. I took a short break to enjoy the sun and continued on.

I was a torn man all morning. On the one hand, I was worried about Dad. On the other hand, the hike was awesome. The land here was gentler than the land along the Kaibab. There were streams lined by green grasses. There were more birds. I went from singing praises to God as I gloried in the beauty of the canyon, to sudden prayers of intercession for the health of my father.

I took a longer break at shady Indian Gardens, where I tanked up on water. But I wasn't there long before the dual prongs of heat and concern forced me to walk again.

I worked up the last section of switchbacks, called Jacob's Ladder, where structures were erected along the way to shelter hikers from the relentless desert sun. I was close, so I just kept going and topped the last switchback at high noon.

Once again, a contradictory set of emotions seized me. I had walked 12.5 miles and gained 5,000 feet in elevation in just over six hours. That was good. I was happy about that. On the other hand, I needed to find my dad; my concern grew thicker the nearer I got to the top. I felt terrible about my leadership. I had failed my sister and father. For the first time in all the hikes I had ever been on, one of my party did not walk out under his own strength. And why? I just hadn't paid attention. I had been thinking too much about myself. And because of this, I needed two rangers, a military man, a helicopter pilot, and a medical team to get my father and my sister out. I knew I was getting weaker. It wasn't just Red Deficit; I was becoming dangerous.

I ran into my family shortly after I completed the trail. Things looked much better, and they had enjoyed the helicopter ride. The hospital topside had okayed dad to travel home.

My feelings on this trail eluded understanding for a long time. Part of me recognized that what had happened was not my fault. My sister and Dad had not sufficiently trained for the trail, even though I had urged them to get serious about their walking on many occasions.

Nor was I to blame for their dehydration. At breakfast the morning of the hike, I had told them to drink at every break, whether they were thirsty or not. I'd told them to drink at such a rate that they would have only a little left when we got to Phantom Ranch. So why was I so upset with myself?

When I first started hiking, all I could think about was myself. My feet were in shivering pain most of the time. I was totally exhausted almost every night. I didn't have enough strength to look beyond myself. I never would have thought that Don's feet might hurt or that Damon might be weary. I didn't have time for that; I was locked and loaded on me. And that's what I had to do at first.

The glory of my first "ascent" was not that I walked 1,200 miles in one summer or bagged Mt. Whitney. The real accomplishment of first ascent was that I began to feel and touch life outside of myself. At first, I connected with nature, then with God, and finally with other people. CMT was not holding me into myself. I broke free of CMT's power and felt the world around me. Other people's feet hurt too. Other people were weary. I had the strength to feel this.

But there, in the inner gorge of the Grand Canyon, CMT robbed me of part of my hard-fought awareness. For the first time since the PCT, I'd had to think so much about me that I'd missed something right under my nose. That was why I was so troubled. I didn't want to lose this awareness. I didn't want to be pushed back into the dismal, lonely world of only thinking about my feet and how tired I was.

CMT was pulling me back in. I didn't want to go.

Chapter 18:
Devil's Lake

I didn't hike for many years after the Grand Canyon trip. Life went on. My family and my church grew. In between these challenging and satisfying pursuits, I didn't find time to walk, much less to backpack, at all. I drove a nail into a stud in my basement and hung up my backpack to collect dust instead of memories. The strength of the PCT still spoke to me. I often used stories from my hiking days as illustrations in my sermons. I watched mountaineering movies, like *Eiger Sanction* and *K2*, and felt connected to the men—I knew what the mountains were about. I still had the heart of a hiker. This was all to change for me in one day.

It was early October 1999, now seventeen years since the PCT. I hadn't done much outside stuff that summer, so I worked out with Rebecca a weekend when I would go up to Devil's Lake in Wisconsin for a little solitude and some real hiking. We had been to Devil's Lake and camped as a family. The park was a pretty place that held some real promise for day hikes, especially the cliffs overlooking Devil's Lake. I planned to log about fifteen miles a day for two days, thus scouring the entire park. No problem.

The fall colors were stunning on the drive up. Reds, yellows, greens, and browns mixed on a palette of life and joy. The entrance to Devil's Lake was so thick with trees that I was lost in a cave of color. Indeed, this was the Midwest's finest hour. Even though pregnant rain clouds dominated the sky, my spirits were high when I drove up to the ranger station to select my camp. School had started once again, and the season for camping was past. I figured that I would have the whole place to myself. No one was around when I entered the station. I walked to the desk and checked out the campground board. A reserved campsite showed a red light, an open site showed green—only about five sites out of hundreds showed green. *What was this? Some kind of maintenance thing?*

I was informed that 1,200 Boy Scouts were on their way for their annual jamboree. By 7:00 p.m. that night, every camp, picnic table, and open area would be filled with scampering, pillaging Boy Scouts. Oh well, so much for solitude. I could still hike. I changed one of the last green campsites to red, got back in my car and, after a short drive, pulled off the road for an easy day hike.

This will be a piece of cake—a 3.5-mile hike up the bluffs over the western shores of Devil's Lake and then back to the car on the Tumbling Rocks Trail that snuggled close to the lake. With staff in hand, I began to make my way.

The trail was steep and soon, within only a few minutes, I was breathing heavily and sweating. I felt clumsy as I walked and had to lean on my staff. After a few hundred yards, I had to stop and catch my breath. People on the trail were blowing past me. Some of them were much older than I was. I started again, only to sweat more and sense a keener loss of breath. As I continued on, I noticed that people were looking at me strangely, like they used to look at me when I'd first started hiking. They were confused, wondering if they should ask if I needed help or if I knew what I was doing. I knew what I was doing.

Finally, I made the 500-foot ascent to the top of the ridge and rested. My legs felt like thoroughly cooked noodles. I was short of breath. I tried to pass my fatigue off and thought that I would be fine once I started walking again. But I wasn't. Along the flat, topside trail, I couldn't keep a stride. I began to suffer power outages in my legs and just fell down where I stood—a crumpled form.

I rested often, but my frequent breaks didn't help. I was afraid to walk; I knew that I was going to fall and I couldn't stop myself. I inched along for a mile or so and came to the descent back to the lake. The mist had now thickened into a rain. As I walked down, the wet leaves under my feet became like ice. I slid everywhere. I fell at least three times in half a mile. My knees were bleeding by the time I got back to the shores of Devil's Lake.

I stumbled along for a few more minutes before I could walk no further. My muscles were not responding and I was scared to walk. I sat down.

There, on a boulder by the shores of Devil's Lake, sadness washed over me like a flood. I could no longer live in a world of delusions. I could no longer deny the damage CMT had worked in my body. I was no longer a hiker—I was a gimp. I was no longer an adventurer—I was old. I couldn't come to a park and have its high places in a rush and move on; I couldn't even walk.

I was cold, so I tried to put my gloves on. I couldn't. They were damp on the inside and I didn't have the strength to pull them over my already wet hands. In frustration, I sat there with my gloves half on. I couldn't even dress myself. And as the rain drenched me, streaks of water flowed down my face. My tears joined this stream and were washed into the lake. I didn't weep. Weeping is for the strong. I could only snivel—a shrunken man.

I sat there for about an hour, fearing to walk lest I fall, fearing to stay lest I fade away. Finally, with emptiness swelling inside me, I very carefully, very slowly walked the last mile back to the car.

I couldn't face the Boy Scouts. I went into town and got a cheap hotel room and took a warm bath. Once more I worked to maintain the delusion. *Maybe today was just a fluke? I couldn't be that bad off. It's just a passing thing. I'll be fine tomorrow.*

So I planned to walk about four level miles instead of the fifteen miles originally envisioned. Four miles is not an impressive hike, but a good hike. I was still a good hiker.

I found the trails covered with Boy Scouts. Their youth mocked me. They bounded around like a bunch of puppies playing in a field, and I stumbled like an 80-year-old man. Hundreds of them passed me. I was nothing to them.

I walked with keen intention. I began to feel ashamed of my lack of ability. I started to wait until groups of people passed by before I worked up a steep section of trail. I didn't want anyone to see me struggle. Then, I got angry with myself for waiting. *They're just kids!*

Toward the end of the hike, I had to descend once more. On a gentle downhill section, I fell again and jammed my knee right into a sharp spur of granite rock. Pain sliced through me like a sword. I couldn't walk. So once more, I just sat there, nursing my pain. Sadness again swept over me.

My wilderness days really were over. I couldn't do this anymore. I had to live an entirely different kind of life. A door closed. The high

157

places were now denied to me. The joy of solitude and beauty was gone. I had no more strength for delusion; my days of hiking were over. CMT had won. I had done a lot with CMT, but now my life had to change.

I managed somehow to finish the trail and came home. I told Rebecca about the trip and fell into a depression.

I thought about how a person can respond to something like CMT.

There are three roads. The first road is defiance. This road denies the reality of CMT. The road of defiance doesn't let CMT stop me from doing anything. I push myself and risk injury. I fight to be normal. Defiance is good because it helps me be the best I can be. I defied CMT on the 1982 PCT. Such brazen defiance had bought me 17 years of active life. But defiance doesn't change CMT. I have CMT. I am not normal. Defiance is also really hard. Defiance takes a lot of work and a lot of time.

I thought about trying to defy CMT again and was immediately even more depressed. I'd worked so hard for so long to prepare for the PCT. My CMT was worse now, and I was older. I had other responsibilities. The path of defiance was just too steep. I didn't have the will or the vision to walk such a difficult road.

The second road is compromise. Compromise recognizes limitation. Everything is not possible, but lots of good things still are. I can canoe, so long as I avoid those pesky portages. I can car camp. There are beautiful places along roads. Put up the backpack for good, be thankful for the memories, and settle down into a less adventurous lifestyle. After all, my life had not been characterized by mountainous adventure the last few years anyway. Didn't sound too bad. But compromise, while realistic, is not inspiring. As a 38-year-old man, the thought of compromise left me cold. What a boring life! Another problem with compromise was that the last road was really close by.

The third road is surrender. Just give up. CMT was going to win. Why not just admit defeat and let go? I was only fooling myself to think that compromise or defiance was possible. Get out the cane. Buy a new house with a single floor. Get the gimp sticker for my car. Dust off the wheelchair. Move to a warm climate and quit the fight. I'd fought long enough.

While there is an aspect of rest on this road, and I knew that someday I would walk the road of surrender, I just couldn't let go. So I didn't know what to do. The path of defiance was too steep. To compromise with CMT left me uninspired, living a boring life. To surrender was not in the cards. I am not ready to punch out. I stayed depressed.

I also thought about my family. I am the father of three young sons. These boys are packed with energy. They want me to play with them constantly—and play the play of boys. Max loves to wrestle. He stands ready to trade blows and tussle on the ground at every moment. Andrew always wants to play catch or go to a park for a baseball game. Grant is a little tike. He still wants to be carried when we walk. He loves to play chase, where I try, emphasis on *try*, to catch him.

What was I to do with this? Could I just sign out on these boys and say that Dad just couldn't do this stuff anymore? The distance between what I needed to be for my sons and the reality that I could deliver got bigger and bigger—especially when I thought about compromise and surrender.

I grew concerned over the future of my relationship with Rebecca. We always led an active life. How would things go if I quit fighting? She was dedicated to exercise and health. We liked to travel. Most of the places we dreamed of going together required some physical ability. If the places we had wanted to go weren't possible anymore, what impact would my weakness have on our relationship? Would we drift apart? To make matters worse, I didn't like the idea of her having to take care of me so soon. When I was 60 or 70—fine!—but I didn't feel comfortable sentencing her to this kind of life now. Yes, she signed on "for better, for worse, in sickness and in health." But was my lack of determination causing this?

I was uncertain about my future as a pastor. What kind of impact would compromise and surrender have on me? I would lose my edge. I would cease to live life fully. I wouldn't be looking ahead anymore. My sermons would suffer. My vision would fade. But could I take care of family, do a good job as a pastor, and still have enough energy to defy CMT? I didn't think so. I'd had to quit school, move to Yosemite, and spend practically all my energy to defy CMT when I was a young man. I couldn't do that now. Something somewhere would suffer.

Days passed into weeks and I asked myself these questions endlessly. But through the mire, one thought began to exert itself. I was not ready to die. I had too much to live for. I still had fifteen years before my youngest son left for college. There was too much joy to be had in being a father; I couldn't punch out. I still felt like I had vision to give to my congregation; I wasn't ready to quit. I still had a life to live with Rebecca; I wasn't ready to rely on memories. Surrender was *not* an option. That much became clear. But what was I to do about defiance and compromise?

I began to think about time. I needed fifteen more years to launch my sons into their adult lives. I would be about 55 at that time. If I opted for compromise, was I sure that I could live fifteen more years before I just gave up? No, I wasn't. In the seventeen years since the PCT, I'd diminished from a 1000+-mile backpacker to someone who couldn't day-hike for four miles. At that pace, I'd be wheelchair-bound by my late forties. I kept thinking about how defiance bought me time. Surrender was downhill all the way; time just marked a steady decay. Compromise wasn't much better. Only defiance bought me time. For every year I defied CMT, another year was granted to me. Even if all I did in one year was stay the same— exercising enough to compensate for the progressive work of CMT— I bought another year. If I was able to get stronger—exercising enough to overcome the effects of CMT—I bought serious time.

In the quiet moments I knew that I had to purchase time. CMT does not affect life expectancy. Wisdom compelled me to think about how my life would look if it ran its course for 75 years. The thought that I would just get off the train for the last 35 years of my life was totally unacceptable. Likewise, the thought that I could find the energy to defy CMT for 35 years left me weary and depressed. I couldn't fight that long.

So, I made myself a deal. I would defy CMT for 15 years. I would give my best shot at being the family man I needed to be. I would choose to fight and fight hard.

At 55, my sons fully grown, I would compromise. Take a pastorate in a multi-staff church where a younger man brought vision. Vacation on cruise ships. Sit in a fluffy lounge chair and watch the world go by.

At 65, let go and embrace surrender. Eat what I wanted and get fat.

Move to Arizona. Watch the sun rise and set from my cushy chair on my flat patio. Maybe write another book called *Sit with Me*.

This deal helped me a lot. I knew I couldn't do the defiance thing forever. Knowing that there was a summit where I could rest helped me to face beginning the climb.

But I still was depressed. There is a point in every mountain ascent when I stare at the summit and count the cost. Is it really worth all this hassle and pain to get there? The bigger the mountain, the harder it is to stare a summit down. I know the cost of defying CMT—constant attention to diet, regular, aggressive exercise, loss of other recreation, loss of time with family and friends, loss of attention to other meaningful pursuits and responsibilities—the list went on and on. Yet I had chose to climb. I had to stare down the mountain.

One of the blessings of middle age is that I know myself fairly well. I know what I like; I know what I love; I know what gets me going. What motivation would inspire me to get up every day and choose to fight? What would make me think twice every time I wanted to stuff my face with cookies and cream ice cream? What would make me get up in the frigid Midwest mornings and exercise, when I like to sleep in my warm bed? Would a general desire to stay healthy do this? Nope. Would a vision to stay healthy for my family do this? I'm sorry to say, nope. But this was no time for games about how I *should* feel and what I *should* do. I need real motivation. Only one thing could give me the desire to defy CMT once again—go back to Lookout Rock and walk the rest of the way to Oregon on the PCT.

I love the Pacific Crest Trail. I love the beauty, the challenge, the solitude, the wonder, and the accomplishment of the PCT. I love her story and the people who walk the PCT's horizon-seeking miles. I know other places are more beautiful than northern California, but beauty is only part of the PCT. The PCT is more than scenery—she is one of my life's few true passions.

What a selfish thing! I can't leave my family for five weeks and go hiking! But if I didn't do this, I will be checking out on my family for a lot longer than that. If I quit living, what good am I? And for every year that I defy CMT, I have another active year with my loved ones.

God placed a love for this trail in my heart for such a time as this. I needed a strong love to work against a strong foe.

161

During an unusually warm November, my family was hiking in the Ryerson Conservation Area about a half hour's drive from my home. The trails are pleasant, meandering through some impressive forest while they skirt the Des Plaines River. At a break along the shore, Rebecca and I watched our sons throw stones into the water. The stones flew for a moment—rockets of power and wonder—only to fall into the dark, cold stream. I was scared to speak. I sensed that a huge balance was before me. Finally, I choked the words out:

"I want to finish the PCT."

"Okay, we'll wait a few years until Grant grows up some more and then . . . "

"No, I want to go before the boys are old enough; I don't think I can wait that long."

"You want to go by yourself? When?"

"I won't be ready by next summer. But I would like to go in the summer of 2001."

Rebecca is a wise woman. She sensed the deep things that were coursing through me: things not said in these few words. We started walking again. Within a few hundred yards, she agreed to my desire. She only asked that I take a partner and not hike alone—again, a wise request.

Winter was coming to the Midwest. Snow, deep cold, and ice were on the way. But instead of being annoyed by winter, now the struggle was part of my training. After all, in twenty months, I will be hiking on the PCT bound for Oregon.

Part 4:
Second Ascent

Chapter 19:
False Start

Okay. Where to begin? I'd done this before. Endurance and wisdom. I had some ideas about what I needed to do. But as winter set in, I didn't feel a compulsion to jump right into some training program. Almost twenty years had passed since I last checked in with the medical establishment about CMT. I wanted to find out if anything new had been discovered or if any new therapies had been pioneered.

I checked the Web. I typed "Charcot Marie Tooth" into the search window and clicked. I didn't expect much and was surprised by the wealth of sites that addressed CMT. I surfed through about five of the most promising. The counsel they were giving wasn't much different from what I'd heard from Dr. Horn as a child—stay in overall good shape, avoid "frank obesity," and remain active. Even though I didn't see much that was new, I felt strangely warmed by the process. I've never met another person with CMT and suddenly I was part of a world where there were chat rooms, support groups, and forums on my condition. If there had been a support group in Chicago, I would have gone. I felt connected.

I made an appointment with my doctor. As his hands touched my tender places, I explained my decline. Much to my disappointment, he speedily agreed. I had lost function in the 18 months since my last visit. He didn't know much about CMT, but my decline was so obvious that he wanted me to take a blood test to make sure that CMT was the only thing wrong with me. He also wanted me to see a specialist at Evanston Hospital to confirm that CMT was the correct diagnosis. I was passed along the medical machine.

After yet another vampire sucked my precious blood from where

God intended it to be, I arrived at the hospital to see Dr. Bernstein, Evanston Hospital's neurological guru. He looked over my legs and poked my feet with the sharp and smooth ends of a safety pin.

"Well, what can I do for you?"

"Do I have CMT? Is this the correct diagnosis?"

"Yes, you have CMT, but your case is not that severe."

That was encouraging. My primary physician had told me that I was getting worse faster than CMT warranted, yet this specialist seemed to think that I had a milder case.

"I've walked hundreds of miles backpacking through the mountains. I want to keep going out into the woods. Can I do this? If so, how much longer can I?"

"I don't know."

"When will I know that it is time to stop?"

"You'll know."

That was discouraging. I wanted something more concrete. I would have felt better if he told me that I couldn't do such juvenile things any more. At least then I could have used his pronouncement as an anvil to hammer out my resolve. If he had said that I was able to hike, I could have used that as a motivation to stay in the game. But this vague statement—"you'll know"—frustrated me. How was I to know? If I had listened to what my body told me, I never would have left Camp Far West Lake.

He gave me a prescription to see a physical therapist for my legs. I was passed along the medical machine.

I strolled into the physical therapy office as gracefully as possible. My posture was exquisite. Surrounding me were small rooms, each a copy of the challenges of the outside world. Among them were a hotel lobby, an auto shop and a grocery store. Each was designed with obstacles to be overcome—door knobs, stairs, checkouts. The rooms were brightly decorated. The rooms had a radiant cheer did not match their primal purpose—survival.

My therapist was named Karen. She was a fit, no-nonsense kind of woman who led me through a battery of tests. We sat down.

"Okay, Martin. What are your goals?"

"I want to increase my walking strength, put on a backpack and walk 400 miles of trail in the summer of 2001."

She considered this. "Well, if you want to increase your walking strength, then you need to walk." A shot of sarcasm cut through me. *I've paid hundreds of dollars, been poked by a vampire, seen two doctors and one therapist and this was the skinny: Walk more!* But I didn't share these bitter thoughts. Instead, I asked, "Are there any exercises that I can do at home during the winter that could help?"

"Not really. If you want to develop walking strength, you need to walk."

Got it. Before I left she asked me to visit the hand therapist for an evaluation. She had noticed some "mass wasting" in my hands and wanted someone to check this out. I was passed along the medical machine.

I showed up for my hand evaluation in a good mood. My legs had always been the focus of my struggle. I had good hands. I was a musician. I was going to enjoy myself.

My new therapist's name was Judy. She was a kind woman with strong hands. During my evaluation we often sat, like lovers, holding hands in the most intimate way and yet she made this intimacy both comforting and appropriate. She was very competent.

Again, we moved through a battery of tests. I squeezed things and arranged things. I pulled things and twisted things. Finally, Judy asked me to grab what looked like a staple gun and squeeze as hard as I could on the handle. I did this with each hand.

"Thanks, I have a good idea about your hand strength now. Your right hand is about a quarter of the strength of a normal man of your age and your left hand is about one-fifth of normal. I am concerned about your left hand. Your grip strength is down in the low twenties. Twenty pounds of grip strength is kind of a threshold: Once you get below twenty, it gets hard to do things like open doors and jars. We're going to have to watch that."

Another revelation. My hands were shot. She scheduled me to come back so that I could be shown an exercise routine and discuss some other options. I left in a haze.

When I came back, Judy showed me how to exercise my hands using theraputty, which looked and felt like playdough. I had to make small balls and squeeze them between my fingers; I had to roll out small logs and pinch them. She showed me a magazine full of stuff that I could get to stay independent. She used that word a lot—independent. All of the pictures in the magazine were of old people.

She recommended a buttonhook to help me with my shirts. I accepted. Lastly, she made small splints for four of my fingers. If I wore them at night my fingers would not permanently claw up. I left the office with my putty, magazine, splints, and buttonhook. I was still in a haze.

I found a place in my drawer for the buttonhook. I wore my splints that night. The following day, around dinner, I sat down to do my exercises. There I was, a grown man, playing with silly putty. As I pinched and squeezed, the meaning of the last few days finally broke through. I felt like America during World War II—we had war on two fronts. For my whole life, I'd focused on my legs and my feet. And that was plenty to contend with. But now my hands were going down too. The parts of me that touched the world were dying.

I looked into my future. Every day, for the rest of my life, I would have to spend a half-hour playing with playdough. CMT has annoyed me and been an embarrassment from time to time. CMT has been a hassle, but I had accepted my struggles as the stuff of life. I was never angry about CMT until that day. But now, I was mad. I was mad at CMT for taking my legs *and* my hands. I was mad at God for giving me this thorn. I wanted to take my gimp playdough and throw it at the wall and walk away. *This was just too much! I can't raise a family, pastor a church, pay my bills, mow my lawn, defy CMT in my legs and in my hands. I can't do this much stuff every day! Where was I going to find time to walk and do these hand exercises? I have to work sometime! And maybe once in a while, I'd like to do something other than work and exercise!* My anger slowly burned away and left weariness. I just sat there staring out of the window. Winter night was coming.

This was the bottom. I stayed there a long time.

As I sat and thought, I realized that there was some resonance to this revelation. *Why couldn't I grab my ice ax on Forester Pass? Why couldn't I achieve any real speed or beauty in my guitar playing? Why couldn't I master the tiny maneuvers of Asteroids? Why couldn't I put on my gloves at Devil's Lake?* Now I knew. CMT was taking my hands as well as my feet. There was a dark sense to this turn.

I believed that my hands were fine—even strong! And yet they were weak—so weak that normal human activity was almost not possible. *Was I that easy to deceive? Were my powers of perception that bad? If I could be so wrong about my hands, how was I to trust my perception about anything else? I thought I was a good pastor—maybe not! I thought I was a good family man—not so sure anymore! Who knows? If I couldn't even pick up that my hands were dying, what good was my insight?*

And how was I to fight CMT when my own perception was so unreliable? Obviously, my feelings about CMT were not accurate. I couldn't trust my own perceptions. I needed something more objective to shape my ascent, something more reliable to measure my progress.

From the bottom, I looked up. I was still mad. I was still weary. I looked at my playdough in disgust. But if I had to fight a war on two fronts—so be it! Bring it on! If I could defy CMT in my legs, why couldn't I defy CMT in my hands? I would find a way to overcome my self-delusion. I could find things that I could trust.

I picked up my theraputty.

Chapter 20:
Acts of Defiance

I needed goals. Concrete goals that I could measure objectively. I decided on an exercise plan that would slowly ramp up until summer 2001. I didn't want to burn out along the way. I planned to lose fifteen pounds so that I would weigh 185 when I started the hike. That way I could carry a fifteen-pound pack and weigh no more than when I began to train.

On April 1, 2000, I began to exercise twice a week. I needed definition. What did exercise mean to me? Rather arbitrarily, I decided that I had to spend one hour on the exercise bike or walk at least four miles to count the activity as exercise. There was a bike trail just across the street from my house that I had never used. I would use it now. I set my van's trip odometer and drove next to the trial until two miles had gone by. There were some benches there. So, on Tuesday and Thursday mornings, I dressed my young son Grant in warm clothes, put him in his stroller and pushed him to the benches and back. On days when rain stopped us, I rode the exercise bike in the basement. I found other four-, six- and eight-mile walks along the Chicago and Des Plaines Rivers.

On July 1, 2000, I began to exercise three times a week. I became thankful for flood plains. For as many locks and dams as they could put on the Des Plaines River, she would not be wholly restrained. During the spring runoff and after unusually heavy rains, her ancient passion was aroused and she broke out of her civilized restraint, spilling onto her flood plain. Builders could not build here. Forest remained. And in this forest, a trail was built. I walked next to the Des Plaines River scores of times. And although I wasn't drawn as a lover, I became familiar with the Des Plaines and enjoyed her moods and gentle voice.

Having walked now for quite a few months, I set out to walk sixteen miles along the Des Plaines in one day. I woke early and got to the trail by 6:00 a.m. I walked steadily, rested briefly and finished by 2:00 p.m. I wasn't carrying any weight and the trail was flat, but I was pleased—a sixteen-mile day is a good walk.

For my birthday on July 11, I asked for a watch with a chronometer. Rebecca and I picked out a Timex Ironman Triathlon. This watch communicated machismo. All kinds of functions and buttons awaited the wearer. It didn't have a normal band; I strapped it onto my wrist with velcro.

I loved that watch. For here was the answer to my lack of faith in my own perceptions: Time. I timed myself every time I walked anywhere. And when I combined the basic realities of distance and time, I had a formula I could trust. If 50 minutes went by before I walked to the benches on Monday and I covered the same ground in 48 minutes on Friday, I was getting faster. If I walked from the MacArthur Woods to Old School Road in one hour and ten minutes one day and then covered the same ground in one hour and fifteen minutes on another, I was getting slower. Where before I wouldn't have been caught dead with a watch in the woods, now I wouldn't go for a walk without one.

On October 1, 2000, I began to exercise four times a week. Devil's Lake was now a year behind me. I had logged hundreds of miles dayhiking over the summer. I needed to know if all this work was helping. I needed a test and I knew where to find one. I had found a pretty good loop trail called the Jordan River Pathway up towards Traverse City in the northern parts of Michigan's lower peninsula. The loop was eighteen miles through hilly terrain. I had hiked this trail twice before. So this was my test: I would put on a pack for the first time in many years. I would take along Max and Andrew, carrying all their stuff on my back. I would walk nine miles a day for two days.

As I drove our van up to the trailhead, I almost turned back. I wasn't at all sure that I could finish this hike. My pack weighed an enormous forty pounds as it strained to hold three sleeping bags and all our other gear. I was endangering my sons.

I assured myself that I would take things slowly and not get injured. I barely convinced myself.

172

I had thought a great deal about how I wanted to approach backpacking. There was no way that I could walk all day at any pace. So I planned to walk for one hour and then rest for a half an hour no matter how I felt. I would experiment with this strategy on the Jordan River Pathway.

At the trailhead, I parked the car and shouldered my pack. An uneasy burden rested on my shoulders. My spine felt compressed. My feet felt like they might explode. I showed my two sons the way to the trail and they were off. I followed.

Day 1 was slow but meaningful. At every break I watched my sons explore meadows and frolic in the river. They were boys in the woods. They could shout, throw rocks, try to catch fish with their hands, get dirty and no one minded at all. As a matter of fact, I was delighted. The bright fall colors matched their joy.

When I walked into camp that night I was tired and achy, but not devastated. I popped four Ibuprofen and, by the time I was through making dinner, I almost felt okay. But my forty-pound pack was too much for me. The next morning, I hid it in some trees next to a road.

Day 2 was most enjoyable. We dayhiked under the fading sunlight of fall. At every turn, diffused light radiated through countless colors and falling leaves. Happy creeks, running clear and clean, met our trail in surprising number and refreshed our way. During our breaks, we sat close to each other sharing our favorite trail mixes and telling funny stories. We laughed.

Our total walk time was ten hours to complete an eighteen-mile loop. I walked a bit slower than two miles an hour, carrying a 40-pound pack for nine miles. But most importantly, I shared two wonderful days with my sons. I was pleased with my progress.

On January 1, 2001, I began to exercise five times a week. The winter months are not kind, so I began to exercise at an indoor walk track. The walk track was like a mezzanine over two basketball courts at our city gym. The track was blue with two white stripes neatly dividing the track into three lanes. If I walked around the track in the center lane eleven times, I could log a mile. Because I was trying to walk four to six miles a day, I had to walk around that track 44 to 66 times. I felt like a gerbil on his run wheel—round and round and round. The management, however, was thoughtful. In order to change the scenery, we shifted direction every day.

Very few middle-aged men came to the walk track. There were young bucks who zoomed around the fast lane making the rest of us look like bowling pins before their speedy onslaught. There were old men clustered in slow groups who spoke of younger days, younger women, money, politics, and their old wives. The old men left me a little uneasy. They seemed deflated, void of the stuff of life. Their eyes were dark and distant, dreamily looking backward.

The older women, however, were another story. They were alive. Their eyes sparkled. Because walking on a track is boring beyond belief, I had to find something to do with my time. When I started walking I'd find an old woman who was walking faster than I was. This was not hard to do; some of those old ladies really truck. Then, when she got about half a lap ahead of me, I'd try to catch her—an ancient pursuit made new.

Walkers, outside of groups of friends who come together, do not talk on the track. Yet I always felt like the lady I chose to chase knew I was after her. These were wise women, schooled in the foolish ways of competitive men. I'd start to catch up and she would pull away. Sometimes, I would pass and there would be this slight shoulder shrug signifying my meaninglessness. But most stayed just ahead of me, never letting me get too close. And when they left the track, still holding the front, for one moment our eyes met; "Gotcha!" they said in a primal sort of way.

One day I had just started to walk. I felt pretty good; I was walking well. I was just about ready to pick my mark, when an elderly woman pulled up beside me, broke all convention, and spoke to me. "You're walking very well today."

Something about the too-gentle way she said this made me wary. I replied, "Well, I can't be doing too well, you're passing me."

Without a pause she asked, "Do you have an artificial leg?"

The fallout from Devil's Lake had spread through every area of my life like a slow, relentless flood. Nothing was left untouched. In the months following Devil's Lake, Rebecca and I began to discuss moving to a warmer climate. I was losing any ability to get around in the snow and ice. The increased number of falls I was taking in the winter were going to lead to injury sooner or later. If I needed to stay active to fight CMT, being in a climate where I could be active more than six months a year would certainly help. I couldn't do the walk track for the rest of my life. Sometimes, when I arrived at the office on a cold day, my fingers would not function and I couldn't type. My productivity was going down. Lastly, I just felt better when I was warm. After seeing the wisdom of such a move, we began to search for a new pastorate. My only geographical restriction was this: NO SNOW. I wasn't going to leave a church I loved, a house I enjoyed and a solid neighborhood for more freezing weather.

After looking around for a while, we got together with a group of people from Dixon, a small town near Sacramento in northern California, who wanted to start a church. I preached, we talked, we ate and we decided to work together.

We needed a bit more space than the trunk of our car, so United Van Lines sent over an 18-wheeler. On March 26, 2001, I loaded my family into our van and moved to California.

Leaving the church that I had spent twelve years building was one of the hardest things I have ever done. I loved the people and they loved my family and me. There were many tears.

As Highway 80 ventured over Donner Pass in the Sierra Nevada Mountains and drew near to Auburn, I began to recognize my homeland. I showed my sons a patch of radiant flowers and said, "These are golden poppies, the state flower of California." As we passed the turnoff to Penryn, I noticed a historical marker sign announcing Griffith Quarry. My childhood wilderness was now a tourist attraction. Due to some timing issues related to the closing on our home, we wound up staying with Dad and his wife in Sacramento—a mere half hour from Dixon—for about six days. I was apprehensive about doing this—we hadn't really gotten along the last time we were there. But the visit was good. I enjoyed being there; I felt welcome, and my sons certainly enjoyed the neighborhood pool. When we left, we talked about getting together again, which was something we all genuinely wanted to do.

A few days later, I took my sons for a walk at Point Reyes National Seashore. We came across a patch of the sun-blessed flowers, so it was time for a quiz. "Okay, guys, what kind of flowers are these?" Andrew, beaming with the Adam-like joy of naming his world, confidently spoke, "Those are golden potties."

On April 23, after we had settled in a bit, I began to exercise six

175

days a week. I weighed in at 185 pounds, my target weight to begin the PCT. Without too much effort, by walking on nearby farm roads and new trails I found in the Coast Range, I was able to do at least 24 miles a week, almost twice as much as I had been doing in Chicago. Nearly every day was sunny. Nearly every day was warm. As I walked among the valley oaks and the buckeyes, I heard the song again.

I was struggling though. The move from Chicago cut out a part of my heart. I missed my friends. Because I was starting a new church, I didn't have an office, a phone number, a computer, or a congregation. I missed my work. Sometimes when I walked, I felt weak. I seemed to be falling more often than usual. And when I fell, my knees hurt a lot more than when I was twenty. At times, I looked through my PCT guide and felt total defeat. There was no way I could walk 438 miles to Oregon, no matter how hard I prepared, no matter how much I tried.

This sense of foreboding got much worse in early June. I was hiking with my three sons in a small wilderness area just outside of Napa. The trail was really steep, and we were all struggling. The sun was hot. Long before we reached the summit of Sugarloaf Mountain, Andrew just gave up and wouldn't walk another step. He had given the ascent his best. I believe that family hiking is supposed to be fun and not torture, so we all turned back. On my way down, my left foot slid on some gravel and my whole body crashed down on my left foot, which crumpled underneath my butt. I usually hurt after I fall, but I can walk off these pains. This time, my foot really hurt and wouldn't stop. I limped to a creek, where the boys happily splashed while I chilled my foot in the cool stream. I rested and took a short nap. I avoided walking as long as I could. Finally, I painfully pushed my foot into my boot and hobbled the last mile back to the car. I had sprained something. My recovery was painfully slow.

I've fallen countless times and never been seriously, or even moderately, injured. Having such a track record left me a little arrogant—I fall, but I always get up. Now I wasn't so sure. As I nursed my foot to health, Dr. Bernstein's words—"You'll know"—floated through my mind like an evil theme in a Wagner opera. A small part of me wanted to play it safe and just not hike anymore. I wasn't at all sure that I could hike the PCT wearing a backpack. I wasn't even sure that my walk was a wise idea. But vision drove me. I would at least get out there and try.

Plan A had been to finish all of California in 1982. I walked a long way, but I didn't see Oregon. Plan B was to finish in one summer—a gonzo 50-day adventure in 2001. Without too much thought, Rebecca and I bonged that idea. Way too much time away from home in one stretch. Plan C was to divide the last section into two summers of about 25 days apiece, getting to Oregon in 2002—twenty years after my first attempt. But now we lived in California. I was three hours away by car from the trailhead to Lookout Rock. I sought to take full advantage of my proximity. I divided the last 438 miles of PCT into nine separate hikes over the next three years. Every time the PCT crossed a road, I would come off the trail and take a break or have someone resupply me. Short trips, long breaks and a light pack—this was Plan D.

The time for planning and preparing was over.

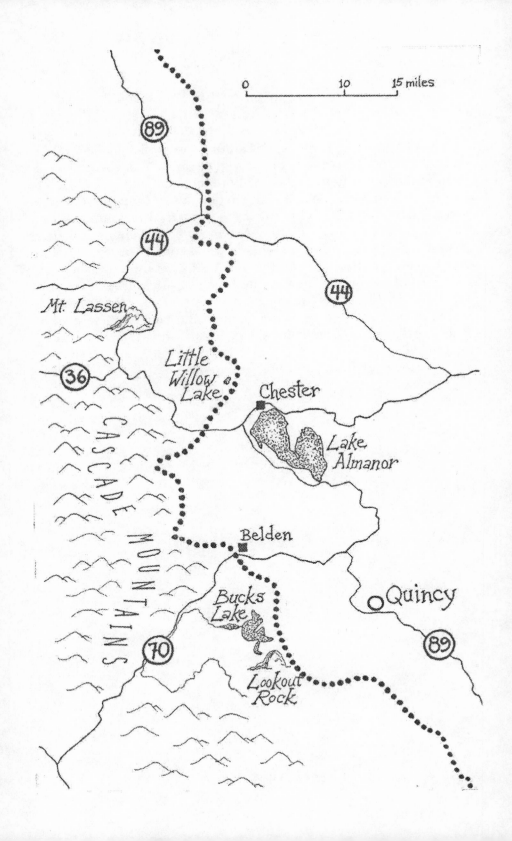

Chapter 21:

The PCT from Lookout Rock to Highway 44

Summer 2001

CNN did not meet me at Lookout Rock. In my fantasies about this day, I imagined Barbara Walters or Larry King greeting me with a camera crew and asking me urgent questions: "How does it feel to be on the trail again? Do you remember being here nineteen years ago?" I answered in eloquent and expansive ways.

My first section back on the PCT was a short one—just a shakedown cruise to see if I could still backpack. All I wanted to do was get back to Lookout Rock and walk some 30 miles over three days to arrive at a very small town called Belden. I had read the trail description scores of times and had the maps virtually memorized.

I had met my partner Brian at my new church. He was young and strong and had done some hiking in the past. He wanted to spend some more time in the mountains. I wanted a partner. We hooked up.

After having a rather difficult time finding exactly where the PCT crossed Big Creek Road, Brian and I said goodbye to my dad and my son Max and shouldered our packs for only a few yards before we hid them in the trees. In order to get to Lookout Rock, we had to walk south on the PCT just over three miles, then turn around and retrace our steps northbound. There was no reason to carry our packs. We had left the bears behind in Yosemite. Our gear would be safe.

The sky was clear. The temperature was pleasant. The trail was snow-free and easy to follow. Stately red firs attended our way as we made a leisurely ascent to Lookout Rock. Although my CNN fantasy was not fulfilled, the reality of being at Lookout Rock was better.

I *remembered* this place—the slope of the canyon leading back to the middle fork of the Feather River, the gracious view of steep forested ridges to the east and distant peaks to the south. I also remembered the kind of shape I was in when I pulled up that last ridge. I was wasted. Even though nineteen years had passed and CMT had pursued its slow course of degeneration, I was in better shape for walking right now than I had been back then.

Takin' a break at Lookout Rock

I had done what I came for—I reconnected with the PCT of 1982. There was no doubt in my mind that I had walked here before. I turned my face north and began to make progress on the northbound PCT for the first time in almost two decades.

As we walked back to our packs, Brian's faster walking speed kept him in front until we were almost back to the hiding place. Brian walked back to me and said, "Martin, there are bears here."

"Did you see any tracks?" We were at a muddy spot in the trail.

"No, I just saw a bear."

Wow! This was so cool! This was why I love the mountains. You just never know what's going to happen. I hurried down the trail a bit to see if I could still see him, and just ten yards off the trail was the cutest little bear you could imagine—a cuddly, light brown bear. I talked to the bear a little bit, but he was blissfully uncaring of my attention. He was perfectly content to walk slowly away.

Brian piped up, "You know, our packs are pretty close. Do you think he got our stuff?"

I hadn't thought of that. We rushed back to the packs and sure enough, Mr. Bruin had ripped open Brian's brand new backpack and put a big hole in mine. Food bags were scattered everywhere. Brian was the first to speak:

"He got all my sandwiches."

"What were they made of?"

"Peanut butter and honey."

No wonder our little friend looked so content. We had just provided him with a royal feast. The score after six hours: Humans 0, Bears 1.

For the first two and a half days of this hike, I felt comfortable and capable in the familiar mountains of the Sierra. My routines worked splendidly. My wristwatch alarm went off at 5:40, and I started walking at 6:00. I enjoyed these cool and solitary walks. I walked for an hour and rested for an hour. I never got overly fatigued and I stayed far away from anything like Red Deficit. I took my boots off at each break to dry out my socks and inspect my feet. The little toe on my right foot was getting pretty red. If I walked for too long, I would get a blister, but my breaks never allowed this to happen. I popped four Ibuprofen at 6:00, 10:00, 2:00 and 6:00, thus reaching the maximum daily limit of sixteen. My muscles never really hurt that bad.

Even though we'd provided a meal for a forest resident, we had plenty of food for ourselves. I "grazed" throughout the day, munching a small amount of trail mix or swallowing a breakfast bar. In this way, I always had energy and was never hungry. Powdered Gatorade mixed into purified water replaced my declining electrolytes. My favorite dessert, instant Jell-O pudding, provided a soothing and tasty way to finish our suppers.

When I walked, I had to think about my feet. I didn't have much time to look around. But when I took my numerous breaks, I enjoyed the creation around me. For someone who had lived in the Midwest for seventeen years, these mountains were most pleasant. I liked to lie down and stare up into the swirling heights of towering red firs. Huge canyons, several thousands of feet deep, were constantly vying for my starved attention. Hummingbirds and bumblebees were everywhere—buzzing about in a flurry of flight.

The fun ended for me on Day 3 at about 11:00 a.m., when Brian and I began a steep, unyielding 4,000-foot descent into Belden. From the top of our ridge, Highway 70 looked like a line drawn with a thin pen. Trucks were ants scurrying to distant destinations. As I looked down this harsh slope, I experienced vertigo and had to keep my eyes on the trail. There was too much air.

My routines failed me. Disciplined breaks did not rejuvenate me, and I fell six times in a few hours. I had fallen only once in the last two and a half days. Resting my feet did not save them. As I took my boots off to inspect my feet, I found blood on my socks. I couldn't stop the relentless downhill pounding from taking its toll on my feet. The top layer of skin on my toe had been completely ripped off. When I put my boots back on, pain cut me. Drugs did not keep my muscles from aching. Gatorade did not stop the heat, which soared higher as we dropped from the high places, from sapping my strength.

But I only had to get to Belden. When I did, my stride was pretty gimpy and I felt pretty bad. That was okay. I had eleven days to rest, heal, and think before I came back to Belden and climbed back up the other side of the north Feather River Canyon for Days 4 through 13 of my 2001 hiking plan. In the mountains, what goes down, must go back up.

Several days passed before I felt remotely whole. My blister, however, was far from healed when I woke up before first light to go to Belden. My foot screamed in pain as I gently coaxed it into my boot. What was I going to do? I couldn't walk for ten days like this. I grabbed a razor cutter out of my toolbox just before my father came to pick us up.

Joining me for this leg of the trip was a man named Paul. Paul was a friend of mine from Evanston, Illinois, who was a lover of the woods. We had canoed together, and I enjoyed his easy company and quiet competence. When we were talking about the trip, his wife looked at me and said, "You take care of Paul out there."

What I said in reply was prophetic, "It's Paul that's going to take care of me."

During our drive to Belden, I put on my boot and noted the exact spot where my blistered little toe rubbed against the side. I took the boot off and, using my razor cutter, carved out a small section of my boot right at the point of contact. When I put my boot back on, I didn't feel a hint of pressure. My foot was happy.

But I was still troubled. I was scared to death of trying to climb back up that canyon. First of all, a 4,000-foot elevation gain seemed impossible. Climbing out of that canyon would be like climbing from the ground to the crown of the Statue of Liberty over fifteen times while carrying a backpack. I also imagined trying to walk up every switchback I had walked down to get to Belden. I didn't think that I had a chance. To make matters worse, the official PCT was washed out due to flooding and an alternate route was being used. I checked some web sites that published hiker journals. Every entry I read mentioned the same thing: The alternate route was really steep. This was not good. The PCT is graded for hikers and horses. Horses require moderate grades. But the alternate route was not a horse trail. Until that day, I had never started a trail where I gave myself less than a 50 percent chance of finishing. I wasn't sure at all that I would see the top.

As we shouldered our packs, I explained to Paul that I only wanted to walk for a half-hour before taking a half-hour break. I didn't think that I had the strength or endurance to walk up that trail for a whole hour. He was fine with whatever I wanted to do. We found the alternate route, and immediately the trail angled severely up the side of the canyon.

My first impression was rather favorable. Even though the route was steep, the trail was extremely well built. Switchback cuts were clean and sharp, usually reinforced by rock walls. Drainage points were well placed and plentiful so that erosion was practically nonexistent. My feet found solid support under every rising step. The trail was wide and free from brush. I hadn't expected an alternate route to be in such good shape. I was encouraged.

But it didn't last. Toward the end of the third half-hour walk, the trail disintegrated. I found myself climbing on all fours to work through about twenty yards of steep, difficult terrain. This extra effort wore me out, and by the end of my scheduled 30 minutes, I was seriously fatigued with thousands of feet left to gain. My only hope lay in the fact that I was nearing the end of the worst part of the climb. I could tell by my map that the land was moderating just ahead. I hoped the trail would too.

The trail did not. After our break we came to a gentler land, but the trail still took an extremely steep and direct route to its distant goal. I was getting more tired. I was also concerned that after making it to the top, after such extreme effort, I would be too tired to walk the next day. I was constantly in tension. *Keep going, you have to climb to the top! Stop walking, you have to walk for nine more days!*

Then we came to hell. Fire had ravaged this forest a few years before. As we entered the burned zone all life ceased. No birds sang. No lizards darted. No ants crawled. Tree trunks were blackened. The burned trunks were all that remained. The fire had devoured the branches, leaving naked black sticks stuck in the ground. They looked like Satan's toothpicks. The ground was ash.

We stopped for a half-hour break here. Paul took out a small compass and thermometer. At about 5,000 feet in the mountains, the temperature soared to 95 degrees. I could see heat waves rising from the ground, distorting the still air surrounding me. It seemed as if the land was having a nightmare about the fire and, in her restlessness, still felt the heat and pain of it. There was no shade. Rest did not replenish my diminishing resources.

The watch ruled us. I walked again for a half an hour, climbing with every step. I fought against weakness in my legs, a trail of ash that crumbled as I climbed, air that parched my throat, and heat that sapped my strength. Because I often reach out and grab trees for support, my hands and shirt were coated black from the burned trunks. And still we climbed. Every step. Every step.

I cared little about how far we walked. I cared a great deal about the elevation we had gained. I kept hoping that the next half-hour of walking would bring a gentler slope. But hope was all it was. Every time we picked up our packs, the trail continued its steep ascent.

As the sun began to set, we still weren't at the top. Because this was an alternate route, our trail was now off of the PCT map. I didn't know where I was or how far I had to go. I critically measured my strength and believed that I had power for one more half-hour walk. Still we climbed.

We finally left the burn and ascended to a creek. The creek gave way to a meadow. The meadow ran up against a small ridge. After climbing an aggressive path up the ridge, our hiking trail suddenly became a jeep trail. I couldn't go any further. I didn't care whether we were at the top or not. I was close to Red Deficit and still had nine days to hike. Besides, I hoped that the jeep trail signified gentler terrain ahead. I said to Paul, "I don't want to walk any more." Day 4 was over. I took off my pack in a clearing and sat down.

As things turned out, we had succeeded in climbing to the top. The next day's walk was a piece of cake. We joined the official PCT and continued north. My leg strength was fine. Walking ten miles to camp almost seemed leisurely.

On Day 6, Paul and I broke out of the trees and walked for several miles right on the crest of the Cascades. No longer in the granitic Sierra Nevada, we now walked in the land of volcanoes. Panoramic views of colorful mountains, glowing red and yellow, and pinnacles, sharp and dizzy, met my thirsty eyes. Mt. Lassen stood proud and prominent, dominating the northern expanse. When I came to this high place, I realized how much I missed the mountains. Not the forests, but the *mountains*. Even though I had enjoyed my hike so far, the scenery hadn't blown me away. I walked in a hush of worship and glory as strong winds swept through my soul.

Having earned the reward of defiance, I also began to pay its dues. I started to get a blister—in a place that I had never had one before. A blister rose up high on the inside of my right heel, almost by the anklebone. I drained the blister and didn't think much of it. But as the day wore on, the pain sent from my foot got stronger and stronger. I changed my gait a bit to lessen the pain.

My folks picked us up on Highway 36 on Day 8 to take us to Chester for a rest break. I was pretty excited about the chance to get a bath and put on some fresh clothes. Much to my dismay, the hotel we selected did not have baths, only showers. Paul suggested that I take one of the plastic chairs from outside our room and sit in the shower. I did so and enjoyed a long, sauna-like shower. I also purchased everything that was available to help me with my feet.

Fresh and clean, we were good to go for the second half of our trip. When we arrived at Stover Springs, our intended camp for Day 9, we found a great many car campers surrounding the spring. One camp had a target set up for archery practice. Another camp was cutting open a watermelon with an enormous knife. The militant spirit of the place was a bit uncomfortable so we filled up our water bottles and pressed on a few more miles into the woods.

I laid down my ground cloth and sleeping bag right on the trail. I had a great view of the sky and decided that this would be the night that I would stay up and savor the cosmic display of stars, planets, meteors, and satellites. Mars glowed red on the southern sky as night fell. I asked Paul to tell me the story of his life, and he wove together a tale of innocence lost and maturity gained. I watched Mars take a speedier course toward the horizon as the rest of the night sky slowly turned around Polaris.

Paul suddenly stopped talking. I quit listening to Paul. The unmistakable sound of twigs breaking under animal feet touched our ears.

I asked Paul, "Did you hear that?"

"Yes."

Then, not more than ten dark yards away from me, many steps were taken. I quickly yanked open the draw string on my bag, reached for a whistle and blew as hard as my fear could blow.

When I stopped all was silent. Paul's flashlight had burned out a few hours ago. There was no moon. Because I had not anticipated bears, I was using my foodsack as a pillow. We were not in a strong position.

I put on my jacket and sat up in my bag. My whistle stayed in my mouth, ready at any moment. I grabbed my staff. My whole body was shaking. Meeting a cute, small bear in the daytime is cause for joy and celebration. Contending with an unseen bear in the dark night is horrifying.

I checked my watch. It was just after eleven. Six or so hours until first light.

I willed my eyes to grow accustomed to the dark. I imagined that my ears were bigger, able to pick up the slightest sound.

Dark.

Cold.

Quiet.

Tense.

Off to my left, twigs snapped and Paul and I broke into our cacophonous outburst. I frantically whistled. He slapped together his sandals, making a sound like a gunshot. We stopped. The quiet was awful by comparison.

Perhaps it is the legacy of CMT. I can't run. Walking in the dark is almost impossible. So when I fight, I simply hold my ground. I don't think much about changing position or flight. I just stand my ground. I don't have many other options, especially in the dark. I was prepared to stay there all night, blowing my whistle against my adversary. I would stay up longer than the bear would want our food. He would surrender before me.

Paul, however, was not content with my passive approach. He got out of his tent and started a fire. We now had visibility to about ten yards. When we discovered that neither of us had packed rope, he tied together extra tent lines and whatever else he could find until he had about fifteen feet of usable rope. He bear-bagged our food, with no assistance from me, and moved our packs away from camp and placed pans on top of them for a basic alarm system.

Once, as he was working, we heard the bear approach. We, quite literally, blew him away.

My watch's glow told me that it was near 1:30. Three times we had repelled the bear. Our camp was prepped for bears. Since the last incident, about half an hour had passed. The fire was burning lower.

We reasoned that our sound blasts should be shorter. If we only blasted for a few seconds, then we could hear the bear's retreat and know some more about his position. We also wanted to see our enemy. The next time the bear came, we would wait until we could see the bear and then I would blow five quick bursts at which time we would both stop and listen.

We waited.

Mars had set.

The stars slowly moved.

Crack!
Snap!

We sat side by side in the diminishing firelight with every ounce of awareness focused on the trees in front of us. This was the exact spot where we had first heard him. He was so close. I wanted to blow my whistle. But I waited.

I sensed movement. In the dim light I saw a brown shape move. Black bears aren't always black; many of them are brown. I saw his side. I saw ribs. I wanted to whistle so badly. I didn't want this bear that close. But something restrained me: I wanted to meet my foe.

His head came from the dark into the light.

My entire body relaxed. Our enemy was a deer.

Our doe moved on quickly. I asked Paul, "Did you see a deer?"

"Yes."

"Well, that's just great! We've been protecting our camp from Bambi!"

Although Paul wasn't convinced that everything we heard was deer-driven, I was. We let the fire die down and went to sleep. We didn't hear anything else.

On Day 10, my blister problem became plural. Because of my change in gait, my other foot rubbed in new places and I got a matching blister on the inside of my heel. When I arrived at Little Willow Lake in Lassen Volcanic National Park to make camp, the pain was excruciating. I told Paul that my condition needed to be downgraded. I couldn't help in camp anymore; I needed to give everything I had to walking on the trail. Paul, who was getting stronger as I was getting weaker, took over camp without missing a beat.

For the next three days I fought a war with my blisters. Every time I passed a trail fork to a nearby road I calculated the time it would take to get me to civilization. Sometimes I was only an hour and a half from a paved road. If I turned, I could stop walking in a very short period of time. At some of those junctions, I really wanted to quit. But I didn't turn.

I kept feeling more and more pain. Blisters sent their most potent pain signals right when I started to walk after a break. At first, I moved from painful to tolerable within ten or fifteen minutes of a new walk. Then, as my blisters got worse, I moved from sharp pain to dull pain. Then I moved from excruciating pain to sharp pain. And every time I took a break, I had to start the cycle all over again. I began to take fewer breaks and walk for longer periods of time in order to avoid the fresh agony of starting over.

The irony of my situation got to me. I had worried about raw strength—my legs were fine. I had worried about falls. I had only fallen once a day since Belden. I had prepared for my back—losing weight and carrying an extremely spartan set of gear. I had thoroughly broken in my boots. While I didn't have the money to buy custom-made boots, I had bought two pairs of differently sized boots to fit each of my feet more precisely. But, nevertheless, I got blisters in places that I had never had them before. The PCT always found a way to get to me.

Day 13 was a nightmare. New heights of pain assaulted me as I began my walk to the intersection of Highways 89 and 44, where my family would meet me and take me home. Every time my foot hit the ground, relentless pulses of pain shot through me. I told myself that my feet would settle down—just keep walking. For twenty minutes I walked in piercing, crippling pain. Slowly, my feet worked through the agony and walking became only very painful.

I knew that I didn't have the will to work through this process again. If I stopped for too long and my feet had to go through all that pain again, I would just quit. So I walked. Thankfully, the trail was a gentle descent. Thankfully, my strength was sufficient. One hour passed. Two hours passed. Paul, who had stopped to fill up some water bottles, caught up with me and proclaimed me the "Energizer Bunny"—I just kept going and going.

At the three-hour mark, I came to a jeep trail that led to Highway 89. I knew I was only about four miles from my destination. I stopped briefly to drink a quart of water, munch some trail mix, and rest my muscles. But I didn't stay long. I got back on my feet and ground out the last four miles in a daze.

As I walked in my trance-like state, one song kept floating through my consciousness—the theme to the old *Mary Tyler Moore* show. I thought for a moment about why this particular song came to mind. Then I grinned as I got to the last line: "You're gonna make it after all." I kept repeating this jingle over and over again. I didn't have a hat to throw in the air when I got to the intersection, but I did make it after all.

I had planned to return to this intersection in October and finish off another 40 miles before winter came. But on September 11, 2001, terrorists crashed hijacked planes into the World Trade Center and the Pentagon. In the aftermath of this attack, America went to war. My partner for this section of the trail was a pilot in the Air Force. He was ordered overseas a few weeks before our start date. I tried to find another partner, but to no avail.

I had walked 120 miles of the PCT. I only had 318 miles left to go. That sounded much better than 438.

I laid my PCT guide on the nightstand next to my bed. Nearly every night I flipped through the pages describing the rest of the trail. Oregon didn't seem that far anymore. I was beginning to believe that I might actually make it.

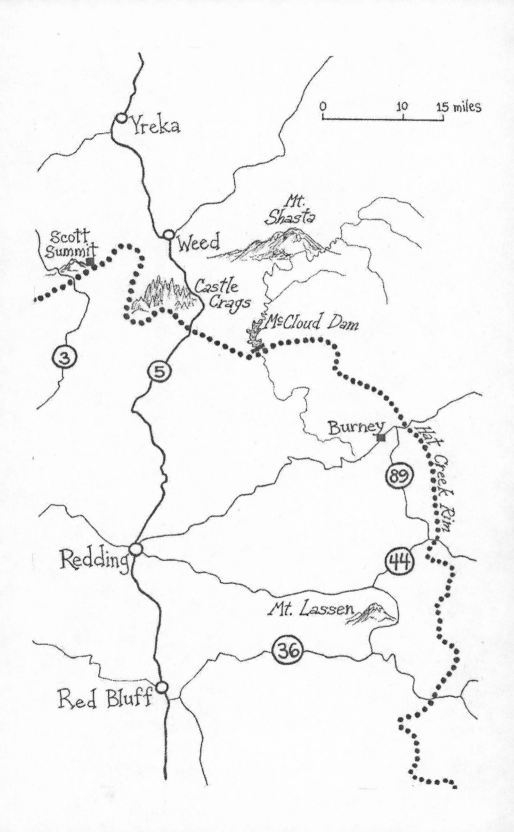

Chapter 22:

The PCT from Highway 44 to Scott Summit

Summer 2002

June 12, 2002, came much too quickly. I wasn't ready either physically or mentally for the PCT.

It was hard for me to get back into an exercise routine after my summer back on the trail. I was tired of the discipline. I had spent over a year and a half getting ready to walk. I also wasn't sure that I needed to exercise. My reflection on the trail left me feeling pretty good about my walking. Strength had never really been the issue. My blisters had been the biggest hassle and I could fix that with a different pair of boots. I'd tried on several occasions to get back in the saddle and start walking, but I'd always fizzled out after a week or so. At best, I'd walked two or three times a week for two to four miles. At worst, I hadn't walk at all. I'd gained weight.

My mind was elsewhere. My church was up and running and all of the challenges that attend such an undertaking were pressing on me—and I enjoyed the pressure. I also volunteered to be an assistant coach for my son Andrew's baseball team and all of my spare time was taken up in practices and games. I didn't have to hit the ball, run or catch. But I did get to yell at the kids. Even though our team had a dismal record (3-12!), I had a blast. It's tough to do better than playing baseball with your son and a bunch of great kids under the warm, California sun.

My biggest problem, though, was with the PCT itself. As I looked over the maps and read the trail descriptions, my determination faded. I couldn't get excited about the trail. First of all, this middle year of a three-year plan didn't have any real meat to it. Going back to Lookout Rock in 2001 and connecting with the 1982 trek had been fun to think about. I was also very motivated by the vision of getting to Oregon in 2003. But my schedule for 2002 was to walk from Highway 44 to Scott Summit on Highway 3—that didn't wow me.

The more I read about this section, the more ambivalent I became. The elevations listed in the trail guide often languished in the 2,000- and 3,000-foot range. I would not walk through high and windy places. Nope, I would spend my summer laboring through flat, hot Jeffrey pine forest. So little natural water flowed through this section that up to 30 miles of trail had to be crossed between man-made water sources. Flies would attend my way in such numbers that I was guaranteed to swallow some. The trail guide likened one particular section of trail to the San Bernardino Mountains of southern California. Did I remember a thing about the San Bernardino Mountains? Not a thing.

Then finally, I had to face the reality of distance. Since I hadn't finished the last section planned for 2001, I had to tack it on to 2002. My plan had been to hike 160 miles in 2001 and about 140 miles in both 2002 and 2003. I figured if I could make 160 miles in my first year, I could lose some strength and still manage the two 140-mile summers. This was not to be. Having only completed 120 miles in 2001, I had to walk 180 miles in 2002. Such a distance seemed impossible. I could barely walk after 120 miles the previous summer. The thought of walking 60 miles more than I had the summer before was horrible to think about. I didn't think I could do it. And even if I could, I didn't know if I even wanted to.

I knew that I only had a handful of years left to backpack. Did I really want to spend one precious summer on such an uninspiring trail? There were trails in Yosemite beckoning me that were high and clear. I could experience glorious places and take along my sons on these shorter hikes. Beauty and wonder were more meaningful than accomplishment. I considered abandoning my quest to reach Oregon. I had accomplished many of my lifestyle goals. Did I really need, or even want, to do this?

This was a brief struggle. I knew that I would regret it if I didn't try to finish. I also knew that this was my last chance. There would not be a third ascent. So, once again, I turned my inner gaze to the north.

But how was I to think about this trail?

Summer 2002 would not be about reconnection or exploration—

nor would completion be its end. No, my 180-mile walk through the broiling, fly-infested hills of northern California would be a battle— a battle of attrition. A battle where my enemy was distance and miles were soldiers killed one at a time. This was neither a pleasing nor motivating thought, but it was the only truthful way I could envision my summer.

So, like a good soldier, I got two new pairs of boots and broke them in. They didn't feel any better than the boots I had worn the previous year. I bought everything I could get for my feet—moleskin, molefoam, Spenco Second Skin, medical tape, scissors and much more—and planned to be as proactive as I could be in the protection of my feet. I simply had to keep my blisters down if I was going to win this battle.

Then, faced with such a grim vision of the trail, I filled my life with more pleasant things.

So one day I was living a normal, full life and the next day I put on a bandana, loaded my pack and hit the trail. Bam!

I got to the intersection of Highways 44 and 89 at 8:30 in the morning. Brian, who had hiked with me the previous summer, was beside me once again. This time he also brought along his wife, Jeanine. I was a little uneasy about Jeanine. She was a very inexperienced backpacker.

Furthermore, there wasn't much water in the next section. We had cached some water up on the trail earlier that morning, but we still had to walk fifteen miles to get to it and another fifteen miles the next day to get to water at a campground. Thirty miles in two days is a long way for anyone. Finally, our trail along the Hat Creek Rim was described as unbelievably hot.

My feet complained when I put on my new boots. I had fifteen miles to walk. It was already hot. I wasn't ready.

Okay, Martin. Let the battle begin. Walk for an hour, rest for an hour. Stay hydrated. One step at a time.

And so we started. Brian and Jeanine walked ahead of me as I tried to focus on my body and set down a decent walking rhythm.

At first we followed old jeep trails through pine forests, but then we started to climb onto the Hat Creek Rim. Here the PCT granted me a lovely gift. The trail clung tenaciously to the edge of a 1,000-foot cliff. There was plenty of air and the revelation of the Cascades was intense and unending. Mt. Lassen, still covered by last winter's snow,

195

loomed in the south, a marker of where I had been. Mt. Shasta dominated in the north, a guide to where I would go. And everywhere in between these two landmarks there were mountains, valleys and forests as far as I could see. Because this trail traced the edge of the rim so tenaciously, these views never went away behind trees or ridges.

It was still a battle, though of a different sort than I had expected. Jeanine got sick. At first she just slowed down, but by lunch, she was obviously struggling. When she took off her pack to take a break, she immediately crawled into a fetal position and slept. Brian and I thought that was good until she woke up and promptly threw up everything in her stomach and began to dry heave. Dehydration is a major cause of physical problems in the woods. We didn't have much water and Jeanine had just lost all of the fluid in her stomach. Brian tried to comfort her as I tried to figure out how we were going to get to our water.

Jeanine's condition was exactly the same as my father's and my sister's on the way down into the Grand Canyon. She needed shade, rest and lots of fluids. I had put a bottle of Gatorade in the cache, thinking that I would need it after a hot day. I was hoping that Gatorade would work the same wonders for Jeanine that it had for my family. But there were still many miles between our cache and us.

Jeanine was able to make a few slower, sun-scorched marches before collapsing 4.7 miles from the lookout. After resting a bit, she looked at me and said, "I'm not going to make it. I think I need to go home."

Cell phones have forever changed the complexion of the wilderness. Don got chicken pox during one of our hikes in Yosemite when we were way out in the Clark Range. There were no options. He hiked out. But with a cell phone, provided that coverage is available, there are plenty of options. Brian carried a cell phone.

"Hey, you may have to do that. But we've still got to get to the water. Hang on, we're almost there."

Finally, baked thoroughly by the sun, we first sighted and then arrived at the Hat Creek Rim Fire Lookout. Brian, who had been carrying Jeanine's pack as well as his own, had gone ahead and a pile of full, clear, cool water bottles and one Gatorade was waiting for Jeanine and me.

As we deeply drank, we decided it was best to get Jeanine out and called her sister in Carson City, Nevada, several hours away by car. They arranged to pick her up on the main jeep trail about a mile or so from the lookout. We asked them to bring more cold beverages.

After a short break, Brian led Jeanine down to the jeep trail to meet her sister and I watched an amazing sunset on the Hat Creek Rim. I was about to crawl into my bag when I saw Brian and Jeanine walk back into camp.

"What happened?" I asked.

"I couldn't find the jeep trail. It was getting dark and I didn't want to lose my way back to the lookout."

Jeanine was exhausted. She had had it for the day.

"There's no more to do tonight. Let's get her some fluids and put her into her bag. Have you been able to contact her sister?"

"No, I can't reach her."

"That's not good."

"No, it isn't."

An hour later, just down the hill, I saw the headlights of a car probing through the darkness. Brian tried to call her but couldn't get through. She just kept driving. So close.

The next morning, Jeanine was not feeling any better and by calling someone we knew in nearby Burney, we were able to get her off of the Rim and hook her up with her sister. When we were back on the trail it was already 9:00 a.m.

"Brian, I'm too tired to push it today. Let's just work the routine, an hour on and an hour off and see how it goes. The last four miles of our route today are on roads, so if we have to walk after dark it's no big deal."

"Hey, I'm beat too. That sounds good to me."

"And Brian…thanks for staying with me. I know you wanted to be with Jeanine."

"I did, but you're welcome."

Day 2 was another hot, beautiful, draining, enlivening day. We stuck to our routine and we were about six miles from camp at 7:00 p.m. when we cooked supper in the shade of some tall manzanita bushes.

I knew what we needed to do. "Let's just walk and keep walking. Maybe I'll take a short break to empty my canteen. But let's grind it out all the way to the campground."

We finished our supper, repacked our packs and set out in the fading light of day. Soon our dusty trail through desert-like brush crossed a paved road. We were now four miles from camp and the sun had set. Despite my pronounced fatigue, I enjoyed this walk. Pine trees began to assert themselves and there was a gentle quiet among them. I was able to see just fine as the light vanished and my night-vision kicked in. The rhythm provided by my boots and staff—step, step, step, tock—was pleasant and mesmerizing. I walked for a long time.

We missed the turn to the campground on our first trip through the tiny town of Cassel, but after referring to our maps, we soon found the right road and made camp for Day 2 in a run-down campground. In a few short moments, I threw down my ground cloth and bag, got out of my clothes and squirmed into my bag. I checked my watch. It was 10:30 p.m.

My body was so wired from walking that it shivered uncontrollably. I used a relaxation technique I'd learned in gimp PE class, settled my body down and slept. I had walked 30 miles in two days.

On Day 3, after a very slow morning filled with complaining, we walked through land remarkable only for its unremarkableness and came to Burney Falls State Park. Despite walking through intense heat and advancing more than my allotted ten miles a day, I felt better at the end of this section than I had after the sections I had done the year before. I had killed 40 miles. And part of it was glorious. Only one thing was bothering me. I had a horrible case of masculine chafing and often walked around like a bowlegged cowboy. But I knew what to do about that.

I came back to Burney Falls in July for Days 4-8 of my summer hiking plan. This time, I was ready. My charming wife, Rebecca, after hearing me complain about the heat, bought me a pair of thin, blue plaid pants with a tie instead of a zipper. They looked like pajama bottoms. I would never have worn them had they been given by a different giver, but…well, you understand. I also added a Ziploc bag full of Gold Bond Medicated Powder to my basic supply. It looked like cocaine. Armed with such additions, I was ready for more of the PCT.

I had a great new partner named Roger. To begin with, he was a strong, big man. I don't like to take help from people when I'm fording a stream or climbing over a fallen tree. I've learned that most people aren't strong enough to handle the kind of load I put on them when I need a hand. After pulling a few people into streams, I'd decided to go it on my own. But Roger was plenty strong enough and his sure hands were welcome at creek fords and difficult points along the trail.

He was also knowledgeable about an amazing variety of subjects. By occupation he was a building inspector, which meant that he had to know all about construction. But he could also converse freely about aviation, all sorts of different music, guns, golf, surfing, rock climbing, fishing and biking. He had competed in several triathlons and was a skilled backpacker. I kept asking him questions in the hopes of unearthing some new field of experience.

He was also patient with me as I waddled through my day. He stayed just ahead of me, where I could not see him, but close enough to stay on hand to help.

Roger's only peculiarity was his snoring. Through a lifetime of roommates, I have never heard such ponderous, sonorous snoring.

For the first few days, our trail passed through a mundane, hot and dusty forest. There were some excellent views of Mt. Shasta and at one point, I got an inspiring look at the Trinity Alps still clad in snow to the west.

Morning near Moosehead Springs

199

There were, however, interesting things going on. Roger and I were passed by tristaters constantly. In the previous year, there was hardly anybody on the trail. On this journey, the PCT felt like a major thoroughfare. And as I chatted with these hikers and watched them speed by, I realized that the entire culture of the PCT had changed since I had first walked it in 1982.

For starters, the nomenclature had changed. Twenty years ago, hikers who sought to walk all the way through California, Oregon and Washington to Canada were called tristaters. Now such hikers called themselves thruhikers.

Thruhikers also used trail names. To simply be Bob or Cindy was unacceptable. Monikers with natural themes were hip, such as Tread Lightly and Wildflower. I thought about using Snail as my trail name, but decided to stick with Martin.

Back in the early eighties, people who assisted hikers were just locals. Now they were called trail angels.

Gear was also different. Trekking poles had taken the place of hiking staffs. Internal frame packs and light loads had overtaken huge, heavy packs. This made complete sense to me. John Muir and I had been packing light for some time.

But one thing was still the same: Thruhikers are maniacs. They cover an extraordinary amount of trail. The physical and mental accomplishment of thruhiking is beyond extreme.

Lastly, the eyes of thruhikers say it all. Their eyes are restless, always looking ahead.

On Day 7, I rearranged my walk a bit to camp on the summit of Grizzly Peak. An abandoned fire lookout still watched over the wilderness for miles around. As Roger and I rested from a hot, long day, a glorious sunset began to take centerstage.

From our summit, the sun hung over the Trinity Alps several ridges over. To the southwest, I could see a sliver of the Great Central Valley stretching out from the Cascades. To the north, snowy Mt. Shasta, dominated the scene. This classically shaped volcano was crowned by dark thunderheads. The rest of the clouds in the sky were mixed. Some were high and light, others straight and thin and still others were thick and low. As the sun set in its leisurely way, the sky was painted a thousand ever-changing, ever-glowing colors. Roger and I sat and watched, enthralled, for 45 minutes.

Mixed into the wonder of this experience came a new feeling, a sadness. I realized that Mt. Shasta would be the last major peak along my way to Oregon. I would be able to see Mt. Shasta from the Oregon border. There would be no more major mountains. All that was left to do was hike to the east a bit and then cut north, with Mt. Shasta always filling the horizon. For the first time, I felt the sadness of completion.

After the last high clouds finished their glowing, like fire coals deep in the night, we got ready for bed. I decided to sleep on the old bed in the fire lookout. The place was pretty messy. I had to take out a pail that someone had used as a toilet—very smelly. There were signs of mice and other small animals all over the floor. But the wind was brisk outside and I figured I could tune out the small sounds of tiny animals. I hadn't thought about the large sounds of big animals.

There wasn't much room for two, so Roger slept just outside.

I was almost asleep when I heard Roger shout, "Hey!" and clap his hands.

"What's up?" I said quickly.

"There's something real big out here. I think it's a buck."

In the quiet, I kept hearing four quick snorts followed by a few moments of silence.

What is that? I've never heard anything like that.

Roger continued, "I can hear him over in the brush."

"Why do you think it's a buck?"

"The way he ran—the sounds he made."

I watched as Roger got out of his bag and moved toward the snorts.

I got out my whistle and Roger and I made a huge racket for a few moments. We stopped. The snorting continued.

Roger began to loft large stones toward the snort. And the snorts continued even after several barrages and whistle attacks.

That's no buck. Any kind of a deer would be long gone by now. But what is it? It has to be a bear.

"Hey, Roger. Give up on the rocks. Let's see if he leaves on his own."

Roger retreated back into his bag and it was quiet.

Just outside the lookout I heard, "Snort . . snort . . snort . . snort."

What is that?

201

Roger was up again. "Martin," he whispered. "You can see him in the moonlight."

A massive buck stood in an open expanse on Grizzly Peak. His defiant snorting continued.

"Well you were right, Roger. That is a buck. I've never heard a buck make that kind of noise before or stick around after being bombarded by rocks."

"Neither have I."

Then I named him. "He is the Psycho Buck."

Roger laughed.

Sleep evaded us. Every time we almost nodded off, the Psycho Buck returned, snorting us out of slumber.

"I know what draws him," I said after yet another attack. "It's your snoring. He thinks it's a love call." This solution perfectly satisfied me.

Roger moaned and moved his bag into the now cramped lookout. We all finally got to sleep. The Psycho Buck was gone the next morning.

I had worried about the descent off of Grizzly Peak. We had to drop almost 4,000 feet to the McCloud River. Memories of the Belden switchbacks swam in my contemplations. I imagined that my feet would be cut to pieces and I would fall several times. My anxiety was in vain. The trail down was well graded with a base of dirt and pine needles. It was a wearying descent, but it was not a painful or difficult one.

Roger's pickup truck was waiting for us by the McCloud Dam. Another sliver of the PCT was complete. As we drove home we managed to get two flat tires in the space of a couple of hours. Even the ever-prepared Roger only carried one spare and we were forced to call a tow truck. This slow path home gave me time for reflection. My walking speed was slowing down. Even on the best terrain, I was no longer making two miles an hour. I had to add more marches to my day. I wasn't making ten-mile camps in five marches; it was taking me six. And on days when I had to walk 10+ miles, I was on my feet a long time. This certainly was a battle of attrition. I had fought for 92 miles of the PCT so far in 2002 and I was beat. Could I fight for 90 more? I sighed.

Time marched on. A few weeks later, I came back to the McCloud

River with Brian and two other friends, Ann and Danette. Within five miles, Ann got sick and started throwing up. We had to go back home. The irony of the PCT flared up again. Here I was, a gimp who could barely haul myself up a flight of stairs, able to stay on the trail and get to camp. Yet normal, healthy people had dropped out on me not once, but twice, in one summer. Was I stronger than I thought? Or was I just more determined? I didn't know. But I did know that even though coming home was the right choice, I was pretty irritated. I was going to have to be much more selective about who I took along.

Brian and I managed to shave out two more days to hike and planned to walk almost 30 miles in 48 hours. I didn't want to hike this fast, but I didn't have much choice. The summer was fading and my next partner was flying in to do the last 2002 section in a few more weeks. I didn't want to take any more time than absolutely necessary.

As our hike drew near, my nose started to run and my throat got scratchy. A summer cold was taking me down. I felt horrible the morning we drove back to the trailhead. My head felt like a lead weight. My body ached and my nose constantly ran. The curvy, mountain drive inspired a dandy bout of motion sickness. I almost told Brian to turn back. It was edgy for me to hike that far when I was feeling good, but to do it when I was sick was nuts. I knew that once that car turned around, I was 30 miles from my ride home.

So once more, I defied my reason. I forced myself to get out of the car, get my pack out of the trunk, put it on and walk.

Within fifteen yards, I knew I had made the right choice. Cool morning air filled my lungs. The energy of walking began to heal my body. My head cleared.

Brian and I got to it. In former hikes, when I needed to bulk up miles, I had tried to extend my walk times rather than shorten my breaks. That plan had not worked well. This time, I only walked for one hour—never more—and shaved my break time. We walked for one hour and rested for half an hour. We climbed 2,000 feet into the Cascades and descended to rest by slow streams. After another climb of 2,500 feet we came to Girard Ridge, where the glory of Mt. Shasta and Black Butte were joined by the majesty of Castle Crags. Things were beginning to look a bit more mountainous. As the sun set, we had worked our walk/rest pattern almost nine times with a few longer breaks to enjoy the streams. Just over seventeen miles of the

PCT was complete. This was a record for me. Even in 1982, I had never walked more than fifteen miles of trail in one day.

The next day, we walked an easy, enjoyable eleven miles to Interstate 5. I was very happy to be there.

My 2002 walking plan climaxed in a six-day, sixty-mile jaunt through the Castle Crags to the threshold of the Trinity Alps. This battle was critical. If I managed to finish it, I was only 134 miles from Oregon—a very manageable distance for 2003. If I didn't finish it, my completion date slipped into 2004. I didn't want to do that.

So I brought everything I had learned to this final hike: how to bulk up miles, how to keep my blisters down, how to manage chafing and how to pack light. My old friend from the Red Deficit hike of 1992, Rich, joined me.

We arrived at the trailhead early and began a cool, mid-September walk through the oak forests of Castle Crags State Park. We ran into several hikers and found plenty of water. As promised, there were so many flies swirling about my face that I did inhale some of them. There were thunderheads in the sky all day. Sometimes they grew to ominous proportions—pregnant, black masses that filled the sky— but no rain fell. At the end of our day, we were confronted with a nasty 2,500-foot ascent. In order to break up the challenge a little, we walked a mile or so up the ridge.

With each ascending switchback, the majesty of Castle Crags intensified. Huge granite spires shot into the cloud-choked sky. Graceful domes dotted the wooded landscape. Cascading streams and bubbling springs blessed the trail. Strange carnivorous pitcher plants, that look oddly like cobras, grew in the seeps. I had returned to the real mountains. And this wonder was bought at a great price.

A regular drip of sweat fell from my bandana as I labored up each steep, granite switchback. My legs grew weary under the strain of carrying a six-day supply up a several thousand-foot ascent. My inner conversation turned to complaining:

Oh man, this is hard.

You're back in the mountains now. Real mountains are steep. What are you complaining about? First, you don't like it because the trail is boring and now you don't like it because the trail is hard. What do you want?

All right, I'll shut up. I've just forgotten how hard this can be.

No more easy walks, buddy. Get used to it.

My shirt was totally soaked with sweat at the end of the day. I shivered as I ate and worked swiftly through the evening's chores. I laid out my bag right on the trail in a steep patch of high mountain brush. The summer was passing and it was dark by 8:00. We were tired and fell asleep quickly.

AAARRRR!

From deep in a dream state, I heard a sound—a very humanlike sound. I reasoned: *There aren't any people up here. It's just your dream.* I turned over and was falling back into sleep.

AAARRR!

That is not a dream! That is a mountain lion!

I ripped my bag open in a surge of sheer terror and yelled, "Rich, there's a mountain lion in camp!"

He stood up and began to yell. I took my staff and began to beat the brush and growled menacingly. We stopped.

AARRRR!

He was only ten yards away in the brush. I got my whistle and began to blow. Rich shouted to me, "Stand up, make yourself look big!"

"I can't," I yelled back. With bare feet, in the dark, I knew there was no way I could get up. *That lion will sense my weakness. The last thing I'll see is a shadow and then I'll be dead.* I growled more menacingly and thrashed the bushes with great purpose. Rich commanded the lion to leave in the name of Jesus. I hadn't thought of that approach before. At the time, it seemed rather fitting. We stopped.

Aaarrr!

He was further away. "That's right! You just keep going! This is our place! You just get out of here!" Our cries echoed through granite canyons and died.

A distant aaarr!

He was retreating. My heart was racing with mountain terror. We yelled some more and began to settle down.

Just then, I felt a drop of rain on my arm.

"Rich, you've got to set up your tent."

205

"Right here? There's no room!"

"We'll just have to make room. I don't think I could sleep outside tonight anyway."

Rich began to set up his tent in the small space provided by the trail. He used rocks when the soil wouldn't hold the tent stakes. He used bushes to tie off guy lines. He did a masterful job.

Once, as he was working, I thought I heard sounds behind us. But it wasn't the lion. At least, I didn't think it was.

Finally, we moved into the tent and closed the flap. I had to sleep on a dreadful slope, but that was okay. The rains never came. The lion did not return. The morning broke clear.

"Was that a lion?" I asked Rich.

"Yeah, I think so."

"The cry was so human—childlike."

"Why do you think he was growling?"

"Maybe he was walking down the trail, saw us and was irritated that he had to go around in the brush. He wouldn't have growled if he had planned to attack us."

"Maybe so."

The picture of a mountain lion turning a corner and seeing me in my sleeping bag in the dark night left me very uneasy. I had always wanted to see a mountain lion, but now I wasn't so interested. It was enough to know that one had seen me.

We continued our wearying ascent toward the Trinity Divide, where the watersheds of the Sacramento and Trinity Rivers part. Gathering thunderheads shaved the tops of surrounding mountains. The air was moist, as if rain was only a moment away.

The Trinity Divide provided a flat space for our camp. Once again, we went to sleep under cloudy skies. This time, however, Rich had a good spot for his tent and set it up before dark.

I don't sleep well in the wilderness. On a good night I might wake up five to seven times to check on noises and look over the camp. On a bad night, that number can go as high as 20. This was a bad night. Memories of our cougar encounter were still fresh. I was troubled by the weather. I kept hearing noises. Every time I woke up, I checked the sky. At first it was mixed, some stars and some clouds. Then it was clear, much to my relief. Then it was pitch black, no stars, all clouds. Thunderheads don't develop at night; they need the heating power of the sun to grow. Only a genuine storm system could move in at night and cover the sky. It was going to rain and rain for a long time, maybe several days.

I hate to walk in the rain. I loathe wearing wet clothes. Sleeping in a wet sleeping bag is close to torture. I thought about different walking plans; how we could maybe cut a day off by walking more or how we could divide up the walk so we didn't get wet more than twice a day. I figured that I could cut a slit in my ground cloth and use it for a poncho. I glided in and out of sleep as I worked out my "rain plan."

Dawn was beautiful. Cloud cover had dropped to just 100 feet above us. Clouds were oozing over mountains and swirling in delicate, soundless patterns. The rising sun glowed yellow through gently meandering puffs. A tender, fluffy feeling permeated the world, as if it were packaged in cotton.

After making an exhausting detour to Upper Seven Lake for water, Rich and I moved on. As the day lengthened, the sky cleared to a radiant, clear blue. Rain ceased to be a threat. The day's walk was pleasant and we found ourselves at Porcupine Lake without incident. There were no thunderheads or mountain lions.

I woke up with a strong sense of determination. In just 2.5 miles, I would come to the highest elevation of my 2002 walking season. After attaining that goal, the PCT gently descended for the next 26 miles. I wanted to get to that point. I shouldered my pack and took off, setting a slow but steady pace. I felt good as I rounded the basin of Toad Lake and saw the high saddle where the trail would cross up ahead. I hit my rhythm and just kept going. At the saddle, Mt. Shasta said hello and the myriad mountains of the Cascade Range stood at attention.

I'm going to make it. I am going to finish this trail. I can do this.

My accomplishment bore me along for several more miles. Then, I hit the wall. I just ran out of gas. The cumulative effect of a summer of hiking caught up to me. I had walked over 160 miles. I had faced the challenges of getting two sick people off of the trail. I had set a record of seventeen trail miles in one day. I had dealt with wild animals. I had spent sixteen days on the trail and had two more to go. I was weary.

I worked my system and kept walking. But I was weakening and fell three or four times a day. And, much to my humiliation, I managed to do so when there were other hikers around. On the night of the last camp, as I was settling in, I heard a distinct growl in the woods. I was sick of dealing with animals and I asked Rich if I could sleep in his tent. He was happy to share. I left my pack outside—I really didn't care if anything got it anyway. The next day was my last day hiking for a whole year. I slept well, uncaring about the camp, our food or my pack.

I managed the last day without too much hassle. My feet weren't in bad shape and the trail only descended about 700 feet to Scott Summit. During this last descent, I enjoyed the glory of the now near Trinity Alps. There were saw-toothed ridges, deep glaciated canyons and soaring peaks just ahead of me.

Next year, Martin. Next year.

Great relief swept over me as I shrugged off my pack. The battle was over and I had won. I was 134 miles from Oregon.

Mission Control, we are good to go for 2003 California PCT completion.

Rebecca picked us up and took us home. As I walked out of the car and into my garage, both of my legs gave out and I fell flat on my face. I sat there, drained, and thought, *"Fourteen more days."*

That's one, two, three, four, five, six, seven, eight, nine, ten, eleven, twelve, thirteen, fourteen more days.

Not that I was counting.

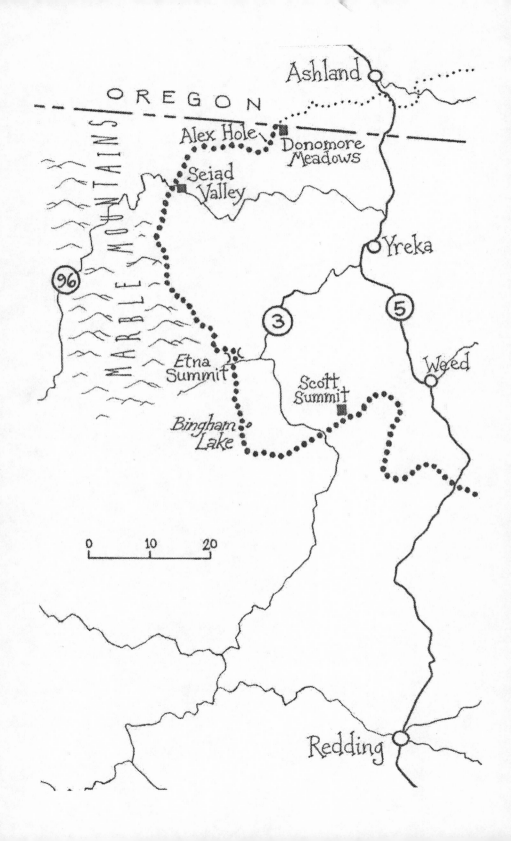

Chapter 23:

The PCT from Scott Summit to Alex Hole

Summer 2003

"Thirteen more days," I said to no one in particular and unbuckled my pack.

I looked over the grassy camp, slapped at a mosquito and smiled. A virulent outbreak of PCT fever had struck Dixon. Including myself, there were eight people settling in for the night.

Ann, who had gotten sick the year before, was working her way deep into her sleeping bag. Danette was drinking from a canteen. The ever-capable Roger worked over a hot stove. A new friend, Steve, rested on his ground cloth. Rich, who had hiked with me to Scott Summit the previous year, experimented with his new super-light stove.

Most pleasing to me was the sound of laughter coming from my son, Max and his friend, Nick, as they fumbled through the setup of their tent.

Max walked up to me, "Dad, do you have any water?"

"Haven't you guys been filling up at the streams?" I asked.

"No, Nick carried a twelve pack of Coke, we've been drinking that. But it's gone."

Such is the strength and folly of youth.

I snickered. *And I was going to be more careful about who I brought along.*

At a planning meeting several months before this trip, I made one thing clear to every hiker. "I need to finish this summer," I said. "If you get injured or sick and can't finish the route, you'll have to work

211

it out among yourselves. I'm going to grab Roger and keep going."

So far, so good.

The Klamath Mountains had welcomed me back to the final summer of my journey. Sculpted canyons and high meadows had graced the trail. Tiny snowbanks still held on against the summer sun. A few wispy clouds had sneaked across blue skies.

I'm going to finish this trail. Just three more days to Etna Summit. Then six more days to Seiad Valley. From there, only four days to Oregon. Yes!

I fell asleep to the chatter of boys, but the ominous tap of first rain woke me up.

"Rich! Wake up! Can you set up your tent in the dark?"

Rich sat up. "Ah. Yeah. Give me a few minutes."

"Can you fit Ann and Danette in there with you?"

"Sure. I think we can make that work."

I turned toward the boys' tent. "Hey, do you have room for me in there?"

"Oh yeah. We've got room."

Roger and Steve were already at work constructing a lean-to.

Dressing quickly, I hobbled into the boy's tent.

I was worried about the others staying dry. But I heard Roger and Steve laughing as they built their shelter. Light-hearted conversation sprang from Rich's tent. As this carefree banter mixed together with the pitter-patter of a light rainfall, I relaxed. All was well with our camp.

The rain had stopped by morning, but the clouds had come to stay. As we walked through the day, these clouds thickened to deep black and the air smelled of rain. Away in the distance, booms of thunder bounced in the canyons.

We came to a road. Max and Nick had only signed on for two days, so we had a friend drive up to take them home. When he stepped out of his van, he exclaimed, "I just came through the worst thundershower of my life!"

As soon as we could get organized, we sent off the boys and made camp. By the time dinner was over, a steady rain fell.

It's easier for me to sleep to the rhythm of falling rain. I slept very well that night.

The morning diminished me.

As soon as my hands were exposed to the cold, wet air, they tightened and became like claws. I worked as fast as I could to get dressed while my fingers were still movable. I managed the clasp on my jeans, but the zipper of my jacket refused to engage under the clumsy attention of my fingers. I decided to leave it open.

I still had enough power to grab my stuff sacks and throw them into my pack. But my hands were useless for any real work.

"Guys, I can't help pack up the camp," I explained. "I'm really cold. I've got to get walking."

They encouraged me to do just that.

When Danette caught up to me, I was resting by the trail under a drizzle. "I don't want to walk in this all day," I said. "Let's all meet at Bingham Lake and look for a camp. Bingham Lake is about six miles."

Danette nodded and set off with a sure stride.

About 20 minutes later, I saw Ann walk out of the mist. She smiled. "I love to walk in the rain," she said. "It's so pretty."

I shook my head. "I'm glad *you* like it. We're all going to make for Bingham Lake and then camp."

"All right," she agreed and moved on.

As my break was ending, the rest of the group came into view. Roger had a concerned look on his face.

"It's going to rain all day," he asserted. "I'm not outfitted for rain. I think we should go back. We can come back on another weekend and finish this section."

I was shocked. There was no way I was going back. A little rain was not going to stop me. I was getting close to the border. Now was the time.

"We can't go back," I reasoned. "The girls are 20 minutes ahead of us. We've got to keep going."

Roger was not pleased, but he grunted and started up the trail. The three of us men followed behind all the muddy way to the outlet stream coming down from Bingham Lake.

Ann and Danette were nowhere to be seen.

I was suddenly exhausted. I had faced the rain all day, hoping for an early camp. I'd planned to eat a hot meal, get into a tent, slither into my bag and get some warm, dry sleep.

That wasn't going to happen. So I just stood on the trail as the rain

213

increased, trying to decide what to do.

The lake was not visible from the outlet. The outlet creek ran under boulders and could easily have been missed.

"I think they walked right over this outlet and kept going," I said.

Roger nodded. "We can't camp here anyway. There's no room."

We were walking on the side of a steep canyon on a trail surrounded by dense mountain brush. There was barely room to walk, much less camp.

I found hope in the PCT guide's description of the upcoming trail: a gentle descent. My hope was swiftly crushed. The trail was horrible. It climbed steeply to granite outcrops only to descend precariously to arbitrary points. The rain continued to gather strength and was almost torrential.

Where are those girls?

Ascend a steep grade.

Briefly rest while standing.

Where will we find room to camp?

Descend meaninglessly.

Hours passed in mist and cloud. Deep fatigue set in. We needed a new plan.

"I'm not going to catch those girls," I said. "Roger, go on ahead and see if you can catch them and make camp."

Roger thought for a minute. "Okay. I'm going."

Rich, Steve and I continued our drenched plodding.

By now, I was well into Red Deficit. I walked by sheer will. My bandana was so soaked that rain streamed down my head directly onto my glasses. As I looked down to see my feet, the streaking water wiggled across my lenses. The earth moved in chaotic patterns.

I'm totally exhausted. Our party is split into three parts. I'm completely soaked and now . . . I can't SEE!

I handed Rich my glasses.

"Can you keep these for me?"

"Sure."

I looked down. The ground was out of focus, but at least it didn't move. I sighed and started again.

How long? I have no idea. I just walked.

I came to another steep section, placed my foot on rock and slipped. Somehow, I managed to stay on my feet, but I lost it anyway.

Anger boiled over. I was mad at everything. The PCT, for steep, stupid trails. The rain, for being wet. The girls, for not knowing where to stop. CMT, for robbing me of my strength. Me, for being such an idiot and trying to finish this moronic trail.

I hated the PCT in that moment. If a helicopter had appeared and I was offered a ride out, I would have taken it and never come back.

I just stared into the clouds and didn't move.

One of the guys asked in a gentle voice, "Are you okay?"

Am I okay? That's a good question. No, I'm not.

But what I said was, "Yeah, I'm okay."

I still didn't move.

"Look. I can't walk much more. Rich, I need you to find a place to camp. If I know you're up ahead setting up the tent, it will keep me going. Roger and the girls will have to work things out on their own."

Rich nodded and moved forward in the mist.

I no longer cared. I couldn't feel my legs or hands. If I had been by myself, I would have sat down and cried.

That is how people die out here. Quit your whining and walk!

Before long, we met an exuberant Rich: He had found a campsite 100 yards ahead. But still no sign of the others.

I walked to the campsite and had Rich undo the buckles on my pack.

"Guys, you're going to have to take care of me tonight," I said. "I can't do anything. I need you to set up the tent."

They did so and I waddled inside.

Okay. Get out of your clothes and into your bag.

I tugged at the clasp on my jeans, but I wasn't strong enough to release it.

Great. Now I need someone to undress me!

This was too much. I would not allow Rich or Steve to unbutton my pants. I sucked in my stomach as much as I could and grabbed the clasp and pulled. My fingers slipped off.

Try it again!

Same result.

Again!

I shook my hands, trying to awaken some strength and pulled again. The clasp opened.

It was the happiest moment of my day.

215

I stripped off my clothes, burrowed into my bag, held my hands in my armpits and waited for warmth.

It was over.

Rich passed me a hot dinner shortly thereafter.

The rain had stopped by morning, but everything was soaked. Tree branches drooped as if depressed. Flowers sagged, unable to rise.

Ten miles and you can rest.

I came across Roger's camp in a quarter-mile.

"How did it go last night?" I asked.

"I couldn't catch the girls and I was getting cold. I had to stop for the night right here. I'm fine. I'm just worried about Ann and Danette."

"Me too. I hope we find them soon."

About a half-mile later, I found Ann and Danette.

There is a radiance to those who face difficult challenges and overcome them. These women were radiant. They had faced one of the most awful days of my entire journey and made it through on their own. Sure, they had missed the rendezvous at Bingham Lake, but they had handled every challenge.

I listened as they told me their story. Ann especially seemed taller and more confident as she explained how they had figured out where they were and how they had managed to arrange shelter and work out dinner.

Amazing. Just last year Ann couldn't walk for five miles on an easy trail. But something had touched her. She had returned home with a vision to get back on the PCT. She had talked with Roger and me about how to train. She had discussed with Danette, an experienced backpacker, how to keep her pack light. Then she actually did what we suggested. All through the year, she had walked, backpacked and reconsidered her hiking strategy. Now here she was, walking ten miles in the rain, improvising shelters and handling challenges. I have rarely seen so complete a transition.

Such is the life-changing magic of the PCT.

When we were ready to walk again, Ann looked at me and said, "You're right about one thing, though."

"What's that?"

"It stinks to walk in the rain."

We arrived at Etna Summit later that day without incident or rain.

I went back home and rested. I bought some new rain gear I and prayed that I would have the strength to finish the next section. I had to walk 56 miles in six days to get to Seiad Valley, where I would be a mere 36 miles from Oregon. But the thought of another six-day hike scared me and, as the hike drew near, my dreams turned to nightmares. I fell into dark, steep canyons. Falling rocks crushed me. Rattlesnakes bit me. It seemed the closer I got to Oregon, the more anxious I became.

I was also uneasy about my partner. My brother had agreed to come out to California and hike the last two sections of the trail with me. While I enjoyed the thought of finishing the trail with someone I had hiked with in 1982, another part of me was wary.

Since 1982, my brother and I have taken decidedly different paths. I became a Christian; he was religiously agnostic. I started a family; he remained single. I stayed with a single career; he worked here and there when it suited him. Our politics were, shall we say, as far as the east is from the west. From time to time, we'd write or talk on the phone, but things went sour fast. From my point of view, my brother was arrogant, pontificating about things that he didn't know about. From his point of view, I had lost my mind, basing my life on fantasies and delusion. I didn't think it was wise to spend so much time together, but there was no other way to make his trip to California from Massachusetts worthwhile other than to hike two sections. This meant that he would live with my family for three weeks between hikes. I imagined some pretty nasty scenes.

It was late already, almost midnight, when I drove to the airport to pick him up. I had waited while his jet deplaned, but I hadn't seen him. I got up to check to see if I was mistaken about his flight status, when I ran right into him. He looked more like John Lennon than like the brother I remembered. His brown hair, combed straight back over his head, had grayed around his ears. His once gaunt frame looked full and healthy. His eyes laughed when they saw me.

We hugged and chitchatted while we got his stuff and headed home for a few hours of sleep before a long drive.

At Etna Summit the next morning, I anxiously pulled on my heavy pack and looked at my brother. He wore the same hat, carried the same pack and still used the same ground cloth he had in 1982. It was a surreal moment watching him hike in front of me. So familiar, yet strange. I knew this man and yet I did not.

The first four days with Pat were great. The Marble Mountains are "classic" backpacking country.

To begin with, the limestone mountains, which give this wilderness their name, gleamed white in the summer sun. Plant communities wholly new to me thrived in the soil scraped from these hills. In contrast to the tedious jeffrey pine forest of the previous summer, the scenery constantly beckoned me forward.

There were no Psycho Bucks snorting at us or cougars pulling us from sleep. Instead, we watched hummingbirds flit between dazzling displays of bursting flowers. We rested as newts and trout danced together in the clear waters of Fisher Lake.

Pat sat on his pack and I laid on my ground cloth. We gazed lazily at a forested scene. My brother is an amazing repository of useless information. During the months prior to the hike, I had saved up some questions for him. Simon and Garfunkel were the category for the day.

"You know the movie, 'The Graduate'?" I asked.

"Yes."

"Well, the Simon and Garfunkel song, 'Mrs. Robinson' seems to be about a women who is being admitted to a mental institution and doesn't seem to have anything to do with the movie. Do you know why they used the song?"

"Nope."

I tried again.

"And what does the song 'The Boxer' mean? Especially the last verse about the boxer and a fighter in a clearing? I don't get it."

He explained to me that the boxer and the fighter were two sides of one man who always got beat up, but couldn't stop fighting. Made sense to me.

Pat wanted to talk politics. Back in 1982, Pat never talked about politics. Now, he talked about little else. He was intrigued by the recall of Governor Davis and constantly commented on it.

I'm bored by politics.

When I asked him to tell me his life story in detail from the 1982

PCT until the present, he declined. "I'd rather let it come out in pieces," he suggested.

And it did. I learned about his summer in Germany working for a dairy farmer, his graduate work in economics, a job with a utility company and his various attempts at playing in rock bands. Pat had stayed with the guitar and was a fine player. After a gig at one bar, someone actually asked him for his autograph.

Certain things about him struck me as odd. In a time of silence, he would suddenly laugh. At first, I asked him what he thought was funny. But he did this so often that I just let it go. He also wanted to eat the food I carried in my pack. This was okay with me. It made my pack lighter and he was willing to share his food when mine was done.

Other things were expected. My brother communicates in a complex system of groans and sighs. His emotional state can be understood by careful attention to sounds and not words. A low, long "hhhhhhhhhhuummmmmmmm" means that he is content. A sharp "hmph" means that he doesn't want to move. He still loves to sleep and eat.

I was attending to the call of nature near our camp on Paradise Lake when I accidentally kicked my plump toilet paper roll down a steep canyon. Thankfully, I had already used it. When I got back to camp, I asked Pat, "How much toilet paper do you have?"

He showed me a tiny clump of about three squares and said, "I can share if you need it."

I laughed. "Oh well. I hope they have toilet paper at Grider Creek Campground."

The trail, though sometimes steep and challenging, rolled away quickly until the fifth day. We were descending from the top of Big Ridge down to the Klamath River at Seiad Valley. A mammoth descent of 5,700 feet.

Things had gone well until I got up for my third walk of the day. My legs were suddenly and completely spent.

Okay. Just go slow. Think about your feet.

I stumbled for a few yards and tried to find some kind of rhythm for walking. Pat had gone on ahead. We had planned to meet at a bridge about two miles down the trail.

You're on your own.

After fifteen agonizing minutes, I had worked out a gimpy stride.

Things were looking better until I suddenly lost all power in my legs and fell. The weight of my body and pack crashed down on my left foot. Sharp pain erupted from near my toes.

I yelled out, "AAAAAHHHHHHH!" and sat there in the dirt.

Is it broken? Did I sprain it?

Gathering my strength, I used my staff to get back on my feet. They hurt, but not badly. I resumed my pained gait.

Within a few minutes I fell again…and then again…and again. Four times in one hour, my body slammed to the ground.

I can't keep doing this! I'm going to get hurt! Why can't I stop falling!

Fearfully, I got back onto my weakened feet.

Think about EVERY step. Think about EVERY motion. Pay ATTENTION! Now WALK!

Very slowly, very methodically, I coaxed my failing frame down to my brother. I threw off my pack, collapsed on the bridge and didn't budge for 75 minutes. When my watch showed it was time to move on, I didn't want to. I knew I was going to fall again and I was scared.

"Stay closer," I told Pat. "I may need your help."

"I'm there."

I needed to go to the bathroom pretty badly. So my world was reduced to this: get up and walk four miles to the campground so you can use toilet paper to do your business.

After about five minutes of cautious limping, I relaxed a bit. The rest had helped me. With electric quickness, my legs failed and I crashed to the ground yet again. My hand released my staff and it rolled into a deep, dry creek bed.

"Pat!" I screamed.

I was so tired, so weary, so spent. My feet hurt from falling and from the relentless pounding of the descent.

My brother caught up to me.

"Can you get my staff?" I pointed to where it had landed.

"Sure."

Come on, Martin! Every time you think that you are doing better and you take your mind off of walking, you fall. You can't think about anything but walking! Lock and load! One step at a time!

I wanted to go to the bathroom, so I got up. I became intensely focused. I allowed nothing to enter my mind but the business of walking. I monitored my legs with steely attention. I made precise calculations for every step. I would not allow myself to fall again.

And I didn't.

In a trance-like state, I arrived at Grider Creek Campground. The bulk of my descent lay behind me. And, most importantly, the pit toilets were supplied with an abundant amount of toilet paper. Ah, thanks be for simple things.

The next morning, as I lurched painfully down a jeep trail toward Seiad Valley, an old truck pulled up next to us. A woman wearing a cowboy hat rolled down her window and asked, "You boys want a ride?"

"Nope," Pat explained. "We've got to walk every step."

"Okay," she replied. "But there's going to be a parade in town. You don't want to miss it. Are you sure?"

"Yes. But thanks. We need to walk," Pat answered.

"Suit yourself," she said and drove away in a cloud of dust.

Still miles from the town, we heard the sirens of police cars and fire trucks making their way along the parade route. The wailing stopped after a few short minutes.

"Seiad Valley must be awfully small," I guessed.

It was. We strolled past a fire station hosting a barbecue. There were potato sack races on the lawn and a man called out bingo numbers from inside a hall. A bright red banner proclaiming "Seiad Valley Days" hung over the road. There were a few small weathered houses, an RV park and a tiny grocery store.

As I watched the clean, energetic children of Seiad Valley run and jump, I felt old, dirty and a little weathered myself.

I touched a post by the Seiad Valley Creek and went home.

Pat was a good guest. He took up residence in our guest room and was easy to get along with. Whatever we wanted to eat and whatever we wanted to do was okay with him. He was respectful of our way of life, going to church with us on Sunday morning and praying with us at meals.

During the day, he read on our back porch, sitting in my favorite chair. Books that took me weeks to read he cut through in one day. He scoured through most of our books.

Rebecca and Pat got along well, much to my relief. Rebecca, who is also a reader, suggested some of her favorites to Pat and he liked them. They enjoyed chatting together after dinner.

One Sunday afternoon after church, Pat and I were alone in the kitchen. He seemed restless.

"I didn't like some of your sermon. Do you think we can talk about it?"

I grimaced. "It won't do any good. You don't like the kind of answers I give."

"I like them sometimes," Pat answered.

"Okay," I conceded. "If you want to try."

Pat accused me of intellectual inconsistency in how I applied Christ's teaching in the Sermon of the Mount. I responded with biblical text. Neither of us budged.

Pat's sarcasm came to the fore, "That was satisfying, wasn't it?"

"I told you it wouldn't work," I chided.

Pat sat for a moment and thought.

"So," he proclaimed, "you think I steadfastly refuse to acknowledge the truth and I think you can't see the nose on your own face."

That summed it up. I didn't see any need to reply.

Sooner than I wanted to, I had to return to Seiad Valley. In six miles, I had to climb 4,000 exhausting feet from the floor of Klamath River Canyon to the summit ridge of Lower Devil's Peak.

Ann, who was anxious to hike more, and a friend named Kurt joined us for the last section.

Fall was near and cold nibbled at my skin as I touched the post by Seiad Valley Creek and trudged west on a road, searching for the PCT trailhead. The others passed me and we began our ascent.

I like switchbacks. They keep the grade of an ascent to a minimum and they also provide attainable goals. A switchback is usually short. Most of the time, I can manage a switchback in a few minutes. And every time I turn that corner—progress toward the goal!

There were lots of switchbacks to like.

We took our first break at Fern Spring. I was glad that Ann was along so that we could work on her map skills. The Bingham Lake snafu had revealed a skill she needed to learn.

I gave her the map. "Now, show me where you think we are and give me three reasons for your choice," I said. "I'll help you a little bit. Your first reason should always be 'Because that's about how far we walk in an hour.'"

"But I don't know how far that is."

"You'll figure that out with more experience. Now, where do you think we are?"

Ann pointed at the words "Fern Spring" on the map.

"And why do you think we are at Fern Spring?"

She pointed to the large spring surrounded by ferns. "Because there's a spring with a sign on it that says 'Fern Spring.'"

"Excellent observations!"

The trail's gradient stayed moderate until the last mile of our ascent. Then, fatigue and a steep trail quickly frustrated me. I wasn't falling, I just didn't have any power or, more importantly, any will left to climb.

I came to a sign that said, "Lookout Spring, ¼ mile." Since this was our goal for the day, I thought the nearness of it might rally me. It didn't. I decided to take a break instead.

I got up again and started to walk through a steep, rocky section and got my legs bent funny and fell. I cut my arm on a sharp rock. Blood dripped from my arm, staining a rock.

Once again, I've given blood to the PCT.

I sat for a long time and stared into the mountains. It felt good not to walk.

You need water. Get to the spring.

I sighed and began my wearied ascent again.

I came to a switchback and knew something was wrong. Lookout Spring was before the switchback on the map.

Did I miss it? Did the others find it? Are they waiting there or did they go on to the top?

I looked up the ridge and saw Kurt. I plodded to the top. "That was hard to do," I said to Pat and sat down. I was almost in tears. "I'm so *sick* of this trail. I'm losing my will to do this."

"That's okay," Pat replied. "You don't need much more."

Pat and Kurt eventually found the spring.

We made our camp right on the trail, just a few yards further along the way.

When morning came, I was exhausted. I had shivered through a near-freezing night. To make matters worse, a front had blown in and the sky was black with clouds. As I loaded my pack, the first raindrops fell.

I stuffed my bag into a trash bag, put on my Gore-Tex rain jacket and set out.

Another day in the rain. I'm not having fun anymore.

But providence smiled on us and the rain did not last. As we rested for our first break, the skies cleared in the west and the weariness cleared from our hearts.

The wilderness opened to receive us. As we made our way toward Cook and Green Pass, we traversed long and stunning ridges and lunched in green meadows by bubbling springs. Beautiful peaks, dashed with limestone outcroppings, stood strong as thin clouds sauntered by.

As the afternoon faded, the clouds gathered and a gentle, healing rain fell from a pillowy sky. A magnificent rainbow, painted with God's watercolors stretched down toward a tree-choked canyon.

About 100 yards from camp, as I mindlessly sang some silly song, my legs simply shut down, without warning or sign, and I fell again. The worst pain I have ever felt from a fall exploded from my left foot.

At least there's a road at Cook and Green Pass. It won't be too hard to hitch a ride out of here.

I tried to move my toes. They hurt even more.

I'm so close. Just try to get up and walk.

After several minutes, I levered myself up, to the complaining of my battered feet. With tiny steps, I began to advance again. I saw the others down by where we would make camp. I hobbled down to them.

Keeping my mind on my feet, I said to the others, "I don't feel very good."

"I can see that," Kurt replied.

We hastily made camp as the rain strengthened. By the time we got into our tent, a vigorous tapping sounded from our rain fly. Our tent not only kept the rain out, it retained some of our body heat and I was encouraged by the prospect of a warm night.

Just two days to go. If I can make it.

During the night, I pushed the illumination setting on my watch to check the time. There was a strange flash and the light quickly faded.

Great. My watch is broken.

First light was sloppy. The ground was wet; the sky was cloud-covered. A weak sunrise brought no warmth.

I crawled out of the tent and uneasily got back on my feet.

"I am vertical," I proclaimed to the morning.

I walked carefully for a few steps. My bones of my feet felt spread out. The tendons holding them together were stretched to the breaking point. It seemed as if the slightest pressure would cause my bones to blow apart, like the pieces of completed puzzle scattered by a child.

I continued to test my injuries, gradually, though fearfully, transferring weight from my staff to my tender feet.

Well, at least it's worth a try.

When Ann heard that my watch got torched, she offered me a small digital watch on a strap.

"Thanks." I needed that watch.

The cold that morning once again transformed my hands into two useless blobs of flesh. I had to have Kurt put the watch on my pack's sternum strap and then help me put on my pack. Not much of me was working.

I looked more closely at the sky and said, "You know, these clouds might burn off. It looks thin, wispy—more like fog."

The morning was dead quiet. The only sounds were the swishing of my clothes as I moved past trailside brush. The cold was heavy on me, so I just kept walking, hoping for my body to warm up, hoping for the sun to break through the clouds.

Light overcame darkness in increments. The sun rose and the clouds thinned. I continued to ascend.

I perceived more movement in the clouds as I approached a gap in the crest of the mountain. Looking up, the rays of the sun were defeating the fog. Visibility increased and periodic splashes of pure light broke through, like spotlights shining on a stage.

The sun's strengthening rays glowed through the thinning fog around me. It seemed as if light could be gathered into my hand. Nearer the ridge top, the morning breezes shot small clouds gushing over the crest so that they looked like steam rising from a geyser. Tiny droplets of water hanging from flowers and trees captured sunlight. Still I ascended.

Finally, I came to a sun-drenched clearing. Checking Ann's watch,

I found that it was time for a break. Only faint memories of cloud and fog remained in the sky. I sat, closed my eyes and turned my face to the sun.

The rest of the day's walk was pleasant. My feet continued to strengthen; my body relaxed as I drew near my goal. I actually managed to walk a bit faster than two miles an hour.

Though the sun was still up, cold had already settled into the mountains when we arrived at a forested saddle near Alex Hole to make our final camp.

I had enjoyed the warm tent the previous night, so I asked Kurt and Pat to set it up again. I brought all of my gear into the tent and imagined getting ready in the morning inside a warm tent.

Ann, who slept nearby in a single-woman tent, wanted her watch for the night. I asked her to wake me up at 6:40. I wanted to be on the trail by 7:00.

She nodded. "You got it."

As Pat and I got ready for bed, we were lighthearted. We were warm and the end was close. Kurt was later to say that we sounded like kids at a slumber party.

Day 170:
Donomore Meadows

September 18, 2003

"Hey, Martin, it's 6:40."

I sat up.

Game on. This is it.

Pat let out a long, low "hhhhhhhhhhhhhuuuuuummmmmmmm."

I understood this to mean, "I'm warm and happy. Leave me be."

The toasty environment of our tent greeted me as I unzipped my bag.

"Man, it feels good in here." I started to pack up my gear.

Pat agreed, "Hhhhhmmm. I think I'm going to become a tent-guy."

I did everything I could do inside the tent before I unzipped the flap and went out into the cold. All Kurt needed to do was put Ann's watch back on my sternum strap and I was off.

The trail kept to the west side of the ridge, so I walked in shadows long after a clear sun had risen. My gloved hands were warm. My stride was resolute. I had ten miles to walk, several questions to answer and many things to remember.

I have often wondered how I would feel on my last day. So, Martin, how do you feel?

I'm thankful.

I felt like I was on a razor-sharp ridge of circumstance. So many things had to be *just so* for me to be walking on that particular day so close to a achieving a near-impossible goal.

Leaving the trail at Lookout Rock in 1982 was key. Sure, 400+ miles of trail to Oregon was a monstrous goal, but finishing was possible. It was worth trying. I don't know if I would have had the guts to pick up my pack again if the distance had been much greater.

The land itself was part of the equation. I left the granitic Sierra Nevada for the volcanic Cascades about 40 miles north of Lookout Rock. These new mountains were much gentler; the trail through them was much softer. I needed this gentleness to begin my hike again. If I had had to walk on harsh, unforgiving granite trail for hundreds of miles, the pain would have been too much for me. Even with a softer trail, my blisters had almost stopped me.

Timing was right on the edge. Both my will and my strength were almost gone. Walking this far had taken all the fight out of me. The desolation of Devil's Lake had awakened me just in time. There are no more summers of major backpacking left in my life.

My churches had been so good to me. The church in Evanston had framed my hikes as a sabbatical of sorts. I didn't even need to use my regular vacation time. My new church in Dixon gave me all the paid time off I needed for the hike and for family trips.

The move to Dixon was pivotal. I can only stay on the trail for about six days before I completely fall apart. If I had stayed in Illinois, I couldn't have afforded the plane fares to come out to California three times a summer. With all of non-freezing America open to me, I wound up right next to the PCT.

I have such good friends. I can't hike by myself anymore. In Yosemite, hiking partners had been hard to come by. I was concerned that I wouldn't find people to walk with me. After all, some of the trail was pretty dull. I have to walk in such a weird way. Yet old friends from the Midwest spent their vacations with me. New friends gladly shared the dusty places of the PCT.

My friends had helped me in other ways. Several people had driven hundreds of miles to get me on and off the trail. Even now, as I walked toward the border, an intrepid elderly woman was driving north in her Volvo station wagon to pick us up at the end of a 20-mile jeep trail.

I was amazed that I had never been seriously injured. When I include every trail I have ever walked, I've logged about 2,800 miles as a backpacker. If I include day hikes in the woods, that number climbs to over 4,000. How many hundreds of times have I fallen? How many hundreds of times did I break through snow? How many times did I strain my ankles to the breaking point?

That I had not been seriously injured seemed almost miraculous.

Most importantly, I was thankful for Rebecca. Since that fall day in 1999, Rebecca has stood by me and encouraged me to finish my dream. While I was out grappling with the PCT, she took care of the kids and managed the household. Then, when I got back, she helped me to rest and get back to my regular life. I couldn't have stayed on the trail without her.

So many things had to come together. If I hadn't married Rebecca, if I had been seriously injured, if several people had not spent their valuable time hiking with me and supporting the trail, if my churches had not opened the way for me to hike, if I hadn't moved to Dixon, if I had waited another year, if I hadn't walked all the way to Lookout Rock, if the land itself had not changed under my feet, I wouldn't be finishing the PCT.

Convergence.

Oh yes, I have much to be thankful for.

As my first one-hour walk drew to a close, the trail moved over the crest to the east and into the sun. From where I rested, I could see all the land we had walked through since Seiad Valley. It didn't look like we'd walked very far.

How did I ever get here from Mexico going so slow?

I was anxious to finish, so I cut short my break and got back on the trail.

I had once joked, "If you look really hard, you can see Oregon." I wasn't joking anymore. A look to the north was now mostly Oregon. California was fading behind me.

So, Martin, do you want to keep going? Is California enough?

There was no doubt in my mind. California was enough for me, more than enough. I felt no pull from the forested mountains and deep green canyons of Oregon.

Okay. But how are you going to stay active without the PCT?

This question troubled me. Twice in my life I have stared down CMT and fought to overcome my condition. Twice I ascended against the downward pull of decay. My motivation in both battles was my love for the PCT. With this goal complete, how would I respond? Would I quit fighting, get fat and let CMT take me? Would I find a new vision? Would I fall into a depression like I did after the PCT is

1982? Would I defy, compromise or surrender to CMT?

I didn't know.

But I did feel change. I was changing. My family was changing. My church was changing. And this change made the future intriguing.

Maybe there's another way to handle CMT.

Our gently descending trail ran through gleaming mica-schist ridges. The glint of fool's gold twinkled around me. Wide clearings surrounded by tall firs framed powerful views of Mt. Shasta.

Goodbye, Mt. Shasta. It's been good getting to know you.

Once again, I walked a bit faster than two miles an hour and came to my second break.

Less than six miles to go.

The group bantered about several subjects, like music and movies. But I didn't pay much attention. All I could think of was: Oregon, Oregon, Oregon!

After a brief rest, I set out for Ward's Gap Fork, a mere three miles from the border.

Everything worked for me. My feet felt great. The pain from my falls had faded. My stride was loose. The trail continued a gentle descent. I could sense the proximity of Oregon.

Still other questions begged to be answered. Ones that had bubbled up several times before, but I had suppressed them, fearing to answer them before their time.

Martin, do you still love the mountains? Do you still hear the song?

These were hard questions. I didn't feel the same way about the mountains as I used to. That was certain. I no longer looked to the hills as a lover. I no longer dreamed of discovering new places and sweet secrets.

Where I once sought out the strong beauty of high passes and sweeping panoramas as food for my soul, now I enjoyed smaller things, quieter places. I had sat by the shores of Paradise Lake and watched steep cliffs cast an early sunset over still waters. Tranquility could be felt, like streamwater running through lazy fingers.

Once, the high places were the only passion I had. Now, I led a rich and varied life. There was a song from my family. How precious to me were my children. How wondrous to watch them grow. To witness miracles.

Above all, I heard the song of God. Age has drawn me toward the

Creator and gently away from creation. The mountains are no longer an end in themselves. They draw me to something deeper.

So, do I still love the mountains? Do I still hear the song?

It seemed to me that the song of mountains was like a single theme in a Bach invention. The mountain's song wasn't the only theme, but to take it out would destroy the music. Wilderness is part of who I am.

Yes, I still hear the mountain's theme in the song of my life.

Yes, I still love the mountains. Not with the passion of youth, but with the deep, resonating love of a husband who can still find mystery and wonder in a woman he has been married to for decades.

During our break at Ward's Gap Fork we watched as flocks of birds glided over trees. Perhaps journeying south for winter.

"I'm so ready to be finished," I said. "I'm so ready for the next phase of my backpacking career."

"What are going to do?" Ann asked.

I rubbed my hands in glee. "Let's see, start at about ten in the morning, long after the sun has warmed everything up. Walk for an hour and stop. Get out my luxurious backpacking hammock and take a nap or read a good book by a stream. Maybe walk for another hour to camp. Set up my hammock and hang out."

Ann shook her head. "That sounds a little boring."

I smiled. "It sounds great to me."

Pat chimed in, "Me, too."

I felt a deep contentment.

"How far to go now?" Kurt asked.

"Three miles. Here's what I'd like to do. I'm going to slow way down and enjoy these last few miles. Let's walk 1.5 miles to Donomore Meadows and take another break. Then we'll walk the last 1.5 to Oregon."

After a pleasant hour had passed, we packed up for the walk to Donomore Meadows.

That was the perfect name—Donomore Meadows. I noticed right away that, if I divided up the syllables, the name became "Do no more Meadows." Do no more Meadows was the last landmark before the border.

The sun was high above me, shining in a deep blue sky. Magnificent trees stood at quiet attention as I walked by. The lapping of Donomore Creek sounded ever stronger as I rounded a knoll and gracefully ascended to Donomore Meadows.

Ann didn't like my new hiking plan. There was a time when such a plan would not have inspired me either. But I'm ready now. I'm ready to let go. Dr. Bernstein was right. He told me I'd know when it was time to stop. It's time.

So much had changed since Devil's Lake. Four years ago, I had sat sniveling on the shores of a Midwestern lake—a broken man. Now I walked north on the PCT after three summers of backpacking more than a hundred miles—a contented man.

California has been good to me.

I enjoyed my new church. Having Dad nearby was great. California's sun loosened my ever-tightening body.

My sons were growing up. Max, who was almost as tall as me, was now in high school. Andrew was a strapping seventh grader. My youngest son, Grant, was in the second grade.

Rebecca and I would celebrate our twentieth wedding anniversary in 2004.

Through tree branches, I saw the others standing on the bridge. They weren't ready for a break yet and seemed anxious to finish the hike. I sat down to soak up my last rest.

"So, are you ready for your triumphant ascent into Oregon?" my brother asked. He began to sing the theme from *Rocky* using the letters "P-C-T, P-C-T!"

I grinned. I didn't feel any kind of triumph or elation. I was immersed in a rich state of well-being.

I let the sun warm me. I inhaled the smells of meadow flowers. I listened to the patient flow of Donomore Creek.

This is all passing. Remember.

I glanced at my watch. "Okay. Let's finish this baby up!"

They wanted me to go first. I appreciated their thoughtfulness.

I had an agenda for my last hike. To say goodbye. My life as a mountaineer was quickly fading. Rather than fight and spit as I completed my journey, I wanted to let this chapter of my life go gracefully.

I worked up a small, open ridge where I encountered a two-point buck and a young doe.

My, what things have these eyes seen! A porcupine at sunrise. A lynx by Yosemite Falls. A weasel in Tuolumne Meadows. A mountain goat in the Grand Canyon. More bears than I care to count. Deer, raccoons, coyotes, eagles, *wild turkeys, a roadrunner, horned toads, snakes. So much more. I have seen more than my share.*

I thought about that cougar snarling in the night at Castle Crags.
I've also heard more than my share.
Thank you, God.
Goodbye.

I walked some more and admired the gentle swells of Donomore Meadows.

And what places have these feet taken me! The moonrise over Antelope Valley. The frozen environs of Forester Pass. How many meadows dashed with columbine and lupine? How many passes? The starry nights. Snow storms in summer. How many streams and rivers have I sat by? How many peaks have shared with me their lofty views? More than my share.
Thank you, God.
Goodbye.

At last Donomore Meadows gave way to a forested ridge. I began my last ascent and sweat gathered on my brow.

And what a price had I paid! So much pain. So many miles. Blisters. So many times it seemed to be over. Muscle strain in Mojave. The ice chute on Forester Pass. Never having enough food in the Sierra. The swelling creek and river fords. My back at Lookout Rock. The endless miles. The unending days.
Thank you, God.
Goodbye.

I looked up from my ascent and saw a wooden bulletin board along the trail just ahead. And so, after dreaming of the PCT for a quarter of a century, after 21 years, six months and one day had passed from its beginning to end, after spending 170 days on the trail, I came to Oregon.

I felt no surge of emotion or sense of accomplishment as I walked across the border with my brother.

I only sensed a deep and resonant fact:
I'm done.

Kurt took a picture of Pat and me.
I'm glad he's here. I'm glad we have the trail.

We still had to walk a quarter-mile to get to a road. The others went on ahead as I strolled along the trail.

Me and Pat at the California/Oregon border

Another 100 yards passed.
What a beautiful day.

The trail arced north.
Are you ready for a new kind of life?

A gaze at the trees.
Yes.

I knew in that moment that CMT would take what is left of my
fading strength. There would be a cane in my future, and, if God

lengthened my days, a wheelchair.

I also knew that every time I saw the majestic Sierra rising above my central valley home, every time I drove along California's north and southbound highways, every time I saw a map of my native state, I would smile. Yes, I have CMT, but I also have California. All 1,700 miles of it.

I don't have to defy CMT anymore.

I turned my face to the sun.
I can live *with CMT.*

The trail met a road. Our ride was waiting to take us home.

I stepped off of the PCT.

A Word of Thanks

I'd like to thank the visionaries who dreamed of the PCT, the people who built it and maintain it, the government agencies who watch over the trail and the many private property owners who allowed me to walk on their land. Kudos to scores of local folks who gave me food when I was broke, a bath when I was dirty or water when I was thirsty.

I would have been lost much more without the excellent *Guide to the Pacific Crest Trail* published by Wilderness Press to guide me. Thanks to you for the care, detail and maps that enabled me to find my way.

A nod goes to the Pacific Crest Trail Association (PCTA), a fine organization with a great website (pcta.org). Their trail updates often came in handy. A membership in the PCTA is a great way to support the PCT.

To the American medical system, I tip my hat. I would never have been able to hike without the phenomenal skill of several surgeons, doctors, nurses and physical therapists. Thanks.

The Charcot-Marie-Tooth Association has helped me to stay in touch with the CMT community. Likewise, a membership to this worthy organization is a way to support research concerning CMT. Visit them on the web at charcot-marie-tooth.org.

Even though I wrote every word of *Walk With Me*, no publisher would have even looked at it without the hundreds of suggestions and corrections made by my readers. My sincere gratitude to:

Bob Anders
Dr. Milton Austin
Dr. Kathy Bogacz
Damon Cline
Don

Larry Eclov
Dan Libman
Pat McCorkle
Renee McLean
Molly McNett
Pat Moeller
Dr. Greg Rutecki
Sally
Kay Shannon
Mike Shea
Andrea Zimmerman

A special word of thanks goes to Pat Moeller. She was the first to believe that my story was worth telling.

Thanks to Michael Muir for his gracious forward. He is president of Driving for the Disabled, USA—a group that brings the joys of horseback riding to the disabled. Check it out at usdfd.org.

I'd also like to mention two authors who were a great help to me—Dave and Neta Jackson. Their support and encouragement has helped me to find my way through the chaos of the publishing process.

Thanks to Karin Richards, who put together my website.

Jana Gittings transformed my horrible scratching into beautiful maps and drawings. Thanks.

The crew at The Printing Shop in Dixon has been a huge help to me in several ways. You folks are the best!

Sincere thanks goes to the staff at Publish America for taking a chance on *Walk With Me*. Thank you.

And thank you, dear reader, for walking with me.

Above all, I would like to thank God. He is the Creator of All, the Composer of the Song and the Savior of my life. Although my clumsy walking could never be compared to that of a deer, the following verse has often inspired me during difficult and solitary walks in the high places:

"The Sovereign Lord is my strength;
he makes my feet like the feet of a deer,
he enables me to go on heights."
Habakkuk 3:19

To contact Martin McCorkle and for more hiking news, photos and CMT updates, visit martinmccorkle.com.

Printed in the United States
30324LVS00003B/34